PHANTOM LIMBS AND BODY INTEGRITY IDENTITY DISORDER

Phantom Limbs and Body Integrity Identity Disorder discusses the conditions of Phantom Limb Syndrome and Body Integrity Identity Disorder together for the first time, exploring examples from literature, film, and psychoanalysis to re-ground theories of the body in material experience.

The book outlines the ways in which PLS and BIID involve a feeling of rupture underlined by a desire for wholeness, using the metaphor of the mirror-box (a therapeutic device that alleviates phantom limb pain) to examine how fiction is fundamentally linked to our physical and psychical realities. Using diverse examples from theoretical and fictional works, including thinkers such as Sigmund Freud, Jacques Lacan, Maurice Blanchot, D.W. Winnicott, and Georges Perec, and films by Powell and Pressburger and Quentin Tarantino, each chapter offers a detailed exploration of the mind/body relationship and experiences of fragmentation, bodily ownership, and symbolic reconstitution. By tracing these concepts, the monograph demonstrates ways in which fiction can enable us to understand the psychosomatic conditions of PLS and BIID more thoroughly, while providing new ways of reading psychoanalysis, literary theory, and fictional works.

The first book to analyse BIID in relation to PLS, *Phantom Limbs and Body Integrity Identity Disorder* will be essential reading for academics and literary readers interested in the body, psychoanalysis, English literature, literary theory, film, and disability.

Monika Loewy, PhD, obtained her doctorate in the Department of English and Comparative Literature at Goldsmiths, University of London. She teaches and writes on film, twentieth and twenty-first-century literature, and psychoanalysis.

PHANTOM LIMBS AND BODY INTEGRITY IDENTITY DISORDER

Literary and Psychoanalytic Reflections

Monika Loewy

LONDON AND NEW YORK

First published 2020
by Routledge
2 Park Square, Milton Park, Abingdon, Oxon OX14 4RN

and by Routledge
52 Vanderbilt Avenue, New York, NY 10017

Routledge is an imprint of the Taylor & Francis Group, an informa business

© 2020 Monika Loewy

The right of Monika Loewy to be identified as author of this work has been asserted by her in accordance with sections 77 and 78 of the Copyright, Designs and Patents Act 1988.

All rights reserved. No part of this book may be reprinted or reproduced or utilised in any form or by any electronic, mechanical, or other means, now known or hereafter invented, including photocopying and recording, or in any information storage or retrieval system, without permission in writing from the publishers.

Trademark notice: Product or corporate names may be trademarks or registered trademarks, and are used only for identification and explanation without intent to infringe.

British Library Cataloguing-in-Publication Data
A catalogue record for this book is available from the British Library

Library of Congress Cataloging-in-Publication Data
A catalog record has been requested for this book

ISBN: 978-0-367-28000-0 (hbk)
ISBN: 978-0-367-28001-7 (pbk)
ISBN: 978-0-429-29912-4 (ebk)

Typeset in Bembo
by Wearset Ltd, Boldon, Tyne and Wear

Cover art by Tom Moglu
Images by Ben Collison

For my parents:
Olivia and Aaron

And my grandparents:
Peter and Annette
and
Alex and Betty

CONTENTS

Preface ix
Acknowledgements xi

PART I
Why psychoanalysis and literature?   1

1 Introduction   3

2 "We didn't ask for this pain": case studies of BIID and PLS   41

3 Science, literature, and psychoanalysis   65

4 Negative hallucination and "The Man from Burma"   76

PART II
Symbolic exchanges and reconstitutions   87

5 The mirror-stage, Blanchot, and "Orpheus's Gaze"   89

6 *The Red Shoes*   106

7 Breakdown: D.W. Winnicott   116

8 *Death Proof*   128

9 Almost artificial limbs: Perec's *W or The Memory of Childhood*   138

10 A psychoanalytic voyage: Perec and symbolic reconstitution   151

11 Conclusion: (…)   166

   Index   171

PREFACE

I primarily decided to write about phantom limbs when I had a dream that my father's wife, who had an untimely death, explained that I should link the concept of phantom limbs to linguistic structure. Although this was only a dream, it was rich, and it lingered. I progressively developed a desire to understand more about the connections between the ways in which we feel physically and psychically fragmented, and how images and symbols can heal fragmentation. Shortly thereafter, I told my father about the idea, who told me an interesting story. His father, Alexander, had been in Auschwitz and survived, though he did not speak of the matter. One day, my father explained, when he was 20, Alexander bent down to tie his shoe and became paralysed. A disc in his spine had snapped, apparently, as a result of the manual labour he was forced to undertake at the concentration camps.

My father told me that he had always felt guilty for not taking care of his father. "Alex would always complain of having pain in his legs, even though they were numb", he told me; he had a phantom limb. Although I was not aware that I knew about my grandfather's phantom limb, perhaps I had unconsciously retained the knowledge, which would explain their recurrence in my dream. I gradually became interested in learning more about a non-normative feeling of pain. This led to my study of Body Integrity Identity Disorder, which interested me because it was an internalised feeling of fragmentation, somehow opposite to, yet paradoxically paralleling, Phantom Limb Syndrome. In both conditions, individuals struggle with a real physical pain that counters material reality.

I had been writing about BIID and PLS for just over two years when I received a call that a tragedy had occurred. My father was in a body-boarding accident and became partially paralysed. He, too, had phantom pains in his legs. He had experienced loss upon loss—the death of a wife, a traumatised father, the loss of a fully functioning body, and underlying all this, the trauma of the Second World War. Although I have been lucky enough to not experience these traumas first-hand,

I have unconsciously learned about feelings of psychical and somatic fragmentation through those around me. Though originally I did not set out to learn about my family's particular experiences, I have studied different forms of psychical and physical feelings of painful rupture, how these are connected to indescribable loss, and how we might begin to work though such experiences.

For me, this monograph acts in a way similar to a mirror-box; it provides a way to begin working through my own perceptions of fragmentation through a (linguistic) reflection. The aim here is to provide a platform for others to contemplate pain, rupture, healing, and how particular exchanges, experiences and cultural works can be useful in this endeavour. I have discovered that certain types of reflection that parallel mirror-box therapy (predominantly psychoanalysis, literary theory, and films and literature about fragmentation) can assist in the reparation process. Writing this book has been an enlightening experience, and the text is offered, in part, as a rethinking of the mind–body connection and an effort to think further about a feeling of fracture that is brought out by Body Integrity Identity Disorder and phantom limbs. As a critical reflection on psychoanalysis, literature, and theory, this text is additionally intended to view the mind–body relationship through a unique lens to open new ways of thinking about the body and its relationship to cultural studies.

ACKNOWLEDGEMENTS

I would like to thank Professor Josh Cohen who served as my PhD supervisor, and who shared with me his great breadth of knowledge, as well as being the one who encouraged and supported me throughout my time spent studying under him. I would also like to thank Professor Naomi Segal, who was my PhD examiner, and whose contribution to this book is invaluable. She also provided me with confidence and knowledge; she is truly an inspiration. I am very thankful to have learned from them both. I would also like to offer profound gratitude to my editors and Routledge for taking on this book. Charles Bath and Ting Baker made this process enjoyable and fluid, and for that, I thank you.

To my family (Olivia, Aaron, Alex, Barry, Natalie, and Phyllis), who have expressed their pride in me, challenged, and supported me, and who taught me to trust the process. And my dad: an ironic inspiration.

I am very grateful to Dr Christopher Lloyd for his loyalty, support, and thoughtfulness. I would also like to thank Tom Moglu and Ben Collison for their brilliant illustrations and Julie Meunier for her thorough translations. Thank you also to Professor Vicky LeBeau, Dr Tiago Gandra, Professor Jane Desmarais, Edward Wall, and Dr Alice Condé for their contributions to the book. Finally, thank you to Joe Mattei, Ananda Grace, Mary Richards (and co.), Victor Sevilla-Diaz, Dr Agnieszka Piotrowska, Dr Christopher Clark, Anna and Jimmy Card, Holly Farler, Charlie Calleja, Slawek Krycia, Donald Underwood, Hanna and Emily Franklin, and the wonderful Nichole Kerman for all of the conversations, to say the least.

Thank you also to my grandparents, and to Laura Paquette and Sue Jordan.

And finally, thank you to those with BIID and phantom limbs who have shared their experiences.

PART I
Why psychoanalysis and literature?

1

INTRODUCTION

> *La suppression radicale d'un membre, ne présentant plus au cerveau que des images […] de bras et de jambes, de membres lointains et pas à leur place. Une espèce de rupture intérieure.*
>
> The radical suppression of a limb, presenting the brain with no more than images […] of distant and dislocated limbs. A sort of internal severance.
>
> Artaud, *Anthology* (1965, 29)

Antonin Artaud's fragmented description of dislocated limbs reflects the focus of this book, which involves experiences of physical, mental, imaginary, and linguistic fracture in relation to illusory limbs. It is the purpose of this book to examine two physical phenomena alongside literary, fictional, and psychoanalytic works, to reground theories of the body in lived, material experience. In so doing, it ultimately raises questions concerning how we are constituted through signs, how this affects our sense of wholeness, and how fiction is fundamentally linked to our physical and psychical realities. Body Integrity Identity Disorder (BIID) is a condition in which individuals desire to amputate a limb because they feel that it does not belong to their body: they feel "incomplete" with four healthy limbs. Phantom limbs occur when amputated individuals feel the sensation that their absent limbs still exist. Thus, BIID and the Phantom Limb Syndrome (PLS) are the inverse of one another. Individuals with both conditions desire to remove an extraneous limb (in BIID an existing limb, and in PLS a phantom) and reflect a similar problem with a feeling of incompleteness and a dissonance between the mind and body. However, while in BIID, the concept of completion concerns a sense of being in bodily excess, a fantasy of destruction, and appears to begin in the mind, PLS involves a fantasy that fills an absence, originates in the body, and can, in certain cases, be healed through a mirror illusion. V.S. Ramachandran invented the mirror treatment in 1996 through what he called the mirror-box (also known as mirror therapy), a box with a mirror in the centre into which amputees place their whole limb on one side, and the stump on the other. When they move the existent limb and look at its reflection, it appears as though there are two limbs, and that their phantom is moving. Consequently, the often uncomfortable or painful phantom sensations can disappear. Thus, a re-imagined version of the self transforms a disturbing experience of rupture, a concept that is also central to certain psychoanalytic, fictional, and literary works. These types of texts, therefore, can provide insight into BIID, PLS, and the mirror-box phenomena, which this book sets out to accomplish. It examines, in other words, how BIID and PLS are representative of a fractured sense of self, and how a certain type of reflection may have a healing effect.

Since BIID and PLS have only been studied through a medical model that fails to find definitive answers or cures, I argue that a theoretical analysis is necessary. Through the use of psychoanalytic, literary, and fictional texts that foreground bodily fragmentation, this book explores various ways of thinking about the fracture and drives towards wholeness experienced by those with BIID and PLS. Specifically, it attends to how a form of possession (the need to control one's sense of being complete) can be mediated by a particular kind of exchange. Since, moreover, mirror therapy takes place through a process of reflection, the mirror-box acts as a metaphor for the structure of this book, which is a linguistic reflection upon BIID and the phantom limb syndromes.

Psychoanalysis provides a starting point for this exploration because, in the words of Marilia Aisenstein,

> if psychoanalysis is unique, and irreplaceable, in relation to other forms of psychological treatment, it is so, in my view, because it opens up thought processes and enables the subject to reintegrate into the chain of psychic events even something unthinkable, such as the appearance of a lethal illness.
>
> (Aisenstein 2006, 679)

Psychoanalysis, therefore, offers new ways of thinking about BIID and PLS, two phenomena that are to a great extent, incomprehensible. This work draws relationships between psychoanalysis and the two bodily conditions, which focus on the fractured psyche and soma. By attending to the body, this exploration will illuminate what is involved in the disorders, while also providing nuanced ways of reading psychoanalytic theories. Naomi Segal states of Didier Anzieu that, "[s]ince Lacan, the stress on language had meant that the body was not being psychoanalytically theorised; yet 'every psychic activity leans on [*s'étaie sur*] a biological function.' Anzieu's aim is to fill this gap" (Anzieu 2009, 44). This thought provides a helpful backdrop for my exploration here, because I am interested in corporeality. However, not unlike Anzieu, I do not only investigate the body, I also foreground the importance of language and the way in which it mediates between the mind and body. In reading the two bodily conditions through a psychoanalytic and literary lens,

I address the importance of linking literature, the body and the mind. As Peter Brooks writes:

> There ought to be a correspondence between literary and psychic dynamics, since we constitute ourselves in part through our fictions within the [...] symbolic order, that of signs, including, pre-eminently, language itself. Through study of the work accomplished by fictions we may be able to reconnect literary criticism to human concern.
>
> (Brooks 1992, xiv)

Studying literature and the psyche together can help elucidate the ways in which we are constituted through fictions, and BIID and PLS both concern fictive versions of the self that involve an imagined sense of unity. Moreover, the mirror-box demonstrates how visualising oneself as a sign (the mirror illusion is a sign of one's phantom limb) can have bodily effects. Mirror therapy acts as a material and metaphorical example of the way in which we are formed through signs, of the way the body is understood and constituted as a language and through language. In drawing these connections between psychoanalysis, literature and the body, this work explores how the fictions through which we are formed can alleviate experiences of fragmentation. To provide a foundation for these analyses, a survey of relevant literature follows.

Body Integrity Identity Disorder

BIID, also known as xenomelia and apotemnophilia, is a condition wherein individuals desire to amputate an existing limb because they feel that it does not belong to their body. Paradoxically, then, the present limb makes these individuals feel incomplete, while the idea of its removal enables a sense of completeness. "The main motivation for the preferred body modification", explains Rianne Blom, "is believed to be a mismatch between actual and perceived body schema" (2012, 1),[1] a disjunction between physical structure and identity. Those with the syndrome complain of feeling that with four limbs they are not themselves and become obsessed with the desire for the removal of a limb. Some who are unable to amputate have a strong urge to commit suicide. Though there are no known cures, some individuals explain that they have found most relief when they are able to amputate the limb. However, many are driven to continue to amputate parts of their body after they have followed through with the original amputation.

According to a survey conducted in 2003 by Dan Cooper ("Fighting It"), who initiated the Internet *Yahoo! Group* "Fighting It", 36% of those with BIID believe it is a neurological problem, while 63% believe it has psychological origins, 44% with the syndrome are straight males, 28% gay males, 13% straight females, 4% gay females, and 8% transgendered. However, Cooper also writes in an email that "[t]hese are informal polls. There is no control over who chooses to participate. Nevertheless, these are probably the best data available" ("Fighting It"). Other studies demonstrate that although the most common request is an above-the-knee amputation of the left leg, BIID may also involve other parts of the body or a desire to remove certain senses (hearing, sight, and so on). The syndrome, moreover, usually originates in childhood, and is often associated with a memory of seeing an amputee for the first time. Amy White explains that in one of the first studies conducted on BIID, Michael First "found that 65% of patients experienced onset of BIID before age eight and 98% of patients before age 16. Some subsequent studies have reported that most individuals with BIID experience early onset" (2014, 231). Since BIID involves the fantasy of losing a limb, it is often confused with (though may still be linked to) acrotomophilia, a sexual attraction to other amputees (as some with BIID are attracted to amputees). In order to self-cure, some sufferers[2] (referred to as "pretenders" in the BIID community) may feign a disability by using devices such as wheelchairs, prostheses or leg braces. The term "wannabes", on the other hand, refers to those who self-injure, self-amputate, or pursue black-market surgery. Some simply want to be disabled, some desire the challenge of living in a disabled body, and others wonder if a physical disability will reduce a felt psychical one. This raises the question as to what a disability means. As one sufferer (Nelson) explains, when he pretended to be an amputee, he "never felt disabled" (2010, 86). Another individual states that he

> crafted and used the term "transabled" to describe someone who has BIID [...]. Transabled means to me that I am in a transitional position, between a body that is not what I need it to be, and hopefully reaching that body at some point soon.
>
> *(Schmidt 2010, 89)*

According to Ferguson (2012), disability studies should "reshape the way that society understands people with disabilities" (72). The field "looks at disability, through politics, the arts, ethics, history, and more recently, phenomenology and personal experiences" (Ferguson 2012, 71).[3] Although it is a wide field that involves the humanities and is largely analytical, it was founded as a predominantly social movement aimed at reducing stigma, calling for changes in healthcare, and bringing visibility to those with disabilities. My study of BIID and the phantom limb is also analytical. However, rather than focusing on a social movement, I embark upon a more detailed discussion that is specifically concerned with issues of fragmentation, wholeness and imperfect bodies.

Though "BIID" was not coined until 2004 by Michael First, and was renamed xenomelia by Paul McGeoch in 2011, documented cases date back to 1785. The syndrome is recently beginning to gain recognition through films such as *Complete Obsession* (2000), *Whole* (2003), *Quid Pro Quo* (2008), and *Armless* (2010), through Ramachandran's interest in the condition, and with the rising popularity of Internet forums, specifically, the Internet *Yahoo! Group* called "Fighting It". This forum is dedicated to "discussion and support for living with or reducing this need [to be an amputee] and understanding its origins" ("Fighting It"). Although I aim to understand the syndrome more thoroughly, I am not searching for a definitive origin or reason. I am interested in learning more about the condition by investigating various theories that pertain to experiences related to BIID. It is this more analytical perspective that differs from those biomedical paradigms currently in discussion.

Although research on the syndrome is limited, what literature exists suggests that the majority of sufferers remember having idolised an amputee at an early age and know exactly what part of their limb must be removed (Bayne and Levy 2005, 11). Reports also reveal that patients feel as though they are not themselves with all their limbs intact, that the primary reason for amputation is the wish to feel complete through a lack (First 2005), and that most fear social stigma and therefore keep the desire secret. Although the condition remains a mystery to medical science, some psychological and physiological hypotheses exist. Sabine Müller writes that

> psychologists, psychiatrists, and neurologists offer quite different explanations for the amputation desire: they discuss whether it is a neurotic disorder, an obsessive-compulsive disorder, an identity disorder like transsexuality, or a neurological conflict [...] which could stem from damage to a part of the brain that constructs the body image in a map-like form.
>
> (Müller 2009, 37)

One psychological study conducted in 2015 examined the role of childhood experiences with BIID, as well as

> abnormalities in parents' behaviour of BIID sufferers, which should be followed up in future research. [...]. Until now, there are no other studies about childhood-related experiences in BIID-people. Childhood experiences have not been subject of [sic] systematic psychological research in BIID context, yet.
>
> (Obernolte 2015, 7)

This book attends to this lack by exploring childhood experiences, albeit from a theoretical, psychoanalytic, and literary standpoint, as opposed to a biomedical one. It does not conduct a survey of individuals' childhood experiences, but rather explores ideas about the way in which infants and children are formed in relation to their environments, particularly through the works of psychoanalyst Donald Woods Winnicott.

In the *Diagnostic and Statistical Manual of Mental Disorders, 5th Edition* (DSM-V, published in 2013), BIID is listed under Body Dysmorphic Disorder (BDD). However, the manual asserts that in BIID, "the concern does not focus on the limb's appearance, as it would in body dysmorphic disorder" (247). Noll writes that "[i]n contrast to body dysmorphic disorder (BDD) is in BIID subjects only a very small tendency to judge the attractiveness of the concerned limb as 'unaesthetic'" (2014, 230). Those with BIID focus on a body image, not the visual aspect of bodily incongruity, and are less "delusional" than those with BDD. Moreover, "[t]hose with BDD have a consuming preoccupation with an ugly body part or parts" (Lemma 2010, 61). They "often describe that they are not seeking an ideal body; they just want to be 'normal'" (Lemma 2010, 83). Another difference between BDD and BIID is that those with BDD associate the ideal body with normality, while those with BIID associate the ideal body with what is considered to be abnormal. Although BIID is also sometimes compared to anorexia, according to White,

> [a] person with anorexia will believe they are overweight despite contrary evidence. Persons with BIID acknowledge that their bodies are healthy, they just identify as a disabled person [...]. It is a mismatch that causes a BIID patient to suffer, not an alleged false belief.
>
> *(2014, 229)*

(though I note that this may not always be the case). Nevertheless, anorexia illuminates another way of viewing BIID: it demonstrates the way in which desiring to erase part of one's body to reach an imagined ideal is not entirely uncommon, as the same principle applies on a lesser scale to disordered eating (or any form of dieting). In this way, there is a gradation between the less radical and more radical forms of desire for bodily removal, a recognition that may allow for a more comprehensive understanding of the syndrome.[4]

BIID is also often paired with Gender Identity Disorder (GID), in which individuals are uncomfortable with their anatomy and desire to alter their body as a result. Both disorders, then, involve a drive to seek out surgery to meet an imagined ideal. Moreover, in both, writes First, "the individual reports feeling uncomfortable with an aspect of his or her anatomical identity" (First 2005, 8). Thus, "[s]ufferers of BIID", writes White, "often describe themselves as being transabled, drawing a parallel with transgendered individuals" (2014, 226).[5] They also display a male predominance, symptoms tend to begin in childhood, and there have been individual case reports and descriptions of MtF transsexuals who have undergone limb amputation. Furthermore, many BIID patients exhibit gender identity issues, are often homosexual or bisexual, and some have reported feelings of wanting to be the opposite sex (Lawrence 2006, 264). This has caused some researchers to ask: "[h]ow can our understanding of GID help us to better understand BIID?" (Lawrence 2006, 154). This book focuses on a similar logic, albeit in relation to psychoanalysis and literary theory.

The field of gender studies is dedicated to the way in which gender and sexuality are represented and constructed as an identity, which is analysed predominantly through LGBTQI or queer studies, women's studies, and men's studies. More specifically, researchers in the field focus on how gender and sexuality are positioned in various discourses in the humanities. Some of the concepts discussed within this field overlap with those in this work, one of which involves the castration complex.[6] It is this kind of psychoanalytic approach that I take, paralleling the neurobiological studies in some ways, though from a theoretical standpoint. These kinds of paradigms are not taken as fact, but are used to illuminate what is at work in BIID. To return to GID, the disorder differs from that in BIID, desires to amputate are directly related to the arms and legs (in most cases) as opposed to the genitals and breasts, and, as one woman who suffers from BIID writes:

> I could have a sex-change operation, but it would not give me the male experience. I would not be a man; I would be a woman with no vagina and an enlarged clitoris [...]. To the contrary, [the] curiosity [of the BIID sufferer] is encouraged by the knowledge that it can be perfectly satisfied.
>
> (Mensaert 2011, 21)

From this woman's perspective, those who desire a sex change are left unsatisfied because they can never completely embody the opposite gender, whereas those with BIID can definitively attain their goal to remove the limb. This is problematic, however, because, first, the statement assumes that there is a specific definition of "gender" (and "sex"),[7] and some individuals with BIID who go through with their desired amputation remain unsatisfied. Those with BIID often emphasise the similarities between transsexuality and BIID for practical reasons, since sex reassignment is legal, while BIID surgery is not. As the aforementioned woman with BIID argues, "sex-change surgery is considered a worthwhile medical treatment because it provides the physical appearance and semblance of function [... and] thereby alleviat[es] great mental torment". She continues,

> I propose that the mental torment undergone by wannabes be recognised as a seriously debilitating condition similar in nature to and as important as *transsexualism*, and that amputation not be ruled out as a reasonable way to treat it, just as gender reassignment is used to treat transsexuals.
>
> (Mensaert 2011, 24–25)

In this way, comparing transsexuality to BIID may allow others to begin to identify with it, accept it, and even perform the desired surgery. However, it must be recognised that "unlike surgery to treat gender dysmorphia, surgery for BIID will leave sufferers physically, and perhaps problematically disabled. Also, surgeries like amputations often are risky and prone to complications [...]" (White 2014, 231–232). Thus, the links drawn between gender dysmorphia and BIID open a way of thinking about and understanding BIID. What interests me about this parallel is that it demonstrates that the core of BIID is not entirely uncommon, and this work is interested in exploring related concepts of the "imperfect" and fractured body.

The syndrome has additionally been compared to various conditions that are believed to be outcomes of tumours or strokes, such as Capgras syndrome, which involves a delusion that someone close to the patient is an imposter. Also falling under this category is alien hand syndrome, in which a stroke causes patients to believe that their hand is alien to them (though only 50 cases have been documented).

Although this parallels the alien limb in BIID, in contrast to these two disorders, patients suffering from BIID "perceive this limb as mere ballast. This difference may explain why one and the same symptom is perceived as a disturbance by stroke or brain tumour patients, but as a part of their identity by BIID patients" (Müller 2009, 39). In short, BIID is more psychically orientated: the condition is a part of the person's identity and does not necessarily originate in the body. There is additionally Cotard's syndrome, in which patients fail to recognise themselves, archaic limb phenomenon, in which individuals feel attacked by their limbs, instances of neurological and psychiatric patients feeling as though they are in another being, and cases in which individuals with paralysed bodies feel that they are functional. These syndromes, like strokes and PLS, are thought to result from physical traumas. And although I do not claim that BIID does not have physical origins, I suggest that the origins are not always known. Thus, BIID calls for a more robust exploration beyond neurology. Rather than asking questions about the possibility of a bodily wound, I am concerned with the way in which the physical and mental sense of self of those with BIID is shaped through more abstract experiences and feelings of trauma. However, the parallel between BIID and these types of neurological conditions have led to neurological hypotheses.

Neurological hypotheses

I now visit some of these, beginning with Ramachandran, who contends that the brain contains a map of the body, which is mismatched in BIID. There is, he suggests, a discrepancy between the body image and the physical body, which creates a cognitive dissonance: the brain fails to incorporate the limb. Since there is no stimulation or a dysfunction of the right parietal lobe, he argues, the limb cannot be felt. Though prominent, his research has been criticised by others in the field because those who desire an amputation often change their preference as to the limb they would like amputated.[8] Though medication prescribed for various mood disorders has (occasionally) worked to reduce suffering, attempts to clarify whether these medications relieve BIID specifically remain unsatisfactory. Alternative psychological and neurological methods are rarely pursued. However, one study conducted in 2015 by Lenggenhager, Hilti and Brugger used the "rubber foot illusion" to test BIID individuals' responses to feeling ownership of a false foot. Those who conducted the study altered the rubber hand illusion (in which the synchronous stroking of an artificial hand and one's own hidden hand leads to an illusory feeling of ownership of the false hand) and created a rubber foot for those with BIID, and those without it. What they found was that both groups experienced the rubber foot illusion in the same way, suggesting that those with BIID have normally functioning senses, and that the integration of visual, tangible and proprioceptive information is intact, again contradicting Ramachandran and McGough's hypothesis. Subjects could feel ownership of an artificial foot, and yet continue to deny ownership of a real one, suggesting that the syndrome is not solely neurological. The scientists who conducted the study wonder if this experiment could be used to alter body representation to allow those with BIID to reintegrate the body part; however, this has yet to be tested. Additionally, in a small minority of cases, a combination of medicine and Cognitive Behavioural Therapy (a psychological treatment aimed at re-training psychological and physical habits) has been helpful in relieving feelings of obsession and depression. However, it does not eradicate BIID. Additionally, Ramachandran states that in very few cases, "merely having the patient look at his affected limb through a minifying lens to optically shrink it makes the limb feel far less unpleasant, presumably by reducing the mismatch" (2011, 257). Though some therapies are in development, most BIID patients report that they only feel better if amputated, and many argue that this is the only cure. Although self-amputation is reportedly more dangerous than, for example, gender reassignment surgery, Noll insists that based on his studies of those who have undergone amputation, "[t]hey listed several disadvantages, but in total they said that the advantage to have reached their goal outbalanced these disadvantages by far" (Noll 2014, 230). Though patients often feel that the only way to relieve BIID is to have the limb amputated, several are open to other possible treatments. Furthermore, the number of individuals who have amputated or undergone therapy is minimal and cannot be accurately calculated. White writes, "[w]hile anecdotal evidence suggests a high satisfaction rate from those who have managed to realise their ideal disabled body, studies are on a very small scale" (White 2014, 227). This is partially due to the fact that "unnecessary amputation" is illegal, and a scarce number of individuals with BIID have publicised their desires. However, "[s]everal individuals find ways to amputate limbs themselves. They may use a wood chipper, a chainsaw, shotgun, or dry ice. Others seek surgery on the black market, one individual suffering from gangrene and dying" (White 2014, 226). Although surgery performed legally can be helpful for those seeking dangerous methods, "sometimes the success is not sustainable: some amputated patients develop further amputation desires". Müller hopes that "less invasive and efficient therapies can be expected" in the future (Müller 2009, 42).

Certain researchers, however, believe surgery to be "ethically permissible because it will prevent many BIID patients from injuring or killing themselves" (Bayne and Levy 2005, 79). In the medical community, this question of ethics is often related to the patient's mental health. On very rare occasions, if the patient can be trusted to make the right decision, they may be permitted to have the amputation. However, this involves a problematic differentiation between the rational and irrational and between mental health and sickness. White explains that "less radical treatment options for BIID should be utilised before a surgical intervention" (2014, 234). Less radical treatments, however, have not been sought, aside from a number of people who have undergone counselling, or have taken medication for accompanying symptoms, or in the case of the experiments mentioned above, all bearing mixed and insubstantial results. Kaur suggests that a medical cure has not been identified because "identity is not located in any simple way in anatomy" (2004, 1). To approach this problem, First calls for more studies that examine psychotherapeutic forms.

Psychotherapy and BIID

Some researchers suggest that psychotherapy can be used as an alternative to, or in conjunction with, medication, because the syndrome appears to be closely linked to mood disorders. According to Bayne and Levy (2005), "psychotherapy is the appropriate response to the disorder" instead of amputation or medication, but "we know of no systematic study of the effects of psychotherapy on the desire for amputation" (11). First (2005) states that in his study, "for none of the subjects did psychotherapy reduce the intensity of the desire for amputation" (7). However, he also notes that a large number of patients never told their therapists about this desire, for fear that the therapist would consider this evidence of a severe mental illness. In addition to this, assessing the success of psychotherapeutic treatment is problematic because "there are very few professionals that are well versed in this particular disorder" (*Body Integrity Identity Disorder* 2014). However, one study conducted in 2011, entitled "Body Integrity Identity Disorder—First Success in Long-Term Psychotherapy", charted the case of a man with BIID for whom two years in psychotherapy proved effective. Another small study found that psychotherapy "can reduce the psychological strain in BIID affected persons" (Kröger et al. 2014, 110). In sum, as Noll (2014), who conducted a study of people who have carried out self-amputation, writes: "there has to be further research on how to improve psychotherapy for people with BIID and to make it more effective" (231).

Thus, neurological, psychological, and psychotherapeutic researchers continue to face difficulties defining terms and finding origins and cures. In my exploration of BIID I am not attempting to find a specific origin or cure, and I do not focus on neurological research. My research aims to understand the more psychical components of BIID, particularly the struggles with imperfect bodies. For this, I turn to literature, psychoanalysis, and fictional texts because they provide insight into what might lie beyond the neurological studies discussed above. I explore human struggles with issues related to BIID that illuminate a more robust understanding of what the disorder entails. Psychoanalysis and fiction are specifically helpful because, as I will soon explain, the kind of psychoanalysis I examine explores the struggles with mind/body dissonance, and how this relates to the way in which we are psychically and physically formed by our environment, experiences, and language. More specifically, these theories foreground how illusion, images and symbols are involved in the mind/body link, a concept that is also central to the phantom limb syndrome. As one apotemnophile, in the film *Whole*, explains, for him BIID is

> like mirrors and prisms and how lenses invert images, and this idea that actually by making something less, you make people more complete, which is the complete opposite to most amputees who perhaps have accidents or disease. By taking that limb away from them they feel less complete. But for us, it's the other way around. By taking it off you make us more complete.
> *(Whole 2003)*

I now want to look at those who suffer from what this individual refers to as the "complete opposite" of BIID: people who have had a bodily amputation that is replaced with a phantom limb. We will soon find that although PLS may seem to be the opposite to BIID, there are many overlapping issues. The next section focuses on PLS, in which a physical lack feels painfully present, as opposed to a physical presence that feels painfully absent. It also explores how mirrors and "lenses that invert images" may, in fact, help to treat those who have phantom limbs.

Phantom limbs

As previously noted, PLS involves the sensation that an amputated limb is still part of the body. While a person knows the limb is gone, she feels that it is still present. The phenomenon pertains to roughly 80% of amputees, including those born

FIGURE 1.1 Phantom limb

without a limb (congenital phantoms).[9] It was Ambroise Paré who first officially documented the syndrome while working with wounded soldiers in 1551. He believed that the phantom pains occurred in the brain, as opposed to in the physical stump itself. Weir Mitchell is also well known for writing about the phenomenon in a story published in 1866 in *The Atlantic Monthly*, which characterised a fictional account of phantom limbs that involved a "quadri-amputee in the presence of others who 'walked across the room on limbs invisible to them or me'" (cited in Schott 2014, 961). The story describes the features of a phantom limb, which he refers to as an "unseen ghost of the lost part" (Mitchell qtd. in Schott 2014, 961). Numerous authors have subsequently written about the phenomenon, including René Descartes, Aaron Lemos, and Charles Bell.

Currently, we know that phantom limb sensations are usually painful and uncomfortable. They may include tingling, throbbing, burning, clenching, and cramping and can fluctuate in accordance with changes in mood and weather. Although phantoms are often felt to move in sync with the rest of the individual's body and revert to a habitual position, they may also feel paralysed or disfigured. This disfigurement is connected to what is called telescoping: a (usually painful) change in size, shape and length, often triggered by material circumstances such as the wearing of prosthetics. One amputee describes a feeling of "'being in contact with every part of my body. Because of the painful itching I know where my legs are, and through the pain I can feel my knees and toes as if they were there'" (Nortvedt and Engelsrud 2014, 602). Another amputee explains "'it's very difficult to explain. It's as if I am lying in a nest of insects, and they're constantly crawling not only outside but inside my body'" (Nortvedt and Engelsrud 2014, 602). "'It's as if the skin of my arm has been ripped off; salt is being poured on it and then it's thrust into fire'", states another (Nortvedt and Engelsrud 2014, 602). What is interesting in these descriptions is that all amputees use metaphors which, Nortvedt and Engelsrud (2014) explain, "provide an inter-subjective perspective that conveys a common dimension of everyday life that could be a significant method for conveying and communicating their pain to others" (602). The use of metaphors to describe physical pain illuminates a theme that will be examined within this work: the possibility and importance of communicating pain through language. The above statements additionally convey that there is a loss involved in translating physical feelings, a loss that is replaced with an image. Although the phantom limb cannot be described, an image (of insects, for example) enables expression and communication.

A variety of treatments have been explored to ease or eradicate phantom limb pain (PLP), including robot hands, vision-based therapies and the rubber hand illusion, in which by stroking an artificial hand one may feel sensations in the absent limb (paralleling the previously mentioned rubber foot illusion). Additionally, the cocainisation of nerves can cause the phantom to temporarily disappear. Some have also reported that after the administration of LSD phantom limb sensations dissolve within three or four hours, for a period of time. And although some hypotheses exist regarding the causes of PLP, "there are many aspects of phantom limb experience that current theories of phantom limb phenomena do not explain, or which cannot be tested under current models" (Giummarra 2007, 224). I attend to this lack by engaging with certain types of dialogue about different sensations, experiences, thoughts, and concepts involved with the predominant issues at stake, several of which align with BIID. To ground this exploration, I shall briefly discuss some key neurological and psychological theories.

Neurological hypotheses

I begin with Ronald Melzack, a neurologist whose work is of interest due to his concern with the mind/body link. Based upon the belief that psychological and physical processes are intertwined, Melzack put forward the "neuromatrix" hypothesis in 1965, which proposes that the brain is prewired to believe that the body it commands has four limbs. When a limb is amputated, therefore, the brain continues to send sensory signals in its place that cause the limb to "feel real". The brain says, "'this is *my* body, it belongs to *me*, is part of my *self*'" (Malle 1991, 94), indicating that a person is neurologically wired to be whole, and that the body shapes the psyche. However, Guimmarra points out that Melzack's theory is "too broad and difficult to be tested empirically" (Guimmarra 2007, 224). Other researchers suggest that visual signals clash when the limb is suddenly absent, and that there are "maladaptive" changes in the primary sensory cortex following amputation. Some believe that an inflammation occurs in the severed nerve endings on the limb, which is misinterpreted by the brain as pain. However, research and treatments for these theories are unverifiable.

Herta Flor is concerned with the link between memory and bodily loss. She suggests that since phantom pain may resemble the pain that occurred before a limb was amputated, "pain memories established prior to the amputation are powerful elicitors of phantom limb pain" (Flor 2002, 877). Though phantom pain usually resembles pre-amputation pain, Flor explains that her theory remains inconclusive, partially due to the influence of the psychical upon the physical. She concludes that "more longitudinal research is needed to test the pain memory hypothesis" (Flor 2006, 878). Ramachandran's research on PLS focuses on the neurological reaction to the trauma of an amputated limb. He theorises that a map of the body exists in the brain, which is suddenly mismatched when a limb is removed, a concept that led to his BIID theory. While Ramachandran suggests that in BIID a part of the brain fails to incorporate the limb, his theory about PLS suggests that the limb part of the brain in the brain map continues to receive sensory information from areas adjacent to it though it is no longer there, which makes the individual feel that it still exists. Though Ramachandran's theory is influential, some have criticised it. For example, Flor found that phantom pain might be triggered by stimulating any part of the body or brain, not just those adjacent to the stump. While Ramachandran's study suggests that sensory input invades the negative space of the absent limb, which causes pain, I am interested in how PLS is formed not only by "physical invasion" but also by psychical impositions of a felt loss, which I shall elaborate through particular psychoanalytic and literary readings. However, Ramachandran's neurological hypothesis is helpful in providing a backdrop, along with his analysis of "mirror neurons".

Mirror neurons, according to Ramachandran, allow a person to understand or empathise with another person on a neurological level. These neurons, he writes, "allow you to figure out someone else's intentions [...] you can see yourself as others see you" (2011, 128). Since these neurons can cause an individual to feel what another is feeling by looking at that person, phantom limb perception must be influenced by physical identification with others who have limbs, and must involve mirror neurons. In support of this hypothesis are his findings that if an amputee sees someone being touched in a particular place, the amputee also feels the sensation. The material world affects the phantom feeling. Additionally, Schilder suggests that since the "hand and foot of the phantom persist longer, [...] those parts of the body which come in close and varied contact with reality are the most important ones" (1950, 64). This neurological concept, along with Schilder's observation, parallels a model of psychoanalysis concerned with how the individual is shaped by the environment, which I will be surveying through object relations theory. Rather than employing a neurological method, I shall examine how the psychical desire to be whole is linked to, not defined by, its physical component: how the limb is an organic reality that has been fantasised.

Psychology and PLS

Though many neurological hypotheses for PLS have been suggested, psychological factors have not been adequately explored. Flor (2006) contends that "psychological factors such as anxiety or depression [...] might well affect the onset, course and the severity of the pain" (874). These factors, she concludes, "need to be explored in greater detail" (2006, 878). Schilder (1950) argues that the phantom limb is

> to a great extent dependent on the emotional factors and the life situation. Probably the way in which the scheme of the body is built up and appears in the phantom has a general significance. It is a model of how psychic life in general is going on.
>
> *(68)*

The body schema to which he refers can be described as a postural figure of the body that arranges and alters new sensations to correlate with the body's habitual movements; it negotiates and represents one's spatial positioning, including the shape and length of the body and limbic organisation. He states:

> we build up a plan for movements [...], we develop this plan in continual contact with actual experiences [...], the motor activity originates from an intention of our inner direction towards a goal, which comes through in the actual movements.
>
> *(Schilder 1950, 70)*

In the case of the phantom limb, the body schema is obstructed by a loss that obstructs habitual bodily movements or intentions. As Vivian Sobchack (2010) describes of her own experience with a phantom limb:

> *looking* at my body stretched out before me as an *object*, I could see "nothing" *there* where my transparently absent left leg had been. On the other hand, *feeling* my body *subjectively* [...], I most certainly experienced "something" *here*—the "something" sort of like my leg but not exactly coincident with my memory of its subjective weight and length.
>
> (53)

Although Sobchack's limb does not physically exist, it exists subjectively as part of her body schema, albeit in distorted form. Her leg's habitual movements may have ceased upon amputation, but the body schema did not. Simmel (1962) suggests that this may occur because the body schema is "not capable of sudden change, [... it] represents something more than is physically present, something more than can currently be innervated. The 'more' is the lost part, and it manifests itself perceptually as the phantom" (63–64). Interestingly, in BIID, the "more" that cannot be innervated is the existent limb, a phantom of absence. As with the phantom limb, one's physical sense of reality contrasts with one's subjective experience, albeit with an unclear cause for the apotemnophile. While the phantom limb fills a lack (perhaps, as Simmel suggested, partially due to the abruptness of amputation), in BIID, the "extra" limb does not fill a perceptible lack which, when related to PLS, suggests that it may be filling a psychical lack, a concept I will return to throughout the book. For those with PLS, the phantom is perhaps necessary to the body schema, as it is (usually) essential for walking with a prosthetic leg. "The brain then begins to accept the artificial leg as though it were a part of the body, able to be used for walking" (Sternburg 2002, 34). This concept of the body schema illuminates the way in which bodily movements, the environment, and the mind are interconnected, and it is this interconnection, which is sometimes overlooked in neurological studies, that will be central to the book.

Most hypotheses in the psychodynamic and psychoanalytic fields today propose that the phantom results from various conscious and unconscious feelings and analytical processes, such as denial and mourning. A patient cited in Nortvedt's (2014) case study expresses these thoughts of mourning, explaining, "I feel that it can be compared with a feeling of grief, the kind of grief you can experience after the loss of a dear, old friend or family member" (603). However, some ascribe the phantom to a wish or need, claiming that although it "has been attributed to the non-acceptance or denial of the lost limb [...] more systematic observations have indicated the inadequacy of a wish or need theory" (Marmor 1968, 241–242). Thomas Weiss (1958), on the other hand, believes the illusion to be the embodiment of a narcissistic desire, and Lawrence Kolb links it to a form of denial triggered by repressed desires to self-harm. Though these psychoanalytic themes will reappear, it is Malcolm MacLachlan's work that parallels my own most closely. He studies

18 Why psychoanalysis and literature?

how a prosthesis can affect a person's self-image, and how it may become "psychologically invested into the self, and hence the person's relationship with it may symbolise how they relate to the world" (MacLachlan 2004, 129). Although I do not focus on prostheses, I explore how the mirror-box is a kind of temporary and illusory prosthesis that raises questions concerning how we react to psychosomatic fragmentation and loss.

Mirror therapy

Ramachandran's "mirror-box" treatment (also called a "virtual reality box", "mirror visual feedback" [MVF] and "mirror therapy") began when he realised that when patients saw the phantom move in the mirror, they also felt it move, which worked to dissipate pain, and allowed them to control phantom movements. For the individual tested, "[t]he sustained level of pain reported" write Ortiz-Catalan et al. (2014), "was gradually reduced to complete pain-free periods". Gawande (2008) suggests that the mirror works because it "provides the brain with new visual input

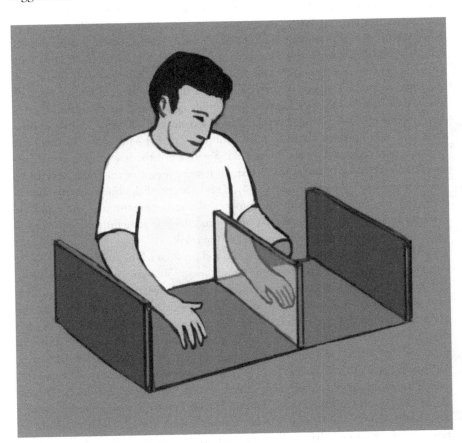

FIGURE 1.2 Mirror-box treatment

however illusory suggesting motion in the absent arm. The brain has to incorporate the new information into its sensory map of what's happening. Therefore, it guesses again, and the pain goes away". This is one of many non-medicinal treatments for PLP. Others include Graded Motor Imagery (GMI), which involves imagining hand movements in order to increase the activity of motor cortical neurons and strengthen the body schema, a method also used for neuropathic pain (Hellman et al. 2015). An alternative form of therapy is the rubber hand illusion, and another involves a cable-driven prosthesis, which may allow users to grasp and manipulate objects. However, many amputated individuals reject these forms of treatment due partially to their inability to alleviate the phantom pain, and to the uncomfortable feeling of an alien body part. Peripheral neural interfaces have also been used to provide proprioceptive and tactile feedback to the phantom limb, which has at times decreased phantom pain. The "Bear Claw" is a sensitised robot hand, created to allow the patient to feel false manipulations of a phantom limb. And finally, CBT is a psychological treatment in which a therapist works with patients to modify their beliefs and alter physical pain. However, CBT is largely unsuccessful at healing

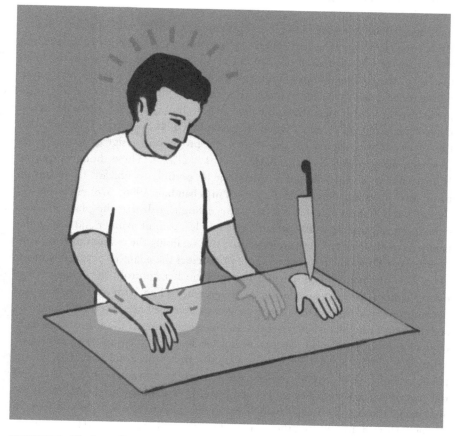

FIGURE 1.3 Illusion of pain

phantom pain. Although, like the mirror-box, it is a way of transforming one's thought processes to help one cope with and accept one's pain, the mirror-box is a physical mechanism that can eradicate pain. It is an object that mediates between the mind and body.

Prostheses have also been used on amputees with phantom limbs, but they do not consistently have healing effects. At times, they even increase pain. Some people, such as Vivian Sobchack (2006), however, have helpfully integrated the prostheses as part of their body schema. She writes that her phantom limb may have adapted to the possibilities provided by the prosthetic, and that "over time, the '*dys*-appeared' phantom may diffuse its self-presenced discretion to become once more the transparent absence and integrity of one's habitual, if self-adjusting, sense of one's lived body" (60). She continues: "[n]ow, having incorporated the prosthetic, I primarily sense my leg as an active, quasi-absent 'part' of my *whole body*" (62). Similar to mirror therapy, the prosthesis allows for a feeling of wholeness. The prosthesis, then, is a physical replacement that allows the individual to walk, while the mirror-box is an illusion of the absent limb that can heal the pain. The mirror illusion is a symbol of the limb that has a physical affect, rather than a physical substitute for it.

Ramachandran developed the idea for the mirror-box by studying "learned paralysis", which occurs when an appendage has been paralysed prior to amputation and causes the same sensation of phantom paralysis post-amputation. He theorised that when the paralysed limb is amputated, the brain continues to tell the felt arm not to move, leaving the individual with a paralysed phantom. The theory is supported by the observation that individuals whose limbs were never paralysed can control phantom movements when first amputated. It appeared, therefore, that the phantom was caused by the brain's pre-programmed signals to the body (Ramachandran and Rogers-Ramachandran 1996, 378). These thoughts spurred Ramachandran to ask whether it "would it be possible to unlearn the phantom paralysis?" (Ramachandran and Rogers-Ramachandran 1996, 378). For this, he thought, the brain would have to begin receiving signals that the phantom does exist and is not frozen, so that it can move in a less painful manner and release the paralysis, an idea that led to the mirror-box. By visualising the existent moving limb superimposed onto the felt phantom, the patient sees the phantom apparently move within her control (though it is not materially in her control); she resurrects her own phantom through an illusion of its presence. The illusion, therefore, can become a physical reality; the mirror image can alter the brain and body. Ramachandran found that after they practised moving their limb in the mirror-box daily over a period of time, most patients' phantoms disappeared completely, and Ramachandran (2011) created what he called the first "successful amputation of a phantom limb" (34). The mirror-box can remove an unwanted limb in PLS, and this can often cause sufferers to feel complete. In the mirror-box, the limb is re-amputated through an image, which erases the phantom and eases the pain of feeling fractured. In this way, the idea of wholeness is challenged, and this paradoxical relationship is important to explore in order to understand more about the issues involved in PLS and BIID, as it also foregrounds a paradoxical relationship with unity.

Some researchers, however, remain sceptical. Tamar Makin associates the treatment with the placebo effect, writing: "I don't believe in magic" (Makin qtd. in Perur 2014). However, phantom limb sufferer Stephen Sumner reported that researchers, doctors and therapists have told him, "'[w]ell, it's not scientific'—simply because mirror therapy looks too simple" (Perur 2014). But, he writes, "I am an above-knee amp. I cured myself with a mirror [… and] I challenge someone in a white lab coat who has never been anywhere where it hurts to tell me otherwise" (Perur 2014). In addition, Stephen highlights the centrality of psychosomatics in the treatment. He states of the physical component, that "[i]t's not in the head, it's in the limb", and of the psychical, "when I finally tried mirror therapy on myself […] it almost had to work. I mean, I needed something" (Perur 2014). Although many researchers are dubious and unsure as to how the mechanism works, it can work, and cannot be confined either to the psyche or soma; it is psychosomatic.

In another case reported in an article in *The New Yorker* entitled "The Itch", Atul Gawande (2008) writes about his experience with a patient who had a tumour removed from his spinal cord, which left him with incurable PLP. He tried various different medications and electrical-stimulation therapy, to no avail, until finally, mirror therapy worked. "For the first time in eleven years, he felt his left hand 'snap' back to normal size. He felt the burning pain in his arm diminish." The patient tells Gawande, "I've never had anything like this before […]. It's my magic mirror". This drug/surgery-free treatment opens possibilities for potential treatments based on the "careful manipulation" of individuals' perceptions (Gawande 2008). It also reveals the flexibility of the mind and provides insight into alternative forms of pain relief. Ramachandran (2011) explains that although benefits are still being discovered, he finds the mirror treatment intriguing because it shows that new pathways can emerge in the adult brain. "The brain", he writes, "is an extraordinarily plastic biological system that is in a state of dynamic equilibrium with the external world" (37). The mirror-box, then, demonstrates the importance of the way in which images and the material world are integral to one's psychosomatic constitution, and this is one of the central concerns of this book. I ask: how do physical and psychical images of self and interactions with the world relate to bodily pain and feelings of loss, and what can the relationship between BIID and PLS convey?

To clarify, then, individuals with BIID and PLS both feel as though they have an extraneous limb that causes them pain. In both syndromes, moreover, individuals strive for a sense of completion through the idea of a removal: they usually believe that their pain will be eradicated when the felt limb is amputated. There is, therefore, a paradoxical drive to fill through removal, a fetishistic disavowal in which both BIID and PLS sufferers know that there is no bodily wholeness, and yet feel that there is. However, while those with BIID want a physical wound, those with PLS have one. It is the mirror-box that is often successful for those with phantom limbs, and although those with BIID often state that they feel better after amputation, the results can be dangerous and are inconclusive. As neither syndrome is completely understood, I am concerned with what we can learn through a theoretical endeavour, and with what the mirror illusion can reveal about how we psychosomatically adapt to rupture. Since in psychoanalysis, "the body tells a story which cannot otherwise be told [... and] the somatic symptom, like all symptoms, 'has a psychical significance, a meaning'" (Yarom 2005, 54), psychoanalysis is a starting point for this exploration.

The hysterical body

Although psychoanalysis is often considered to be a theoretical discipline, it began with the body, with Freud's study of hysteria. Currently, hysteria is regarded as "the designation for [...] a vast, shifting set of behaviours and symptoms limps, paralyses, seizures, coughs, headaches, speech disturbances, depression, insomnia, exhaustion, eating disorders" (Showalter 1997, 14). It was originally considered a medical condition particular to women, caused by bodily disturbances of the uterus. Freud (and before him, Charcot and Breuer) found that the cause of hysteria did not reside in the body, but in the mind. Something arises, he suggests, which is refused access to the mind and becomes inscribed onto the body; hysteria is "a neurosis caused by repression, conflicted sexuality, and fantasy" (Showalter 1997, 38). Freud's theory was spurred by his interest in the work of Jean-Martin Charcot, who suggested that the symptoms of hysteria result from a traumatic accident. According to Charcot, when his patients were in a hypnotic state he could remove their hysterical symptoms, thereby leading him "to the very border between neurology and psychology. The preliminary condition for the successful execution of any movement is, he argues, 'the production of an image, or of a mental representation'" (Fletcher 2013, 21). For Charcot, bodily symptoms were not only physical, they were connected to the mind and imagination, a concept central to my argument that PLS and BIID are not only biomedical phenomena. Freud and Breuer proposed a new theory about the origin of hysteria, which hinges upon the concept of conversion: that bodily symptoms convey disturbances in the mind.

Hysterical symptoms might contain "*symbolic* meaning: they express repressed ideas through the medium of the body" (Laplanche and Pontalis 1996, 90). These ideas have been repressed because, Freud suggests, unbearable traumatic experiences have been barred from the conscious mind and transformed into somatic symptoms. The body is the carrier for a psychical wound, "the memory of the trauma acts like a foreign body which long after its entry must continue to be regarded as an agent that is still at work" (Freud 1962, 6). The trauma itself cannot be remembered, but appears in different forms, meaning that it is the memory of the trauma which invades the patient's body. In this way, the symptom is both physical and mental; it is located in the body and psyche simultaneously. The relationship between conversion and the phantom limb is clear: the phantom limb can be seen as the memory of a traumatic loss, whether sudden, gradual, or congenital, that has been transformed into a foreign bodily feeling. However, while in hysteria the traumatic experience cannot be known, the phantom limb begins with a physical and perceptible wound. Moreover, the symptoms are clearly psychosomatic. They are felt but cannot be seen. BIID parallels hysteria more closely in that its origins are unknown, and in this way, it resembles a neurosis. However, unlike hysteria, in BIID the symptom does not organically arise on the body. Though the body feels broken, it functions "normally". Moreover, those with the syndrome desire a physical wound that is reflective of what the hysteric may want to remove.

For Freud, somatic symptoms can ostensibly be remedied through the linguistic exchange that takes place in analysis. Here, bodily symptoms carry unconscious symbolic meanings that, when articulated and analysed, can be brought towards conscious thought. "Understanding the idea behind the feelings", writes Juliet Mitchell (2001), "can bring the conversion symptom to an end" (206). The mirror-box, I contend, parallels the psychoanalytic process of symbolising bodily symptoms through a linguistic exchange, because it involves a process of healing through a symbol of the phantom limb. It allows a subjective feeling to be consciously visualised. I examine the way in which the mirror-box is a type of symbol that, paralleling language, can helpfully link subjective to objective experiences. I am interested in how the image of a phantom limb has a healing affect, and how this is related to language. It is important to survey different conceptions of symbolism to understand what kind of symbol this is and how it works.

Symbolism

Ernest Jones addresses the difficulties involved in defining symbolism, noting that the term "has been used to denote very many different things, some of them quite unconnected with one another" (Jones 1961, 88). One argument, however, is that symbols can be traced back to "the bodily self" (Jones 1961, 116) and are therefore useful in interpreting physical expression. Symbolism is valuable because it may helpfully allow individuals to express the thing that has been repressed. Since both BIID and the phantom limb involve an inexplicable feeling, I suggest that finding ways to symbolise the two disorders can provide new understandings of sufferers' experiences. To clarify, I do not consider the phantom limb and BIID as symbols; rather, they are bodily conditions that illuminate notions of somatic and psychical fragmentation when explored through symbolic media. Language and the mirror-box are two forms of symbolisation that can convey more about the disorders. For this exploration, I focus on object relations theory, because it foregrounds the kind of symbol that is structurally reflective of language and the mirror-box, as it involves a simultaneous absence and presence, and is thought to connect subjective and objective senses of self.

Although object relations theorists have many different conceptions of symbolism, Melanie Klein "described the capacity to symbolise unconscious frightening, sadistic aggressive feelings for the object as an important step in ego development"

(Auchincloss and Samberg 2012, 256). Hanna Segal follows Klein's work, theorising that "the word 'symbol' comes from the Greek term for throwing together, bringing together, integrating" (Klein 1946, 397), and, as BIID and PLS foreground psychosomatic dissonance, I will suggest that a symbol can have the effect of appeasing psychosomatic pain. Winnicott proposes that a type of material object that also carries a symbolic meaning is called a transitional object, which can helpfully bridge subjective feelings to an objective environment, a concept of symbolism that most closely correlates with the one I use throughout this book, and which acts as a template. These objects can be linguistic; they are, he writes, "symbolical of some part-object, such as the breast. Nevertheless, the point of it is not its symbolic value so much as its actuality" (Winnicott 1971, 8). In this way, the symbol does not only stand for something, it is "actual". It is both illusory and concrete, and thus functions in the same way as language and the mirror-box. These tools can, like the transitional object, lead to a feeling of psychosomatic integration, a topic I shall briefly survey.

Psychosomatics

According to Winnicott (1989), there have been "failures to classify psycho-somatic disorders" along with an "inability to state a theory, a unified theory of this illness group" (111). However, Joyce McDougall (1989) describes the central feature of psychosomatics: "we all tend to somatise at those moments when inner or outer circumstances overwhelm our habitual psychological ways of coping" (3). If something intrudes upon the psyche, the body reacts. She suggests that what underlies the interconnection between the body, mind and communication is that "[s]ince babies cannot yet use the words with which to think, they respond to emotional pain only psychosomatically" (9). It is the body that speaks, a process that extends in later life to psychosomatic illnesses in which the body expresses what cannot be thoroughly explained. As McDougall writes, "the body has a language of its own" (12), and it is my intention to open a dialogue about what the body in PLS and apotemnophilia reveals. Since both conditions demonstrate problems with psychosomatic fracture, I will focus on theories of fragmentation and splitting, such as those explored in the Paris School of Psychosomatics.

The "Paris School of Psychosomatics highlights a split between the mind and the body" (Birksted-Breen and Flanders 2010, 438).[10] Their theories, therefore, offer ways of thinking about the mind/body dissonance involved in BIID and PLS. Several members of the Paris School are concerned with bringing theoretical analyses back towards the bodily experience, and with discovering what the body reveals about the psyche. Dana Birksted-Breen writes that in this kind of French psychoanalysis, "somatic illness was discovered to be the consequence of a failure to *mentalise* experience, the body offering up an organ to bind disintegration, a progressive disorganisation which was seen as the product of an overwhelmed and disabled psyche" (Birksted-Breen and Flanders 2010, 35). Although this echoes Freudian theory, one central difference is that the focus here is on bodily fragmentation. French psychosomatics will be useful in opening a dialogue about the somatic fracture central to both conditions, and in particular, the bodily destruction involved in BIID.

I will also focus on Winnicott's thoughts on the mind/body relationship, because they allow for a more thorough understanding of how symbolic objects play a role in linguistic and non-linguistic communication and psychosomatic discord. For Winnicott (1989), psychosomatics involves a split "that separates off physical care from intellectual understanding; more important, it separates psyche-care from soma-care" (105). My discussion of Winnicott will focus on the impact of the carer's role in forming this split, and in how symbolic objects are involved in the healing process. The symbolic object can be helpful to patients with psychosomatic illnesses, he suggests, because, although they may experience a split, they are "in touch with the possibility of psychosomatic unity" (114). Indeed, this simultaneous split and drive towards unity echoes the experiences of those with PLS and BIID, as BIID sufferers believe that amputation will result in a feeling of completeness, and phantom limbs fill a physical incompleteness with a sense of unity.

This paradoxical relationship with fragmentation and completion parallels Freud's concept of a fetish, and to understand more about this, we must return to the castration complex. Freud (1955) writes that "in so far as one can speak of determining causes which lead to the *acquisition* of neuroses, their aetiology is to be looked for in *sexual* factors" (257), which can be traced back to the Oedipus complex. In the Oedipus complex, the child desires the parent of the opposite sex, and in reaction to these desires, suffers from castration anxiety. However, as noted earlier, this concept is problematic, partially because it is based upon the false assertion that females are (symbolically) lacking or un-whole. In this way, the underlying problem with the castration complex parallels BIID itself, as BIID involves a discomfiture with a whole body, which is believed to be ruptured. In both circumstances, therefore, one's conception of unity is located in the mind. Through the mirror-box, an illusory object can appease the feeling of un-wholeness in PLS, which echoes Freud's notion of the fetish, which I shall now discuss.

BIID, I have suggested, echoes Freud's concept of a neurosis because it seems that a psychological wound is felt on the body, but it also differs from it, in that in BIID there is no physical wound. The phantom limb, I suggest, resembles psychosis more closely, because the psychotic rejects a "present reality and replac[es] it with a delusion that contains a grain of truth from some reaction to a past historical 'event'" (Mitchell 2000, 263). And the phantom can be considered a partial delusion based upon the idea of a once present limb (aside from congenital phantoms). However, "psychoses", continues Mitchell, "tend to express themselves, among other ways, in delusions and hallucinations which are fully believed in" (Mitchell 2000, 263). The difference between the phantom limb and psychosis can be found in the latter part of this statement: delusions in psychosis are fully believed in, while individuals with phantom limbs know that the phantom is not objectively "real". In this way, the phantom limb can be more closely aligned with a fetish, particularly when relating the phantom limb to the male genitals.

26 Why psychoanalysis and literature?

> For Freud, a fetish is a substitute made by a child for his mother's missing penis. The fetish alleviates a son's castration anxiety by restoring [*sic*] the mother's penis. The boy thereby preserves the delusion that his mother has a penis.
>
> *(Segal 2003, 159)*

In relation to this, as Adam Phillips (2010) writes, the phantom limb

> is a loss at once acknowledged and invisible [...]. Like Freud's account of fetishism in which "only one current" in a person's life had not recognised the disturbing fact of there being two sexes, while "another current took full account of the fact", the two states of mind "exis[t] side by side".
>
> *(105)*

Indeed, the phantom limb involves a simultaneous disavowal and acknowledgement of a bodily loss, and similarly, in BIID, sufferers acknowledge that their limb is present, and additionally believe that it is (subjectively) absent.

In a different way, the mirror-box echoes Freud's notion of the fetish, as it involves a loss that is at once acknowledged and denied. It both preserves the illusion that the phantom limb is part of the amputee's body, and simultaneously demonstrates that it is absent. The mirror illusion allows two states of mind to exist side by side; however, unlike the fetish and the phantom limb, the mirror image, like the psychoanalytic exchange, can enable a reparative process. I will argue, therefore, that mirror therapy is a metaphor for and embodiment of psychoanalytic transference, where a reparative process takes place through an illusion experienced simultaneously with a material reality. While the analyst and the room exist, the memories and actions that take place in transference are distortions and re-enactments. Mirror therapy, like transference, "creates an intermediate region between illness and real life through which the transition from one to the other is made" (Freud 1958, 155), through language, illusion, or, as Peter Brooks calls it, fiction.

Brooks (1987) writes that psychoanalytic transference

> succeeds in making the past and its scenarios of desire live again through signs with such vivid reality that the reconstructions [...] achieve the *effect* of the real [...]. [T]hey rewrite its present discourse. Disciplined and mastered, the transference ushers us forth into a changed reality. And such is no doubt the intention of any literary text.
>
> *(345)*

Transference, like certain literary texts, may allow the individual to alter the way in which the past is embodied by (re)enacting it through signs. Similarly, in mirror therapy, a sign of the phantom reconstructs the absent limb, thereby altering the amputee's felt reality to achieve the effect of the real. "The transference", writes Brooks (1992), actualises the past in symbolic form so that it can be repeated, replayed, worked through to another outcome. The result is, in the ideal case, to bring us back to actuality, that is, to a revised version of our stories.

(344)

The mirror-box acts as a metaphor for transference and certain types of literature in this way, as it actualises the past (the absent limb) in symbolic form and repeats the movement of the existent limb, which enables a revised version of the phantom, a changed sense of reality.

In both psychoanalysis and literature, as Peter Brooks (1994) suggests,

> change is produced [...]. [T]he textual reader, like the psychoanalytic patient, finds himself modified by the work of interpretation and construction, by the transferential dynamics to which he has submitted himself. In the movement between text and reader, the tale told makes a difference.

(Brooks 1994, 72)

In this way, literary texts and psychoanalysis share an important relationship: they may create a certain kind of self-modification through a symbolic exchange. And similarly, the mirror-box modifies the amputee's sense of self through a symbol of her phantom limb. Thus, the mirror-box, literature, and psychoanalysis involve a symbolic exchange that can alter feelings of psychosomatic rupture. In order to unpack these links between literature, psychoanalysis, and trauma, I turn to the field of trauma studies.

Trauma studies

Freud argued that traumatic experiences are delayed and distorted forms of an occurrence that was too powerful to comprehend at the time. An incident, he found, might trigger the memory of the "original" trauma: as he writes, "a memory is repressed which has only become a trauma by *deferred action*" (Freud 1966, 356). Again, Freud's account indicates that the effects of a trauma cannot be experienced directly, but only belatedly. This theory is foundational to trauma studies, a field of study established in the mid-1990s and concerned with the idea of trauma as an un-representable event. Trauma theorists approach the concept through psychoanalysis and poststructuralist thought, suggesting that the inability to represent trauma is connected to the inadequacy of language to express trauma. The field was popularised by Cathy Caruth's analysis of trauma as a crisis of representation.[11]

Drawing upon Caruth's project, Shoshana Felman and Dori Laub (1991) also examine how gaps in literary and fictional works reveal what cannot be known about history. They trace the relationship between "literature and testimony, between the writer and the witness" (xiii), to examine the way in which literature contains and bears witness to unknown trauma. Following Caruth, Felman and

Laub argue that the postmodern crisis of representation is linked to the inability to witness a trauma. Since trauma cannot be represented, and since text cannot represent it, the text itself becomes traumatic. While Felman and Laub's views of trauma differ from Caruth's, due to their interest in "the therapeutic sense of working-through trauma, as opposed to its endless repetitions" (Crownshaw 2010, 10), they also share similarities, such as their interest in the connection between trauma and psychoanalysis, and postmodern literature's concern with the difficulty of linguistic representation. All three theorists also share the view that trauma can be registered through linguistic gaps.

However, their theories have been critiqued because there is a certain generalisation in a poststructuralist approach to the notion of the "crisis" of language, as it devalues individuals who have experienced real historical trauma. Although this poststructuralist concept of trauma that language is unable to capture reality and subjectivity is important to this book, I do not conflate postmodernism with traumatic experiences. I do not suggest that BIID and PLS can be understood completely, or that psychoanalysis, fiction, and literature can allow a reader to feel or comprehend sufferers' individual experiences. I discuss the syndromes in relation to these theories in order to open up new ways of thinking about them, and about the struggle with fragmentation and unity. Some critics, such as Ruth Leys and Amy Hungerford, have argued that if, as Caruth suggests, traumas can be felt through gaps in language, this means first, that the text is synonymous with the author, and second, that the reader is experiencing the same trauma that was felt by the original victim, problematically undermining the victim's trauma. In *Trauma: A Genealogy* (2000), Leys contends that Caruth's account of trauma exemplifies a postmodern approach that precludes representation. In Caruth's version, in which the trauma is registered as a blank, the witness is "devoid of potential interpretive agency and has become the mere carrier of trauma" (Leys 2000, 6).

In *The Holocaust of Texts* (2003), Hungerford also criticises movements in trauma theory that collapse actual and fictional individuals, literature and personal traumatic experience. Both Felman and Caruth, Hungerford writes, imagine "texts as traumatic experience itself, thus transmissible from person to person through reading" (20). Here, the importance of embodiment is neglected, "when embodiment is exactly what situates us in history and makes us vulnerable to oppression" (Hungerford 2003, 21). If literature about the Holocaust is shaped through a postmodern focus on the crisis of representation and its relationship to trauma, she argues, the particularity of people, events and experiences is overlooked. I attend to this problem of generalisation by focusing on specific bodily traumas. While I read these particular experiences of trauma though a theoretical discussion about fragmentation, I am careful not to generalise, as I do not suggest that the texts I discuss are traumatic in themselves or can transmit traumatic experiences. I explore thoughts about physical fracture and wholeness through postmodern theory to open a discussion about BIID and PLS. In this discussion, I am also interested in how mirror therapy illuminates what Dominick LaCapra calls a "working-through" trauma.

Contrary to Felman and Laub, LaCapra asks if the collapse of persons and text can be avoided through a particular kind of writing and thinking about the Holocaust. He is concerned with discovering ways in which to write about the past productively, by paying attention to the interactions between writer and reader, theory and history, individual and collective. He states,

> [o]ne crucial undertaking for postmodern and poststructural approaches may [...] be to address the issue of specificity as a complex mediation between the particular and the general. Such an undertaking may further an understanding of how to attempt to work through problems without either bypassing their traumatising potential or endlessly and compulsively repeating it.
> (LaCapra 1994, 223)

To approach this, LaCapra examines how the relationship between history and theory is integral to understanding and representing the Holocaust. Though this cannot be avoided entirely, it can be resisted, he explains, by linking history and theory to social concerns, partially through a theoretical language that relates the text to the reader instead of distancing it from them.

Psychoanalytic theory is particularly helpful here, because it is concerned with studying relationships between individual and society, the present, and the past. LaCapra (1994) explains: "I maintain that what Freud termed 'working-through' has received insufficient attention in post-Freudian analysis, and I stress the importance of working through problems in a critical manner" (xii). Although in his analyses LaCapra is influenced by postmodern thought, he wonders if it can be used without trying to exceed linguistic binaries with a "generalised conceptual blur" (11). Psychoanalysis, for him, can enable a more productive forward movement. I do not follow LaCapra in specifically analysing the relationship between the present and past or exploring history, and although the Holocaust underpins the analysis of George Perec's *W or The Memory of Childhood* (1989 [1975]),[12] I do not discuss it specifically or historically. I examine how the author-narrator's psychosomatic experience of trauma can be "worked through" within the text. In so doing, I aim to discover more about how poststructuralist theory can help us to more thoroughly understand BIID and PLS. In this way, I move away from a "generalised conceptual blur" by attending to specific bodily syndromes, and individuals' experiences with these syndromes.

Postmodernism

To return to the individual's statement in *Whole* that for him, BIID involves an

> idea that actually by making something less, you make people more complete, which is the complete opposite to most amputees who perhaps have accidents or disease. By taking that limb away from them they feel less complete. But for us, it's the other way around. By taking it off you make us more complete.

What this man seems to be saying is that those with BIID oppose the standard concept of normality: while others feel whole with four limbs and incomplete with three, those with BIID only feel complete with three limbs. They are, in this sense, aware of, interested in, and (to a degree) accepting of their unconventionality, while still experiencing the pain involved. Postmodernism and, connected to this, poststructuralism (which is interested in the absence of meaning and uncertainty of questions) parallels this interest in unconventionality. As Catherine Belsey (2002) puts it, poststructuralism "offers a controversial account of our place in the world, which competes with conventional explanations" (6). Some poststructuralist and postmodern literature is, moreover, concerned with how language and the body are interrelated. It is thus important to investigate postmodern theory concerning corporeal fracture, in relation to BIID and PLS. I examine the way that postmodern theorists write about the fractured body, individual, and text, and how this can help us think about the experiences of those with BIID and PLS.

Alphonso Lingis (1994) is interested in how the body and theory are interlinked, and he explores the ways in which contemporary thinkers discuss the body through physiology, social technology, psychoanalysis, and ethical theory. Within a phenomenological framework, he examines how bodily perception is linked to culture, identity, and philosophy. Lingis asks that if a tool is an extension of one's body, "[i]s it not also an exteriorization of that organ a separating from our body of its own organ?" (ix). Although his thoughts about technological organs seem particularly pertinent to prostheses and amputation, I do not focus on this relationship. I am more interested in the mirror-box as an illusory extension of the body.

Ihab Hassan's exploration of the postmodern condition focuses on the limits of language and literature, including what lies beyond postmodernism, and addresses the question, "what kind of self, in its society, is adequate to our postmodern world, a world caught between fragments and wholes, terror and totalitarianism of every kind?" (Hassan 1987, xiv). Integral to postmodern thought, in Hassan's account, is the fact that we cannot choose between binaries, but must instead "reopen [...] terms to constant negotiations" (Hassan 1987, xvii), which we must approach by attending to linguistic silences. It is this preoccupation with silence that interests me, and it is discussed at length in *The Dismemberment of Orpheus* (1971). Hassan defines silence as the disruption of language and examines the work of modernists who abandon "traditional elements of fiction such as character, plot, metaphor and meaning" (Woods 1999, 52). He uses the Greek myth of Orpheus as the starting point for his discussion, because Orpheus's dismemberment anticipates the postmodern rupture of linguistic meaning. When Orpheus's broken body continues to sing, explains Hassan (1971), it holds "a contradiction between the dumb unity of nature and the multiple voice of consciousness that the song itself longs to overcome" (6). Orpheus allegorises the human conflict between the desire to destroy and the search for unity and meaning, because he is simultaneously torn and vocal, he expresses his fragmentation. And, as I discuss later through analysis of Blanchot's essay "Orpheus's Gaze" (1982), BIID and PLS both raise questions about the paradoxical search for unity through rupture.

Hassan is also interested in the topic of schizophrenia, suggesting that, if schizophrenics speak symbolically rather than logically, Orpheus's condition also reflects that of the schizophrenic. He theorises that linguistic discussion is to be uprooted by resisting discourse, and so we must consider the schizophrenic mind-set. He writes: "if the fall of human consciousness is into language, then redemption lies in puns and metaphor, holy derangement, the re-sexualisation of speech, babble or silence" (Hassan 1971, 16). For Hassan, literary fragmentation and non-coherence is integral to change. This idea of listening to a unique perspective from those concerned with psychosomatic fracture underlies this book. BIID and PLS provide insight into the "non-rational". These conditions resist complete linguistic explanation, so it is important to explore theories concerned with the silences within language and with physical expression. In developing these ideas, I focus on the work of Maurice Blanchot, because, as Hassan (1971) writes, "Blanchot understands the authority of the negative; he dwells constantly on the limits, the impossibility of literature" (19). I am not alone in drawing links between phantom limbs and postmodern thought, as the following analysis of literary limbs demonstrates.

Literary limbs

In his article "Archive Trauma" (1998), Herman Rapaport argues that Derrida's "*The Post Card* may well be *Archive Fever's* phantom limb, something essential that has been cut off and that haunts the text" (69). Rapaport proposes that if we read Derrida's writings on archives while keeping the "phantom limb in mind, archives occur at that moment when there is a structural breakdown in memory" (Rapaport 1998, 69). Put another way, archives, like the phantom limb, are products of trauma. Rappaport suggests that archives, for Derrida, are thereby fragmented, bordering on a madness that, like the phantom limb, cannot be explained: "[i]t is an insanity that defies anything like an essentialist (but also constructivist) explanation" (Rapaport 1998, 80). While intriguing, Rapaport's reading is somewhat problematic because there is a certain conflation between phantom limbs, archives and texts. By suggesting that "*The Post Card* may well be *Archive Fever's* phantom limb", and that *Archive Fever* has "phantom textual limbs", Rapaport suggests that texts are not analogous to, but synonymous with, phantom limbs. Although a text may act as a metaphor for a phantom limb, the syndrome is a specific bodily problem. While I make links between texts and limbs, I do not suggest that the work itself is a phantom limb, or the limb a text. I aim to explore the way in which the absences and histories behind certain literary works relate to the semi-presence and absence that is the phantom limb. In this way, the phantom limb is not only a metaphor for certain texts, but also an experience that relates to a certain kind of interaction with language.

James Krasner allegorises PLS through literary examples in his article "Doubtful Arms and Phantom Limbs: Literary Portrayals of Embodied Grief" (2004). Krasner examines the way grief is represented through a "framework of tangibility" (Krasner 2004, 220) in relation to embodied grief. He asks how literature can bring about "discomfort by allowing us to participate in the illusions of physical presence to which the grieving are prone, placing us in the midst of an irritatingly and cripplingly present grief" (Krasner 2004, 220). Literature produces something similar to what is conveyed through the phantom limb syndrome: a feeling of bodily discomfort that stems from grieving a loss. Krasner investigates how grief can develop into a variety of bodily actions, by tracing various theories of embodiment including those found in the works of Merleau-Ponty, Derrida, and Freud. Krasner develops the concept of embodied grief through analysis of Virginia Woolf's *To the Lighthouse* (1927), in which the widower Mr Ramsay reaches out for a brief moment, expecting to find his wife's body. Like the phantom limb sufferer, the protagonist does not feel the body, but "the 'place' where that body belongs" (Krasner 2004, 226). Here, "[l]iterary portrayals of grief that emphasise embodiment present the bereaved with compromised bodies, [... failing] to adjust to the physical postures and environments their losses have left to them" (Krasner 2004, 226). Krasner's article is helpful in foregrounding a more general view of how an environmentally imposed loss can affect physical existence. However, while Krasner focuses on the loss of loved ones, I do not explicitly discuss grief. I am concerned with the splits between fragmentation and wholeness, and the mind and body, which Elizabeth Grosz discusses in *Volatile Bodies: Toward a Corporeal Feminism* (1994).

Grosz weaves the phantom limb example into a discussion of how the body incorporates its material surroundings. The phenomenon, she writes, "attests to the more or less tenacious cohesion of the imaginary anatomy or body schema" (41), which is also apparent in hysteria, hypochondria and sexuality. She emphasises the fact that the "biological body, if it exists at all, exists for the subject only through the mediation of an image or series of (social/cultural) images of the body and its capacity for movement and action" (Grosz 1994, 41). The phantom limb, in her account, raises questions about the continual transformation of the body image. She also points out the contrast between body image and the lived body, in experiences such as sicknesses, in adolescence, within gender roles, and in relation to neurosis, psychosis, and hypochondria. Grosz discusses the phantom limb and castration, asking whether "women have a phantom phallus?" and whether "women experience the castration complex as a bodily amputation as well as a psychosocial constraint? If so, is there, somewhere in woman's psyche, a representation of the phallus she has lost?" (73). Like Grosz, I ask how the phantom limb disorder exemplifies a continual transformation in body identity and how the body exists through the medium of images. Since according to Grosz, the phantom limb demonstrates that the biological body exists for the subject only through the mediation of an image, I ask what this means for those with BIID, who are often tortured by the fact that their biological body does not match their image of self? I am interested in what mirror therapy conveys about how we cope with this rupture in "imaginary anatomy", in how images and language affect one's sense of physical wholeness.

David Evans also examines the connection between language and BIID in "CUT! ... Flannery O'Connor's Apotemnophiliac Allegories" (2009). Evans's article considers how BIID may facilitate an interpretation of imperfect bodies in

Flannery O'Connor's writing, and hinges upon the question as to how BIID elucidates O'Connor's portrayal of imperfect bodies. He uses the phenomenon to examine the content and form of O'Connor's fiction, stating that "[t]he link between O'Connor's narratives and apotemnophiles' bodies is that they can both be considered texts that demand interpretation and in so doing put in question our reflexive valorisation of wholeness, our default preference for faultlessness" (Evans 2009, 309). Lastly, a parallel is drawn between incompleteness in BIID and the gap between a sign and its meaning, which is a concept central to modern, postmodern and poststructuralist thought. This notion of an irresolvable gap between sign and meaning and its relationship to apotemnophilia also underpins my discussions of literary theory, literary works and psychoanalysis. However, while Evans explores the theme through the specific example of amputated individuals in O'Connor's work, I take a psychoanalytic perspective, and offer a more detailed investigation of how bodily composition is related to the way in which certain fictional works are composed and embodied.

In *Prosthesis* (1995), David Wills works from memories of his father's phantom limb pain. The question he asks in relation to this is how nature relies on artifice, which he approaches by overlapping his own memories with a variety of fiction, art, psychoanalysis, film, and literary theory. He aims to show that "prosthesis is concerned as much with the practice of writing as with the writing of theory. The enfolding of one within the other, their cutting and pasting, simply reinforces the fact that the two are resolutely coextensive" (Wills 1995, 28). Writing, for Wills (1995), is prosthetic because it is artificial and fragmented. A prosthetic leg, he explains, is made of some alloy, and yet it is still called a wooden leg, which demonstrates that

> [t]he wooden leg is not really wooden. Language has already taken leave of reality, the literal taken leave of itself. By the same logic, that of the stand-in or supplement, which is that of language itself, a language that has always already taken leave of itself, by that same logic it is probably not a leg either.
> (26)

Wills suggests that language replaces the thing, referencing the postmodern crisis of representation. The wooden leg is not a leg to begin with. And even if the prosthesis were a leg, he explains, saying this would not make it so. For Wills, therefore, just as the prosthesis supplants the leg, language is always at a remove from what it represents.

Although I refer to the notion of an irresolvable gap between signified and signifier, I do not suggest that writing and a limb (phantom or prosthetic) are coextensive, because an amputation is a corporeal condition. I am interested in the way that the phantom can be undone by a kind of illusory prosthesis the mirror image and it is this image that serves as a metaphor for language. However, I do not contend, as Willis states above, that language has taken leave of reality, but rather, that language is undifferentiated from "reality", that the mirror limb is a symbol reflective of language that can alter pain. For me, then, the linguistic and somatic are interrelated, as Segal writes, texts "invoke the movement of eye or hand towards something one ought to be able to caress" (2009, 120). Texts and language, in this way, can have physical effects. I argue that analysing certain kinds of texts that are concerned with somatic and linguistic fragmentation can thereby illuminate the way in which the body is conceived of in BIID and PLS. To approach this, I will combine four types of material: individuals' descriptions of BIID and PLS, psychoanalysis, literary theory, and fictional works.[13]

To begin, the next chapter takes two individuals, one with BIID and one with a phantom limb (who uses mirror therapy), investigates their experiences of psychosomatic discord, and surveys how these kinds of experiences will be discussed throughout the book. The mirror treatment prompts questions about how we are formed through images and symbols, which I address in Chapter 3 by unpacking the relationship between psychoanalysis and literature. This opens a dialogue about the reparative possibilities of language, which is elaborated through a discussion of two psychoanalysts: André Green and Marilia Aisenstein. Their interest in tracing split-off parts of the self (evident in BIID and PLS) through gaps in speech is developed in Chapter 5, through the works of Jacques Lacan and Maurice Blanchot, and in Chapter 6, through the example of Powell and Pressburger's *The Red Shoes* (1948). Questions are raised here about the physical impact of images and symbols in relation to fiction, literature, and the mirror-box. Chapter 7 explores how images and symbols can be helpful in integrating a traumatic split through D.W. Winnicott's theories of "breakdown" and the "transitional object", which are developed in Chapter 8 through Quentin Tarantino's film *Death Proof* (2007). The closing discussion about repair is then exemplified in Chapter 9 and 10 through the example of Georges Perec's semi-autobiography *W or The Memory of Childhood* to demonstrate how a painful drive towards wholeness, as reflected in BIID and PLS, may be altered through a symbolic reworking.

Notes

1. According to Paul Schilder (1950), a body schema is "the immediate experience that there is a unity of the body [...] it] is the tri-dimensional image everybody has about himself" (11). In the case of BIID, there is a loss of unity in one's body schema.
2. Though not every individual with BIID or PLS can be considered a sufferer, I use this word to differentiate those who have the conditions from those who do not.
3. The debate as to whether the syndrome is considered to be a psychosis also acts as a backdrop to this study. For some psychologists, such as Bayne and Levy, First, Schlozman and Blom, apotemnophilia poses a conundrum because the sufferers' beliefs differ from "normality" and "reality". However, unlike in psychosis, patients do not hallucinate: they acknowledge their intact limb.
4. From a psychoanalytic point of view, Thomas Ogden (1989) suggests that an anorexic person may have an "unconscious fear that he does not know what he desires" (214); there is no exact goal. Though this is to some extent true of those with BIID, the majority of sufferers believe that they know precisely what they want: the removal of a particular limb. Lemma (2010) hypothesizes that the body may "have to be denied, or visibly modified to create an experience of ownership of the body" (94). Again, this

parallels BIID in that perhaps, the desire to self-amputate is related to an experience of controlling and owning one's own body, a concept I will develop, predominantly through the thoughts of Winnicott. Winnicott believes that anorexia is "an illness of [the patient's] *mind*" (1989, 108), which brings us to one key factor in the similarity here: BIID involves a problem of the mind, and thus, to discover more about BIID, we must discover more about how the mind is involved in the disorder. As Sebastian Schmidt (2010), a BIID sufferer, explains, it is "not about the functionality of the limb but about the 'feeling' of having or not having it" (80).

5 For more on current discussions regarding the conceptual vocabularies for transgender studies, see Robert Phillip's article "Abjection", in *Transgender Studies Quarterly*, vol. 1, nos 1–2, pp. 19–21.

6 The castration complex is a Freudian notion that individuals are driven by an anxiety that begins in childhood: for men, that their genitals will be castrated, and for women, that they are born with a physical lack (of the male organ) and have "penis envy". The girl assumes "that at some early date she had possessed an equally large organ and had then lost it by castration [...], whereas the boy fears the possibility of its occurrence" (Freud 1961, 665). The castration complex is problematic, as it is founded upon a concept that women are structured through a loss. Moreover, as Karen Horney states, it "treats the penis, as, in many ways, the fulcrum of human identification, for males and females alike" (Horney qtd. in Hook 2007, 49). Horney also links the castration complex to her concept of womb envy (the male desires a womb), which provides a different perspective on BIID. While the BIID drive to rid oneself of a limb (particularly in males who are predominant among those who have BIID) might be paired with a desire to control castration, it also might be paired with the desire for female genitals, or the womb. From this perspective, in other words, a male might unconsciously wish to amputate a limb to resemble the female body, which can bear children. The parallels between the castration complex and BIID will be further developed.

7 For more on this differentiation see *The Psychology of Gender* (1993) by Alice H. Eagly, *Different but Equal* (2001) by Kay E. Payne, *Biology at Work* (2002) by Kingsley R. Browne, or *Language and Gender* (2003) by Penelope Eckert and Sally McConnell-Ginet.

8 Furthermore, as Alicia Johnson points out, those who have self-amputated often report that they feel phantom limbs. Johnson explains: "if the limb could not be felt at all, as Ramachandran suggests, subjects would not feel a phantom limb or want to replace it with prosthesis post-amputation" (13). These phantom feelings, writes Noll, "contradict the theory of BIID as a limb not embedded in the brain's body-schema" (222). Those with BIID are not numb in the specific limb, as Ramachandran suggests, but rather (almost in contrast to Ramachandran's theory) feel that the limb is an excess appendage. Though this illuminates an overlap between the phantom limb and BIID that I will later discuss, for now I remain focused on neurological discussions of BIID.

9 For purposes of clarity, I focus on non-congenital phantoms in this book.

10 Those affiliated with the Paris School include Pierre Marty, Michel de M'Uzan, Christian David, and Michel Fain.

11 The "crisis of representation" refers to the crisis of representing historical events in the wake of the Second World War. Thinkers such as Theodor Adorno and George Steiner considered how to create art after Auschwitz, how to speak about the unspeakable, and how to represent the un-representable. Thus, the Holocaust is integral to the field, and though it is not the focus of this book, it is featured in many of the texts. The underlying connection here centres upon conflicting ideas of unity and fragmentation, and how this relates to violent physical rupture.

12 I refer to Perec's semi-autobiography as *W*.

13 Although I do not discuss these analyses due to the pertinence of the arguments, some other fascinating insights have been made about the phantom limb syndrome. In *On Balance* (2011), Adam Phillips suggests that "[j]ust as there are phantom limbs there are phantom histories, histories that are severed and discarded, but linger on as thwarted

possibilities and compelling nostalgias" (105). Here, the phantom limb acts as an allegory for ideas and words that create possibilities through their absence. Unique to the previous analyses of the syndrome, Naomi Segal's *Consensuality: Didier Anzieu, Gender and the Sense of Touch* (2009) relates the phantom limb to an angel or imaginary friend: those lost objects that, like the phantom limb, are not exactly lost. However, she writes, "[u]nlike an imaginary friend, the phantom limb is a externally projected part-object and, as with the lost love object, it is hard to know what exactly is meant by saying 'it' hurts" (Segal 2009, 224). The phantom limb is subjective, and in this way is responsible for the pain is placed elsewhere, on some "it". What happens, she wonders, after a betrayal occurs in a relationship when two people become lost to one another, when someone is unrecognisable? In this situation, she proposes, we are the one causing the betrayal and carrying the pain: "we become their phantom limb" (2009, 227). Shawn Huffman's "Amputation, Phantom Limbs, and Spectral Agency in Shakespeare's *Titus Andronicus* and Normand Chaurette's *Les Reines*" (2004) uses the phantom limb example to explore how sense is a performance and how action is a projection, which he calls, "spectral agency". To do so, he analyses amputated characters in Shakespeare's *Titus Andronicus* and Normand Chaurette's *Les Reines*, asserting that "[t]he phantom-limb phenomenon manifests itself through texts. Literature haunts the body, providing it the modified means through which it may interact with the world" (77). In this instance, a lost body part equates to a lack of communication, which is performed through the text. These examples thus reveal "the impact of literary discourse in shaping subjectivity, body image and perception" (Huffman 2004, 78).

"Phantom Limbs: Film Noir and the Disabled Body" (2003) analyses a variety of noir films in which an individual with disabilities plays a supporting role, which "serves as a marker for larger narratives about normalcy and legitimacy" (Davidson 2003, 57). Michael Davidson uses the phantom limb to signify a "residual sensation of narratives that film cannot represent or reconstitute" (58); the phantom limb again stands for a work's (though this time filmic) incompleteness. While studies of the phantom limb generally refer to a desire for a whole body based on a Freudian lack, states Davidson, he sees the phantom limb as body "still under construction" (71), and when read in light of these noir films, it stands for, more simply, otherness. Lennard Davis's "Nude Venuses, Medusa's Body, and Phantom Limbs: Disability and Visuality" (1997) concerns the way in which representations of the body usually portray a dialectic between the normal and the disabled, and how disabilities involve a space that the body cannot occupy. Two examples of bodies in culture are used to fortify his book: the Venus de Milo statue, and Pam Herbert (a woman with muscular dystrophy who is widely pitied). She writes, in relation to the Venus de Milo that in

> the case of the art historian, the statue is seen as complete with phantom limbs and head. The art historian does not see the lack, the presence of an impairment, but rather mentally re-forms the outline of Venus, so that the historian can return the damaged woman in stone to a pristine state of wholeness.
>
> (Davis 1997, 57)

References

Aisenstein, Marilia. "The Indissociable Unity of Psyche and Soma: A View From the Paris Psychosomatic School." *International Journal of Psycho-Analysis*, vol. 87, 2006, pp. 667–680.

Artaud, Antonin. "Description of a Physical State" [Description d'un état physique, 1925]. *Antonin Artaud Anthology*. Edited and Translated by Jack Hirschman, San Francisco: City Light, 1965. Epigraph Translation by Julie Meunier.

Auchincloss, Elizabeth L., and Eslee Samberg. *Psychoanalytic Terms & Concepts*. New York: American Psychoanalytic Association, 2012.

Bayne, Tim, and Neil Levy. "Amputees By Choice: Body Integrity Identity Disorder and the Ethics of Amputation." *Journal of Applied Philosophy*, vol. 22, no. 1, 2005, pp. 75–86.

Bell, Charles. *The Anatomy of the Brain Explained in a Series of Engravings*. London: T.N. Longman and D. Rees, 1802.

Belsey, Catherine. *Post-structuralism: A Very Short Introduction*. Oxford: Oxford UP, 2002.

Birksted-Breen, Dana, and Sara Flanders. "General Introduction." *Reading French Psychoanalysis*. Edited by Dana Birksted-Breen, Sara Flanders, and Alain Gibeault, London: Routledge, 2010, pp. 1–51.

Blom, Rianne M. "Body Identity Integrity Disorder." *Open Access*, vol. 7, no. 4, 2012, no pagination.

"Body Integrity Identity Disorder." *Biidorg*, 19 August 2014, www.biid.org/possible-causes-biid.

Brooks, Peter. "The Idea of a Psychoanalytic Literary Criticism." *Critical Inquiry*, vol. 13, no. 2, 1987, pp. 334–348.

Brooks, Peter. *Reading for the Plot: Design and Intention in Narrative*. Cambridge: Harvard UP, 1992.

Brooks, Peter. *Psychoanalysis and Storytelling*. Oxford: Blackwell, 1994.

Crownshaw, Richard. *The Afterlife of Holocaust Memory in Contemporary Literature and Culture*. Basingstoke: Palgrave Macmillan, 2010.

Davidson, M. "Phantom Limbs: Film Noir and the Disabled Body." *GLQ: A Journal of Lesbian and Gay Studies*, vol. 9, no. 1–2, 2003, pp. 57–77.

Davis, Lennard. "Nude Venuses, Medusa's Body, and Phantom Limbs: Disability and Visuality." *The Body and Physical Difference: Discourses of Disability*. Edited by David T. Mitchell and Sharon L. Snyder, Ann Arbor: U of Michigan, 1997, pp. 51–71.

Descartes, René, and John Cottingham. *The Philosophical Writings of Descartes*, vol. 3. Cambridge: Cambridge University Press, 1996.

Diagnostic and Statistical Manual of Mental Disorders: DSM-5. American Psychiatric Association, 2013.

Evans, David. "CUT! ... Flannery O'Connor's Apotemnophiliac Allegories." *American Literature*, vol. 81, no. 2, 2009, pp. 304–330.

Felman, Shoshana, and Dori Laub. *Testimony: Crises of Witnessing in Literature, Psychoanalysis, and History*. New York: Routledge, 1991.

Felman, Shoshana, and Dori Laub. *Jacques Lacan and the Adventure of Insight: Psychoanalysis in Contemporary Culture*. Massachusetts: Harvard UP, 1987.

Ferguson, Philip M., and Emily Nusbaum. "Disability Studies: What Is It and What Difference Does It Make?" *Research and Practice for Persons with Severe Disabilities*, vol. 37, no. 2, 2012, pp. 70–80. doi:10.1177/154079691203700202.

"Fighting It." *Yahoo! Groups*. http://groups.yahoo.com/group/fighting-it/. Web.

First, Michael. "Desire for Amputation of a Limb: Paraphilia, Psychosis, or a New Type of Identity Disorder." *Psychological Medicine*, vol. 35, no. 6, 2005, pp. 919–928.

Fletcher, John. *Freud and the Scene of Trauma*. New York: Fordham UP, 2013.

Flor, Herta. "Phantom Limb Pain: A Case of Maladaptive CNS Plasticity?" *Nature Reviews Neuroscience*, vol. 7, no. 11, 2006, pp. 873–881.

Flor, Herta. "Phantom Limb Pain: Characteristics, Causes, and Treatment." *The Lancet Neurology*, vol. 1, no. 3, 2002, pp. 182–189.

Freud, Sigmund. "Studies on Hysteria" [*Studien über Hysterie*, 1895]. *The Standard Edition of the Complete Psychological Works of Sigmund Freud*, vol. 2, 1893–1895. Edited and translated by James Strachey, London: The Hogarth Press and The Institute of Psychoanalysis, 1955.

Freud, Sigmund. "The Dissolution of the Oedipus Complex" [*"Der Untergang des Oedipuskomplexes"*, 1924]. *The Standard Edition of the Complete Psychological Works of Sigmund Freud*, vol. 19, 1923–1925. Edited and translated by James Strachey, London: The Hogarth Press and The Institute of Psychoanalysis, 1961.

Freud, Sigmund. "The Psychical Mechanism of Forgetfulness" [*Zum psychischen Mechanismus der Vergesslichkeit*, 1893–99]. *The Standard Edition of the Complete Psychological Works of Sigmund Freud*, vol. 3, 1893–1899. Edited and translated by James Strachey, London: The Hogarth Press and The Institute of Psychoanalysis, 1962.

Freud, Sigmund. "Project for a Scientific Psychology" [*Entwurf einer Psychologie*, 1895]. *The Standard Edition of the Complete Psychological Works of Sigmund Freud*, vol. 1, 1886–1899. Edited and translated by James Strachey, London: The Hogarth Press and The Institute of Psychoanalysis, 1966.

Freud, Sigmund. "Remembering, Repeating, Working-Through" ["Erinnern, Wiederholen und Durcharbeiten", 1914] *The Standard Edition of the Complete Psychological Works of Sigmund Freud*, vol. 12, 1911–1913. Edited and translated by James Strachey, London: The Hogarth Press and The Institute of Psychoanalysis, 1958.

Gawande, Atul. "The Itch: Its Mysterious Power May Be a Clue to a New Theory about Brains and Bodies." *New Yorker*, June 2008. www.newyorker.com/magazine/2008/06/30/the-itch.

Giummarra, Melita. "Central Mechanisms in Phantom Limb Perception: The Past, Present and Future." *Brain Research Reviews*, vol. 54, 2007, pp. 219–232.

Grosz, Elizabeth A. *Volatile Bodies: Toward a Corporeal Feminism*. Bloomington: Indiana UP, 1994.

Hassan, Ihab. *The Dismemberment of Orpheus: Toward a Postmodern Literature*. New York: Oxford UP, 1971.

Hassan, Ihab. *The Postmodern Turn*. Ohio: Ohio State UP, 1987.

Hellman, Randall B., Eric Chang, Justin Tanner, Stephen Tillery I. Helms, and Veronica Santos J. "A Robot Hand Testbed Designed for Enhancing Embodiment and Functional Neurorehabilitation of Body Schema in Subjects with Upper Limb Impairment or Loss." *Frontiers in Human Neuroscience Front. Hum. Neurosci*, vol. 9, no. 9, 2015, no pagination.

Hook, Derek. *Psychoanalysis, Sexual Difference and the Castration Problematic*. London: LSE Research Online, 2007.

Huffman, Shawn. "Amputation, Phantom Limbs, and Spectral Agency in Shakespeare's *Titus Andronicus* and Normand Chaurette's *Les Reines*." *Modern Drama*, vol. 47, no. 1, 2004, pp. 66–81.

Hungerford, Amy. *The Holocaust of Texts: Genocide, Literature, and Personification*. Chicago: University of Chicago, 2003.

Jones, Ernest. *Papers on Psycho-analysis*. Boston: Beacon, 1961.

Kaur, Dosanjh H. "Producing Identity: Elective Amputation and Disability." *Scan Journal*, vol. 1, no. 3, 2004 http://scan.net.au/SCAN/journal/print.php?journal_id=38&j_id=3.

Klein, Melanie. "Notes on Some Schizoid Mechanisms." *International Journal of Psychoanalysis*, vol. 27, 1946, pp. 99–110.

Krasner, James. "Doubtful Arms and Phantom Limbs: Literary Portrayals of Embodied Grief." *Postmodern Language Association*, vol. 199, no. 2, 2004, pp. 218–232.

Kröger, Katharina, Thomas Schnell, and Erich Kasten. "Effects of Psychotherapy on Patients Suffering from Body Integrity Identity Disorder (BIID)." *American Journal of Applied Psychology*, vol. 3, no. 5, 2014, pp. 110–115.

LaCapra, Dominick. *Representing the Holocaust: History, Theory, Trauma*. Ithaca: Cornell UP, 1994.

Laplanche, Jean and J.B. Pontalis. *The Language of Psychoanalysis*. New York: Karnac Books, 1996.
Lawrence, Anne A. "Clinical and Theoretical Parallels Between Desire for Limb Amputation and Gender Identity Disorder." *Archives of Sexual Behavior*, vol. 35, no. 3, 2006, pp. 263–278.
Lemma, Alessandra. *Under the Skin: A Psychoanalytic Study of Body Modification*. London: Routledge, 2010.
Lenggenhager, Bigna, L. Hilti, and P. Brugger. "Disturbed Body Integrity and the 'Rubber Foot Illusion." *Neuropsychology*, vol. 29, no. 2, 2015, pp. 205–211, doi:10.1037/neu 0000143.
Leys, Ruth. *Trauma: A Genealogy*. Chicago: University of Chicago, 2000.
Lingis, Alphonso. *Foreign Bodies*. New York: Routledge, 1994.
MacLachlan, Malcolm. *Embodiment: Clinical, Critical, and Cultural Perspectives on Health and Illness*. Maidenhead: Open UP, 2004.
Malle, Bertram F. "Phantom Limbs, the Self, and the Mind-body Problem: Comment on R. Melzack." *Canadian Psychology*, vol. 32, no. 1, 1991, pp. 94–95.
Marmor, Judd. *Modern Psychoanalysis: New Directions and Perspectives*. New York: Basic, 1968.
McDougall, Joyce. *Theatres of the Body: A Psychoanalytical Approach to Psychosomatic Illness*. London: Free Association, 1989.
Meckel, Philipp Friedrich Theodor, and Aaron Lemos. *Dissertatio Inauguralis Medica, Quae Dolorem Membri Amputati Remanentem Explicat*. Officina Batheana, 1798.
Mensaert, Alex. *Amputation on Request*. London: lulu.com, 2011.
Mitchell, Juliet. *Mad Men and Medusas: Reclaiming Hysteria*. New York: Basic, 2001.
Mitchell, Juliet. *Psychoanalysis and Feminism: A Radical Reassessment of Freudian Psychoanalysis*. New York: Basic, 2000.
Müller, Sabine. "Body Integrity Identity Disorder (BIID) – Is the Amputation of Healthy Limbs Ethically Justified?" *The American Journal of Bioethics*, vol. 9, no. 1, 2009, pp. 36–43.
Nelson. "Living a Life with BIID." *Body Integrity Identity Disorder (BIID): Störungsbild, Diagnostik, Therapieansätze*. Weinheim: Beltz, 2010.
Noll, Sarah. "Body Integrity Identity Disorder (BIID): How Satisfied Are Successful Wannabes." *PBS Psychology and Behavioral Sciences*, vol. 3, no. 6, 2014, p. 222.
Nortvedt, Finn, and Gunn Engelsrud. "'Imprisoned' in Pain: Analyzing Personal Experiences of Phantom Pain." *Medicine, Health Care and Philosophy Med Health Care and Philos*, vol. 17, no. 4, 2014, pp. 599–608.
Obernolte, Catharina. "The Role of Specific Experiences in Childhood and Youth in the Development of Body Integrity Identity Disorder (BIID)." *American Journal of Applied Psychology*, vol. 4, no. 1, 2015, p. 1.
Ogden, Thomas H. *The Primitive Edge of Experience*. London: J. Aronson, 1989.
Ortiz-Catalan, Max, Nichlas Sander, Morten Kristoffersen B., Bo Håkansson, and Rickard Brånemark. "Treatment of Phantom Limb Pain (PLP) Based on Augmented Reality and Gaming Controlled by Myoelectric Pattern Recognition: A Case Study of a Chronic PLP Patient." *Frontiers in Neuroscience*, vol. 8, 2014.
Perec, George. *W or The Memory of Childhood* [*W, Ou, Le Souvenir D'enfance*, 1975]. Translated by David Bellos. London: Collins Harvill, 1989.
Perur, Srinath. "The Mirror Man." *Mosaic the Science of Life*, 2014. No pagination. http://mosaicscience.com/story/mirror-man.
Phillips, Adam. *On Balance*. New York: Farrar, Straus and Giroux, 2011.
Phillips, Robert. Abjection. *TSQ*, vol. 1, nos 1–2, 1 May 2014, pp. 19–21. doi: https://doi.org/10.1215/23289252-2399470

Ramachandran, V.S., and E.M. Hubbard. "Synaesthesia – A Window Into Perception, Thought and Language." *Journal of Consciousness Studies*, vol. 8, no. 12, 2001, pp. 3–34.

Ramachandran, V.S., and D. Rogers-Ramachandran. "Synaesthesia in Phantom Limbs Induced with Mirrors." *Proceedings of the Royal Society B: Biological Sciences*, vol. 263, no. 1369, 1996, pp. 377–386.

Ramachandran, V. S. *Tell-tale Brain: a Neuroscientist's Quest for What Makes Us Human*. New York: W.W. Norton, 2011.

Rapaport, Herman. "Archive Trauma." *Diacritics*, vol. 28, no. 4, 1998, pp. 68–81.

Schilder, Paul. *The Image and Appearance of the Human Body: Studies in the Constructive Energies of the Psyche*. New York, NY: International Universities, 1950.

Schmidt, Sebastian. "My Life with BIID." *Body Integrity Identity Disorder (BIID): Störungsbild, Diagnostik, Therapieansätze*. Weinheim: Beltz, 2010.

Schott, G.D. "Revealing the Invisible: The Paradox of Picturing a Phantom Limb." *Dorsal Column*, vol. 137, no. 3, 1 March 2014, pp. 960–969.

Segal, Naomi. *Consensuality: Didier Anzieu, Gender and the Sense of Touch*. Amsterdam: Rodopi, 2009.

Segal, Robert A. "Psychoanalyzing Myth: From Freud to Winnicott." *Teaching Freud*. Edited by Diane E. Jonte-Pace, Oxford: Oxford University Press, 2003, pp. 137–165.

Showalter, Elaine. *Hystories: Hysterical Epidemics and Modern Media*. New York: Columbia UP, 1997.

Simmel, Marianne L. "The Reality of Phantom Sensations." *Social Research*, vol. 29, no. 3, 1962, pp. 337–356.

Sobchack, Vivian. "A Leg to Stand On: Prosthetics, Metaphor, and Materiality." *The Prosthetic Impulse: From a Posthuman Present to a Biocultural Future*. Edited by Marquard Smith and Joanne Morra, Cambridge, MA: MIT, 2006, pp. 17–42.

Sobchack, Vivian. "Living a 'Phantom Limb': On the Phenomenology of Bodily Integrity." *Body & Society*, vol. 16, no. 3, 2010, pp. 51–67.

Sternburg, Janet. *Phantom Limb*. Lincoln: U of Nebraska, 2002.

Trilling, Lionel. *The Liberal Imagination: Essays on Literature and Society*. New York: Viking, 1950.

Weiss, Samuel A. "The Body Image as Related to Phantom Sensation: A Hypothetical Conceptualization of Seemingly Isolated Findings." *Annals of the New York Academy of Sciences*, vol. 74, no. 1, 1958, pp. 25–29, doi:10.1111/j.1749-6632.1958.tb39525.x.

White, Amy. "Body Integrity Identity Disorder Beyond Amputation: Consent and Liberty." *HEC Forum*, vol. 26, no. 3, 2014, pp. 225–236.

Whole. Directed by Melody Gilbert. Performance by Michael First. Melody Gilbert, 2003.

Wills, David. *Prosthesis*. Stanford: Stanford UP, 1995.

Winnicott, D.W. "Psycho-somatic Disorder." *Psycho-Analytic Explorations*. Cambridge: Harvard UP, 1989, pp. 103–118.

Winnicott, D.W. "Transitional Objects and Transitional Phenomena" (1953). *The International Journal of Psycho-Analysis*, vol. 34, no. 2, 1971, pp. 89–97.

Woods, Tim. *Beginning Postmodernism*. Manchester: Manchester UP, 1999.

Yarom, Nitza. *Matrix of Hysteria: Psychoanalysis of the Struggle between the Sexes Enacted in the Body*. London: Routledge, 2005.

2

"WE DIDN'T ASK FOR THIS PAIN"

Case studies of BIID and PLS

One man with a phantom limb writes: "[s]ometimes [I] feel as if the fingers on my amputated hand are moving uncontrollably, which is both extremely painful and embarrassing" (Nortvedt and Engelsrud 2014, 602). And in his self-published book *Amputation on Request* (2011), a man with BIID named Alex Mensaert explains that the "need for amputation is an obsession that keeps a wannabe the whole day busy [*sic*] till he gets his wanted limb(s) amputated" (44).[1] Mensaert later states that the vast majority of the individuals he spoke to who are determined to self-amputate are aware that 80% of (BIID) amputees suffer from "severe phantom pains", and that "their answer to the question [as to] what could be the reason they were not perfectly happy immediately [after amputation] is clearly; [*sic*] 'because we didn't ask for this pain'" (Mensaert 2011, 54). Here Mensaert is referring both to the torment of BIID and the phantom pain after the amputation. Already there is a certain paradox: the BIID sufferer desires to be in the physical shape of those with phantom limbs (missing limbs), and those with phantom limbs desire to be in the physical shape of those with apotemnophilia (with all limbs intact). Although they oppose each other in this way and involve seemingly different types of pain (the physically generated phantom versus the psychically orientated BIID limb), they undergo a very similar struggle, and, in a sense, mirror one another. Individuals with both syndromes want to amputate what feels like an extra limb.

In what follows I will be unpacking the similarities and differences between these phenomena through the stories of two individuals' struggles. First, I examine the story of Peter, a man with BIID, and second that of Stephen, whose phantom limb was healed through the use of mirror therapy. Both individuals convey a feeling of helplessness, a difficulty with psychic and somatic fragmentation and wholeness, and a dissonance between subjective and objective senses of self: with how they feel and how they are perceived.[2] Both desire to feel psychosomatically integrated, accepted, and complete. However, their experiences with these feelings differ on many accounts.

An additional connection between Stephen and Peter is that they struggle to comprehend their sensations. For both, language is an insufficient tool with which to completely understand and allow others to understand their feelings. This is particularly harmful for Peter, as he is thought to be mentally ill by some people who are close to him and is insufficiently supported at times. Interestingly, it is, in fact, support from friends and family that both Stephen and Peter find integral to their improvement. Peter was able to begin accepting and sharing his struggle through the help of internet research and by communicating with others who have BIID, though these communications were often fragmented and ambiguous. I will suggest that this ambiguity facilitates the expression of non-logical sensations. A similar point will be made about the importance of the fictional aspects of Peter's story, the telling of which was beneficial to his recovery. In relation to this concept of fiction, the mirror therapy parallels a certain notion of language, because it involves a fictional representation of something that is not materially present. In drawing these links, I will establish how both Peter and Stephen use language and communicate to recreate themselves, and how this is manifested in the mirror-box, which Stephen uses to integrate his mind and body. In this chapter, I will introduce the ways in which I will be using the selected texts within this book to understand more about how Peter and Stephen's cases can be explored beyond a medical approach. In what follows, both case studies will be evaluated and related to the themes in the book in order to map out the ways in which I will be exploring the experiences of those with BIID and phantom limbs.

Peter

In *Amputation on Request*, Mensaert discusses his own experiences with BIID, while also sharing interviews and letters from other apotemnophiles. Amongst these letters is one from Peter, who is a man of unknown origin, and who tells of his struggle with the syndrome. His letter is written in broken English and chronicles how his long-standing desire to amputate his left leg above the knee has affected his life, relationships, and body.[3] Peter's story will be used to develop an understanding of BIID that is separate from the biomedical approach. My intention is to introduce the way in which Peter (who serves as an example for others with BIID) has experiences that are related to the theoretical concepts in this book.

Peter's struggle with BIID began when, at the age of seven, he saw an amputee named Helen and he was fascinated by her. Unable to stop thinking about her, he grew obsessed with the desire to lose a leg. Though he was too embarrassed to share the obsession and did not understand it, he secretly cut off his arteries with ligatures, which he describes as being both painful and pleasurable: though it caused him pain, he also enjoyed the feeling of paralysis. This act was ultimately unsatisfactory, however, and Peter desperately went on to freeze his calf in order to have it amputated. When the attempt failed, Peter was left with four limbs, a family who didn't know what he was going through, and a feeling of loneliness and helplessness. He then began to research his condition online and was delighted to discover that others shared his feelings. This allowed him to reveal the secret with his wife and close friend (who was also his doctor). Although they did not completely understand, they primarily learned to accept his struggle and need to amputate. Soon thereafter, he found a "German wannabe" online who explained that he had amputated all of his toes and who told Peter how to self-amputate in a painless manner. When he followed through and amputated a small toe, his wife and friend were unsympathetic. As he continued to remove parts of his body, Peter also removed himself from relationships with the people closest to him and found others who he felt understood him. Though his wellbeing increasingly improved as a result of these new relationships, he remained discontented with his physical form. Gradually, Peter severed all the toes on his left foot. Although he enjoyed the feeling of the stumps, he wanted his entire leg to be amputated. He then froze his left leg and injected it with a "self-made infection", which consisted of "urine, death flies and other garbage" (Mensaert 2011, 68). This, however, was unsuccessful, and he was thereafter sent to a mental institution. Peter explains that he was treated by doctors who rather than listening to him defined his problem as a suicide attempt and a form of self-mutilation, a diagnosis that angered him and left him feeling increasingly alienated. He explains that he then escaped from the institution but returned as a result of his former wife's encouragement. Eventually, he explains, he was granted the right to leave, after which he contacted a doctor on the internet who had BIID. He travelled to "a neighbouring country" (Mensaert 2011, 70) to meet this doctor, who gave him anaesthesia to facilitate the desired amputation. Under the anaesthetic, Peter "chopped off [his] foot with a hammer" (Mensaert 2011, 70) and had his left leg, below the knee, amputated in a hospital thereafter. When others asked what had happened to him, he told them that he had been involved in an accident, which, he claims, they believed. In spite of these bodily modifications, Peter remained unfulfilled, and finally fooled a surgeon into amputating his left knee by confabulating that he had terrible stump pains. Finally, Peter explains, he was able to start a "new life", but remained angry at the inability of those in the medical world to understand his struggle.

This story is dubious in many ways, but it is true to Peter, and what it does suggest is this: that there is a strong link between Peter's desire to remove parts of his body and to remove people in his life, that written texts play an important role in his ability to share and alter his feelings, and that a non-medical analysis may be helpful.

Peter's doctor was also his good friend, and when he finally decided to reveal his secret, Peter explains that his doctor would not "talk to [him] about it, and that was just what [he] wanted, someone who wanted to listen to [him]" (Mensaert 2011, 65). Although the doctor primarily accepted that he had the condition, Peter explains that he ultimately felt betrayed by him, a person "who I trusted and knew for fourteen years, a man who promised me to never change my wannabe feelings" (Mensaert 2011, 69). Although the doctor attempted to help Peter by providing

44 Why psychoanalysis and literature?

him with painkillers and sending him to a mental institution, he was unable to sufficiently understand or treat the problem. Peter was also angry about the way he was treated in the institution. He explains, "I was some kind of *state property* without any rights. [...] On the forms made by the psychiatrists stood all lies, according to them I was someone who thought about nothing else but suicide and self-mutilation" (68). These doctors, though presumably with good intentions, further stigmatised and defined Peter, causing him to feel increasingly misunderstood.

Peter's having been labelled as suicidal exemplifies the way in which professionals in the medical field sometimes respond to cases like Peter's. They can attempt to categorise those with BIID in order to facilitate treatment, which is necessary and beneficial in some ways, but can also lead to a limited and problematical treatment. In Peter's case, this categorisation further alienated him, as he writes, "[i]t was terrible hearing this, knowing I didn't want to die, I only wanted a leg off" (Mensaert 2011, 68). Eventually he was released from the institution on the condition that he saw a psychiatrist. The

> crazy psychiatrist told me he thought that *internet-thing* was some kind of *sect*, and internet was the cause of me—continuing my plans to get rid of my leg. I always kept saying that I didn't want to loose [sic] my leg anymore; just to get rid of him.
>
> (69)

Here, Peter conveys that he not only felt misunderstood by the psychiatrist, but also encouraged to abandon the very thing that allowed him to feel most successfully understood: the internet. However, the internet sources were often dangerous, as some suggestions about how to self-amputate were hazardous. This raises the question of whether there is an alternative way of understanding his dilemma, and I contend that consideration of the connections between the body, language, and fragmentation can contribute new insight. Since Peter's story demonstrates that textual media play an important role in his struggle with BIID, I now want to investigate the ways in which Peter engages with and is affected by various types of text.

Throughout the story, Peter's actions are influenced by various texts (including conversations, posts, and threads on internet groups) that advance his understanding of BIID and provide a platform from which to discuss the condition with those close to him. These texts also help Peter feel less alone, and it is this feeling that allows him to open up to others. After learning that others suffered from BIID, Peter was able to use medical texts to explain his condition to his friends and family. In this way, texts affected Peter's life by enabling him to begin to accept and communicate his experiences with the syndrome. His actions were also shaped through a textual medium when he read about how to tie his limbs with an elastic ligature, and when the "German wannabe" and "internet doctor" taught him how to paralyse his toe and leg. Although these texts did not necessarily engender physically healthy outcomes, they informed actions. Texts played a large role in facilitating

Peter's communication with others, and with the process of self-amputation, a theme explored in the chapters that follow.

Peter and the texts

Chapter 4 discusses one specific case study in which a psychoanalyst, Marilia Aisenstein, works with a patient who has a psychosomatic condition. Paralleling Peter's experience in some ways, the patient (Mr L) does not explore the meaning behind his physical disorder, and Aisenstein is concerned with this lack. However, she does so with the intention of processing it psychically so that it ceases to be caught in the realm of the somatic, and in this way differs from Peter's internet dialogues. In her article "The Man from Burma" (2009 [1993]), Aisenstein suggests that the patient had physically registered a trauma that had been erased from the psyche, and by attending to the absences in his language she was able to repair his physical illness. In relation to the ideas brought forth in Aisenstein's case study, in this chapter I am interested in what might be hidden within Peter's story. However, in my reading I am not creating a psychoanalytic interpretation. I am introducing the concept of how hidden aspects within language might be illuminated. I pay particular attention to how the psyche, language, and the body are interconnected. Chapter 5 is interested in the ways in which the body and language affect one another, albeit, from a literary perspective; and in how the desire to possess an absence, as seen in BIID, can be mediated by language. This is related to a discord between subjective and objective notions of self. Though I develop these concepts in Chapter 5, I will introduce them now through the works of Sigmund Freud and Maurice Blanchot.

The most fundamental notion for Blanchot (1995) is that language is structured around a void. According to Blanchot, the linguistic system is an incomplete yet necessary one that is used for communication. What interests Blanchot is the way in which writing involves an experience of erasure. This mirrors BIID, I will suggest, in that those with the syndrome are interested in experiencing and expressing feelings of erasure. In relation to this, for Blanchot, engaging with a text is a bodily experience involving negation. Blanchot's thoughts elucidate the ways in which Peter's testimony demonstrates an overlap between language and the body. This link also illustrates the ways in which a deficiency in expression might be connected to a bodily deficiency. As noted, Peter faces difficulties in articulating his hidden feelings of fragmentation with others. When he first tells his wife of the syndrome, for example, it is in an ambiguous manner. He writes: "[i]ndirectly I tried to talk about it with my wife [...]. I printed out the medical texts I found, and gave them to her as a sign [...]. We didn't talk much about it" (Mensaert 2011, 65). Perhaps this ambiguity can be attributed to a difficulty in completely expressing feelings. He conveys that he must communicate through texts and signs, through a fragmented dialogue that suggests a linguistic deficiency. Blanchot is interested in what underlies fragmented exchanges, and in illuminating what language cannot reveal, what a word cannot express.

Blanchot's "Literature and the Right to Death" (1995) discusses what is referred to as the *two slopes of literature*, which will be elaborated in Chapter 5. Briefly, these slopes "constitute the poles of [literary] ambiguity" (Critchley 2004, 49), as theorist Simon Critchley writes, "[l]iterature always has the right to mean something other than what one thought it meant" (Critchley 2004, 49). I will concentrate on the first slope of literature in order to illustrate the way in which it parallels Peter's plight. The first slope of literature involves a notion of abstraction in the service of meaning. It is, according to Blanchot, "meaningful prose. Its goal is to express things in a language that designates things according to what they mean" (1995, 332). However, language cannot completely express thought or sensation, as Peter cannot completely express his feelings. Furthermore, Blanchot contends that language "murders" the "thing:" when something is named, it is negated. Thus, language involves an experience of death and erasure. Blanchot (1995) explains:

> [f]or me to be able to say, "This [*sic*.] woman," I must somehow take her flesh-and-blood reality away from her, cause her to be absent, annihilate her. The word gives me being, but it gives it to me deprived of being. The word is the absence of that being, its nothingness.
>
> *(322)*

When the woman is named she is erased, because language is at a remove from the physical, the "flesh-and-blood". Put another way, when "things" are translated to conscious thought they are negated. Literature, writes Blanchot (1995), "is *my* consciousness *without me*" (328). Peter's disorder can be seen, therefore, as a failure to function on the "first slope:" language distances us from ourselves. From another perspective, perhaps his amputational drive is a kind of failure in the connection between what Freud refers to as thing-presentation and word-presentation.

Like Blanchot's first slope of literature, the thing-presentation comprises visual (ambiguous) images in the preconscious, while the word-presentation brings images to conscious thought. Freud (1961) writes that "[v]erbal residues [...have], as it were, a special sensory source. The visual components of word-presentations are secondary" (633). The preconscious, in which the thing-presentation resides, is closer to the sensory, but as the image becomes conscious through a word-presentation, it is distanced from the sensory. Perhaps Peter is trapped in the "thing-ness" of his limbs (the preconscious "thing-presentation"), as he is unable to render them linguistic entities. His feeling of absence must be represented through the body rather than through language. While Peter's expression must occur somatically, in Freudian psychoanalysis the sensory drives can ostensibly be distanced from the body through language. In Blanchot's thought, this removal from the sensory also occurs through language, though not in a curative sense. As Blanchot (1995) writes, "I say my name, and [...] I separate myself from myself" (324). From this point of view, Peter is unable to adequately grasp or comprehend what is involved in his desires and is driven to experience them physically. His subjective feelings of deficiency cannot be vocalised or comprehended linguistically: he is trapped in the "thing-ness", in that failure to function in the first slope of literature and use language to mediate bodily absence.

After having amputated a toe for the first time, Peter explains:

> I wanted to feel the good amputation feeling. I wanted to feel my stump. I decided to amputate another toe, this time without informing my wife. I thought that when this time I would cut off my big toe that I would be able to enjoy the feeling of amputation.
>
> (Mensaert 2011, 66–67)

First, Peter desires to physically feel an absence, one that seems nearly impossible to obtain. Just as language—as Blanchot conceives it—cannot completely convey sensations because it is lacking, Peter cannot completely obtain his felt absence by enacting it. Moreover, since he did not tell his wife, the above sentence suggests that a lack of communication is connected to the amputation. This again illustrates, in relation to Blanchot's theory, a clear connection between a lack of expression and a physical absence, specifically, a partial bodily death. Blanchot believes that death involves a possibility and impossibility: individuals understand death because they experience the loss of another, and are also unable to understand it, because it cannot be consciously apprehended. This can be related to Peter's desire for a partial "death". Blanchot is also interested in how the human relationship with death involves a desire to grasp the impossible. The man that Peter encounters online exemplifies this notion, as he tells Peter that he has frozen and saved his ten amputated toes. Although he does not want to die, the man needs to grasp a part of his dead body (the frozen toes), and in this sense experience a kind of death. This reflects the literary writer's plight as Blanchot perceives it. These concerns with the desire to experience death and with being driven by something unknown are also central to Freud's concept of the uncanny.

Peter's story begins with the statement that upon seeing Helen at the age of seven he was stricken with "a strange inner feeling". "Why", he asks, "isn't it me who is lying there in the hospital with one leg off?" (64). It is precisely a strange feeling that Freud's essay "The Uncanny" (1919 [1955]) explores, a double self that one may not recognise but that is always buried within. Freud states that it is "a special core of feeling [...] that class of the frightening which leads back to what is known of old and long familiar" (1955, 218–219). From this perspective, Helen represents a kind of double self that is buried within Peter, and that continues to invade his body and mind throughout life. Moreover, for Freud, the uncanny is a feeling of rupture and death that cannot be controlled, and that can manifest itself psychosomatically. Speaking of the incident when he froze his calf before attempting to amputate, Peter writes that his calf was "black and dead", he "didn't knew [sic] how it happened, it was suddenly there" (Mensaert 2011, 64). Interestingly, then, although he froze it, Peter claims not to know how his calf became black and dead, suggesting that he both knew and did not know. Or, as one of Freud's patients Lucy R. states of her symptoms of hysteria, "'I didn't know or rather I didn't want to know'" (Freud 1955b, 117). Peter's denial that he caused the limb to turn "black and dead" can be seen as a kind of disavowal, a failure to recognise and a simultaneous recognition of the appendage.[4] As Peter later states in response to his psychiatrist labelling him suicidal, "I didn't want to die, I only wanted a leg off" (Mensaert 2011, 68). Though he does not want to die, he is driven to experience and possess a partial bodily death. And indeed, according to Freud, "[m]any people experience the feeling in the highest degree in relation to death and dead bodies" (1955a, 13). Also reflective of the uncanny, a part of Peter's body feels foreign to him it feels as though it should be absent and he is repeatedly driven to remove it. For Freud, it is by tracing what is hidden in one's speech (the unconscious) that the experiences and ideas behind this drive may begin to be revealed (in psychoanalysis). In Chapter 7 I expand upon the psychoanalytic interest in the hidden self, focusing on trauma and psychosomatic rupture through the works of D.W. Winnicott.

Winnicott is interested in the way communication and language are related to feelings of fracture, and I focus on his thoughts about how a linguistic exchange might enable a reparative integration between the mind and body, the self and other. Winnicott's essay "Fear of Breakdown" (1974) explores a particular type of trauma in which, due to an absence experienced in infancy, a child is left with an incommunicable feeling of emptiness, reflective of Peter's struggle. In Winnicott's theory, if the infant's carer leaves the infant for too long, it experiences a feeling of anxiety, of being split between the mind and body. These traumatised individuals embody something that resembles Peter's description of having a "strange inner feeling" from a young age that cannot be understood, and that materialises in various psychical and somatic forms. Since in infancy the feelings that relate to being left cannot be comprehended linguistically, Winnicott contends that they are registered in the body, and these individuals physically carry their mental traumas, as reflected in some of Peter's statements such as the previously noted one: that he *was* a lie. Peter also, as noted, told his doctor "what feelings [he] was walking around with" (Mensaert 2011, 65), indicating that his body physically carries a psychical wound, and it is this type of wound that Winnicott analyses in "Fear of Breakdown". Although this does not suggest that Peter is traumatised precisely in the way Winnicott describes, Winnicott provides a helpful model with which to understand BIID more thoroughly.

Winnicott theorises that these traumatised subjects will, for the remainder of their life, endure an unconscious desire to return to a primitive state and re-experience the feeling of traumatic fragmentation in order to gain control and restructure themselves. Therefore, at times, they engage in self-destructive acts. Traumatised individuals, in other words, may be unconsciously driven to reintegrate their feelings of being split and empty, and to feel as though they are "gathered" together. However, Winnicott suggests that they may also fear re-experiencing this traumatic state. Here there is a paradoxical split in which the individual both fears and desires to experience fragmentation. Since Peter removes parts of his body in order to feel better, he reflects the traumatised individual who is driven to return to his early trauma to survive and restructure himself in order to feel integrated. Moreover, the traumatic state of rupture in Winnicott's theory relates to the absence of another individual (a carer), and Winnicott suggests that reintegration must be approached through the help of another, such as a psychoanalyst.

Peter demonstrates a desire to be supported by another individual, thereby paralleling the traumatised patient in need of reintegration through the help of another. We see this when he goes online and seeks the help of a German wannabe in order to amputate his toe and bind his wound. However, rather than finding the supportive figure that Winnicott's theory calls for, it is another pained individual who teaches him how to "ti[e] up the wound": to gather together his feelings of fracture through another's support. While for Winnicott, a traumatised patient attempts to experience a breakdown in order to feel more thoroughly integrated, in Peter's case a similar kind of attempt proves insufficient. When read alongside Winnicott's paradigm, this can be related to the notion that traumatic experiences have been stored in the mind rather than the body, so the mind is where integration must take place. Or, as Winnicott states, a traumatised subject might be "sending the body to death which has already happened to the psyche" (1974, 93). The patient must experience a psychical, rather than somatic annihilation, in order to safely re-experience the trauma and subdue feelings of fragmentation. Peter also illustrates an attempt to restructure himself through stories about "false accidents", as he explains that he created stories about how he lost his limbs in order to convince others that his amputations were accidental. From Winnicott's point of view, he may be attempting to reform his identity in order to decrease feelings of rupture.

Winnicott offers an alternative concept of repair in which an analyst helps traumatised subjects re-experience past trauma through a supportive and reparative linguistic and physical exchange. When Peter states that he "didn't want to loose [sic] my leg anymore: Just to get rid of him [the psychiatrist]" (Mensaert 2011, 69), he demonstrates that a desire to remove part of the body is closely connected to a desire to remove unsupportive people in his life. Throughout the majority of his life, Peter feels unsupported by his doctor and wife. However, he eventually is divorced and finds a girlfriend who he "got to know better and who understood me and tried to listen to my wannabe-feelings" (Mensaert 2011, 67). Peter's process of psychical recovery and bodily destruction is aligned with the search for support. I contend that the kind of support this new girlfriend provides parallels what Winnicott calls for in his model. Peter explains that she "[l]istened to me, not that she approved of what I wanted; having my leg off, but at least she paid attention to me. We fell in love and kept coming closer to each other more and more" (Mensaert 2011, 67). In Winnicott's paradigm, the psychoanalyst is able to provide a certain amount of distance that allows the patient to accept others' absences. Though Peter's girlfriend does not completely approve of his decisions, she remains present. Although this does not stop him from self-amputating, it does enable him to feel stronger. This does not suggest that she replaces an analyst, but that a certain type of support is important.

Peter's interaction with the internet doctor also parallels the psychoanalytic process in Winnicott's theory. Just as Winnicott suggests that the analyst and analysand are to enable healing by re-living the past in the present, Peter and this doctor devise a story as to why he had an accident. Here, rather than creating false accidents alone, Peter is assisted, and, according to Peter, a surgeon believes him.[5] However, since the internet doctor helped Peter self-amputate—rather than, for example, helping him linguistically undo feelings of absence—this is not an exact parallel of Winnicottian psychoanalysis, but a demonstration of a similar kind of support. Although Peter's repair was attributed to a bodily removal, I suggest that it was intertwined with having felt supported by others. The novelist George Perec (1989) explores a process of psychosomatic reparation through a fictional self-reconstruction in *W or the Memory of Childhood*, and Peter's story can be related to Perec's experience as it is reflected in this text. Although unlike Peter, Perec's pain stems from the loss of his parents in the Second World War (and is not to be conflated with Peter's struggle), this literary example demonstrates how language and the body interconnect. I shall first examine the ways in which Peter and Perec convey a similar experience of feeling psychosomatically broken, misunderstood, and alienated from society. For Perec, language has a reparative effect, and I want to explore how language also plays a role in Peter's life. Specifically, Perec engages in a process of rewriting himself by fictionalising his past and identity through a text. In relation to this, the possibly fictional elements in Peter's story might be linked to his processes of bodily and psychical healing.

Peter's story begins with a description of having felt psychosomatically broken from an early age, and in *W*, Perec writes of a similar feeling; however, his feelings result from the loss of his mother. Although, like Peter, he never precisely understands its origins, Perec searches for them through the processes of psychoanalysis and in writing *W*. *W* is founded upon the premise that the past cannot be accurately remembered. It is not an autobiography, but a semi-autobiography: it is aware of and plays with its fictional elements. Through metaphors, descriptions of photographs, and borrowed memories and stories, Perec shares the way in which his traumatic past affected and shaped him. He was physically weak throughout his childhood and felt lonely and estranged from wider society. Similarly, Peter has feelings of incomprehensible fragmentation and estrangement. Though their experiences and circumstances differ drastically, Perec's journey illuminates Peter's. Like Perec, Peter feels as though he was defined by a lack from an early age, which he attempts to repair through the physical means of self-amputation. They also both encounter a struggle with the definitions that have been imposed upon them by society, which are related to false concepts of truth and "wholeness".

In describing what occurred at the mental institution, Peter states that one patient was "one-hundred percent *nuts*" (Mensaert 2011, 68). Here, his language highlights his feelings about mental illness, suggesting that he uses the very definitions he fears. He continues to explain that this "old fool [...] had millions of dollars hidden under his pillow, and he had to guard it all night long" (Mensaert 2011, 68). First, "one-hundred percent" might suggest that for Peter, systems of wholes are closely related to sanity (100% represents a whole that suggests a concept of truth). Possibly, some individuals who feel un-whole and use language in this way are attempting to (perhaps defensively) exclude others and validate themselves. Peter states:

> [w]hen I was 26, I got internet. I found medical texts about wannabeisme, I discovered I wasn't the only person in the world who wanted to lose an arm or leg. This feeling gave me new courage to continue my search for perfection.
> (Mensaert 2011, 65)

From this angle, the "search for perfection" may not only be related to bodily incongruity, but to a feeling of social inadequacy. Peter explains: "I tried to get my friends to understand it" but "heard from others they were laughing at me behind my back" (Mensaert 2011, 69). Perec also describes several instances of feeling isolated from social confines, which he illustrates through a fictional island called "W" that serves as a metaphor for society. Physically weak individuals are sent off this island and essentially tortured, while the "perfect" individuals strive for a "united" community on the island. It is this kind of social structure, Perec indicates, that contributed to his own feelings of rupture. Similarly, when Peter was sent to the mental institution he was not only socially ostracised, he was physically removed from society and heavily medicated. This demonstrates how feelings of being (physically and mentally) cut off are intertwined with the environment. Peter and Perec convey in different ways that this is partially because language is formed through a system of wholes: a notion that will be discussed in relation to poststructuralist theory throughout this book.

Both Peter and Perec demonstrate a need to use a fragmentary and ambiguous form of language to communicate. Since upon sharing his syndrome with his wife, Peter "printed out the medical texts [he] found, and gave them to her as a sign", he displays a need to communicate in an ambiguous and detached manner. Later, when he tells his friend that he is an apotemnophile, "without thinking", his friend explains that the root of the word, "apotemno" suggests "that it had something to do with amputation, he studied and knew the meaning of the word apotemno" (Mensaert 2011, 65). What Peter remembers of these moments, therefore, involves fragmented and more abstract linguistic forms. Perec's text is concerned with a similar type of communication and is written in a ruptured form. Perec indicates that a linear language based on a system of wholes is insufficient for expressing feelings of incompleteness. As a child, before he was aware of a problem with linguistic expression, Perec drew pictures to convey his incommunicable feelings, which echoes Peter's experience with BIID.

Peter explains that when he told his old friend (and doctor) about his condition, his friend stated that he should have known because "[d]uring all our friendship he saw me often enough make drawings about amputees" (Mensaert 2011, 65). This form of expression through drawing may signify a frustration with communication and comprehension, as drawing involves a visual element that may be able to portray something more subjective than words can convey. Drawings are generally more abstract than language: they do not directly explain that Peter has BIID, but rather can depict the images and feelings involved. Interestingly, Perec also drew pictures of fragmented bodies from a young age, which denotes that Peter and Perec share similar difficulties with expressing feelings of rupture linguistically. Therefore, a less direct form of communication may, in some cases, more adequately express experiences of brokenness.

Perec (1989) acknowledges, moreover, that his past cannot be remembered accurately, shared objectively, or understood completely, either by himself or by others. It is because he is able to recognise this that he distorts and obscures his past. In this way, linguistic form echoes a drawing (in its obscurity). However, language is more successful in expressing the specificity of Perec's feelings. By writing in this manner, I contend, Perec is able to begin rewriting his identity in order to more comprehensively understand, share, and begin to repair his painful fracture. He is able to do this by, primarily, recognising the fictional aspects of his life and identity. I now want to return to Peter's statement about the patient at the mental institution (that the "old fool" "had millions of dollars hidden under his pillow, and he had to guard it all night long"), because it suggests that for Peter, individuals who are unaware of the fictional nature of their own stories are "mad". This "old fool" *had* millions under his pillow, rather than *claiming* to have it. Although it is obvious that Peter means to say that the man claimed to have millions of dollars, his neglecting to use this word suggests that Peter is knowingly mocking the delusional man and is therefore not "mad". He himself is aware that his leg is objectively attached to his body. When related to his statement about the man being "100% nuts", Peter's use of wholes, logic, and sarcasm seem to suggest that he is attempting to prove that he is sane. Moreover, this statement indicates that for Peter, health is defined in part by individuals' abilities to recognise the fictional nature of their subjective feelings of reality, and to recognise that they are not objectively shared.

Tracing the possible fictions within Peter's narrative further illuminates the ways in which Peter feels misunderstood. There are some tenuous aspects of Peter's story. First, the assertion that he escaped from the mental institution is questionable, as this is a highly unusual occurrence. Second, various amputations that Peter describes, such as cutting off his foot with a hammer, are dubious. Another unrealistic claim is that towards the end of his struggle, people in Peter's life believed that his foot amputation was the result of an accident. Since at this point people were aware of his BIID condition, it seems unlikely that they would unquestionably believe the story. We cannot, of course, know the absolute truth (and, as I shall argue, this does not exist), and this is not my interest here. Rather, I am concerned with what some of the (partial) fictions discussed here and elsewhere in this book can reveal about concealed thoughts and experiences. In connection to Perec's experiences of writing a semi-fictional narrative, I suggest that illuminating the fictional (though, ostensibly, subjectively true) aspects of Peter's autobiography can allow for an alternative kind of listening. Towards the end of his story, Peter explains that after amputating his foot,

I told another story and made everyone believe I had an accident. Fortunately, everyone believed me, and the next day I woke up with my left leg amputated under the knee. Finally, at least I reached my goal, or at a least for a large part.

(Mensaert 2011, 70)

Though this relief coincides with a dangerous self-amputation, it is by attending to the other aspects of Peter's experience and story that we can begin to understand this kind of a fragmented and painful relationship between the psyche and soma, self and other, language and the body. He continues to explain that when his third surgeon believes his story and amputates his left leg, he starts a "new life". Here we see how Peter's repair is closely linked to a fictional reconstruction of the self, and it is a different kind of fictional self-reconstruction that has reparative and healthier effects in Stephen's experience of having a phantom limb, which I will now survey.

Stephen

On the website www.reddit.com, activist and amputee Stephen Sumner shares his experience of having a phantom limb. His posts were written 11 years after having lost his left leg in a "horrific" motorbike accident, after which he suffered multiple traumas and fell into a coma. However, his only lasting pain, he explains, was a phantom limb. After roughly five years, Stephen was introduced to mirror therapy,[6] which he used for two years, until his pain disappeared. He explains that after his pain disappeared:

> It dawned on me that I was, basically a very lucky dude to have had all these circumstances collude to give me back my life and places on Earth where peeps, for myriad of reasons, are not nearly so fortunate […]. So I set about forming a one-man humanitarian organisation aimed at using Mirror Therapy […] to help relieve the suffering caused by PLP in these traumatised places.[7]
>
> *(Sumner 2015)*

He travelled through various impoverished countries in Asia with mirrors and taught individuals how to use them to help with PLP. As those on Reddit proceed to ask questions about the experiences involved, Stephen describes the phantom limb pain as a relentless feeling of "strangeness" and "agony". The pains, he writes, "tend to hit you in very specific spots" and are "SUPER-intimate", involving sensations such as crushing, cramping, pins and needles, restless leg syndrome, burning, and (most painfully) electric shock. The only sensation he was unable to eradicate was the burning, although, he explains, it is mild, and in one spot. It is "nothing", he writes, "next to the smoking, black-out electrical spasms I used to host". Although medicine was unable to "touch the pain", by sticking to a routine of mirror therapy he was able to "rewire" and alter his sensations. Though he asserts that the sensations are impossible to completely describe, they were, he writes, "comforting", "cool" and "uncanny", "kinda like a homecoming". When he first gazed into the mirror, Stephen was "suffused with a sense of calm completion", and a "very vivid feeling of 'activation' in the gone leg. It was there again and it was comforting", and after five weeks, the pain was almost completely eradicated. Ultimately, found the strength to improve his condition through the support of his family and friends, who believed that he was "a big strong guy", and who offered "a huge amount of very quiet assistance". By keeping an open mind, looking at his reflection, and engaging with his imagination, he explains, Stephen was able to "move" his phantom and it eventually vanished. He also states that he "really like[s] to help folks", and as he teaches them to use the mirror, he tells them to practise moving, touching, and looking at their existent limb. It was through communal support and a psychosomatic process, then, that Stephen's PLP was eliminated.

Many people with phantom limbs find medication to be unhelpful, and as Stephen explains, although opioids and Neurontin reduced the "panic element" that accompanies phantom limb pain, medication (a medical approach) was ultimately useless. However, a psychical approach was also unhelpful, as Stephen demonstrates in his statement that he endured the pain for four or five years "thinking that I could 'man up' or 'mind-over-matter it,' but no dice. It was bigger than me". Paralleling the medical physical approach, this attempt was also unsuccessful in healing the psychosomatic pain. Stephen writes: "from a neuroscientific view the guy you want to search [... is] VS Ramachandran" (Sumner 2015). Rather than healing the body through medical intervention or taking the "mind-over-matter" approach, mirror therapy involves both the psyche and soma. Stephen demonstrates the ways in which the therapy relates to both his mind and body in his statement that when introducing it to others in the world, he "inculcate[s] this mantra: LOOK, MOVE, IMAGINE". Indeed, this mantra involves an interaction between the physical acts of looking and moving, and the psychical act of imagining. For Stephen, then, the only way to heal a psychosomatic injury is through a psychosomatic mechanism, suggesting that since the physical feeling involved in the phantom is located in the psyche, it must in this case be treated through the psyche. The mirror-box works because it is not only psychical or physical: like the phantom, it is both at once. There is a paradox here that relates to the way in which Stephen uses language to describe phantom limbs, and in what follows I will explore this by returning to the theory of Blanchot. What is essential is that Stephen is frustrated with the inability to understand an absence, and it is precisely this kind of a difficulty that concerns Blanchot.

Stephen and the texts

PLP, writes Stephen, was "bigger than me". The burnings and electrical shocks "totally beggar words", and the mirror experience is "impossible to describe" (Sumner 2015). Although he states that the sensations cannot be described, they are nonetheless described as being "strange, uncanny, and cool". Here, language can and cannot communicate: though the sensations can be partially expressed, they ultimately escape definition, reflective of Blanchot's first slope of literature. Stephen's paradoxical experience with language echoes Blanchot's notion of language because, for Blanchot, a thing is murdered by its description, sensations cannot be captured in language. This concept echoes mirror therapy in that, as Blanchot writes, "real things [...] refer back to that unreal whole" (1995, 330), just as the real loss of the original limb creates an imaginary whole: the phantom. In other words, language involves an illusory whole that is necessary for communication. Critchley explains that for Blanchot, literature "negates reality and posits a fantasized reality in its place" (2004, 52). Similarly, the mirror Stephen uses negates the real feeling of the phantom limb, replacing it with a fantasised reality, the mirror image creates a new subjective reality. The word "gives me being, but it gives it to me deprived of being. The word is the absence of that being, its nothingness" (Blanchot 1995, 322), as the mirror image gives Stephen control of the phantom by erasing it. The image kills or negates the felt phantom: the mirror is a metaphor for and embodiment of language as Blanchot conceives it. In this way, the body and language do not only parallel one another, but are connected: they affect one another. Moreover, similar to the way in which Peter states that he "was a lie", Stephen conveys a conflation between language and the body. The phantom limb, he writes, left him feeling "ripped-off", a statement that indicates a similar collapse. What Stephen presumably means is that he felt cheated; however, the language also indicates a literal and physical ripping off. From this point of view, it is important to explore what the body and language can convey about one another, and it is this relationship that psychoanalysis investigates. In Chapter 5 I examine this relationship through Lacan's (1977) concept of the mirror stage.

In the mirror stage, an infant identifies itself in its mirror image, which is an imaginary whole (the infant looks complete in the mirror) that contradicts the fragmented and ever-changing subject. Lacan contends that here a divide is formed between the fantasy mirror image, and the uncoordinated physical baby. The mirrored reflection is thought to act as a blueprint for the subject's relation to images and language, which is related to the split that those with phantom limbs may feel: a bodily discord that contrasts a fantasy whole (the amputee's image when they use the mirror-box). As Stephen explains, during mirror therapy "I was literally suffused with a sense of calm, completion". He continues:

> you gotta look right in the eyes and it is incandescent and unmistakable and is, truly, that LOOK, the reason I continue [...]. The first instant that I gazed into a mirror at a sound limb that was bending and waggling and all, in place of this epicentre of electrical storms.
>
> *(Sumner 2015)*

Like the baby in Lacan's mirror image, Stephen is delighted and transformed upon recognising himself in the mirror. Lacan writes, "[we] have only to understand the mirror stage *as an identification*, in the full sense that analysis gives to the term:

namely, the transformation that takes place in the subject when he assumes an image" (1977, 2). Stephen explains that the mirror image allowed him to feel complete, and thereby relieved. Similarly, in Lacan's theory, the infant feels fragmented and "caught up in the lure of spatial identification". However, when it identifies with its mirror reflection, the "fragmented image of the body [... transforms to a] form of its totality" (1977, 5). This results in the creation of "an identity that will mark [... its] entire mental development" (Lacan 1977, 5), which echoes Stephen's statement that identification with his mirror image "rewires" his brain. In both scenarios, then, the subject is shaped through a split between an illusory wholeness and a felt fragmentation. A double is thus formed, which, as discussed in relation to Peter's double self, is reflective of the uncanny.

As mentioned, Peter experienced a "strange" uncanny feeling upon seeing an amputee at a young age, which, I suggest, relates to Stephen's experience with PLP. Stephen writes that "strangeness or the accountability is a really big part of the trauma [...]. Your arm or your leg [...] is GONE. Yet it's still agonizing you?" (Sumner 2015). However, for Peter, this feeling is instigated by the observation of another, while for Stephen, it is based on his own sudden and traumatic bodily amputation. Moreover, as we see in Freud's notion of the uncanny, for Stephen, it is not what is there that causes pain, but rather what is not there. Freud suggests that an uncanny feeling is rooted in the unconscious, in which traumas from the past continue to haunt the subject.

Viewed thus, the phantom limb is not only an allegory for the unconscious, but an embodiment of it: it is a lingering pain with no present source, often derived from a trauma, an invisible part of one's past self (in non-congenital phantoms) that returns in a ghostly form. However, one difference between the traumas discussed in Freud's work and the phantom limb is that although the limb pain is located in the psyche, it definitively stems from a physically, rather than psychically, orientated trauma. It is, moreover, a visible absence, while the traumas Freud writes of are often ambiguous in nature. Nevertheless, in both cases, the subject is left with a feeling of discomfort without a specific and present treatable wound. As Stephen writes, "the itches are the worst cuz you truly can't scratch them" (Sumner 2015). Although Stephen cannot scratch an itch because there is no body part to scratch, Freud suggests that disturbing feelings similar to these can be treated in psychoanalysis, which is itself an uncanny experience "laying bare [...] hidden forces" (1955a, 14). Language, in psychoanalysis, can scratch an invisible itch.

In Freudian psychoanalysis, the analyst and patient relive traumatic pasts in a different form and through this process, the terror of the old experience can be recognised and become less terrifying. Similarly, for Stephen, the mirror therapy experience is "both cool and uncanny. It's also deeply comforting". The mirror can be envisioned as a manifestation of the analytic encounter: an uncanny "old" and "familiar" experience becomes comforting through a process of self-reflection. For Stephen, it is mirror therapy that "scratches the itch", that allows him to "touch" and "command" the pain, while in therapy it is ostensibly appeased through the patient–analyst dynamic. Therefore, Stephen begins to find relief through a mirror reflection, just as in Freudian thought the patient can be healed through verbal reflection. Although these two modes of reflection (language and mirror therapy) are different, they are closely interlinked, share a similar process, and even share a similar structure. Language, in other words, is a type of mirror, and just as the mirror can physically affect amputees by replicating the real existing limb, language can affect the patient in psychoanalysis by replicating a (typically) ambiguous trauma (though distorted) in the present moment. This relationship is clarified through a discussion of Winnicott's "Fear of Breakdown" (1974), which suggests that the analyst and analysand can recreate a kind of experience that happened in the past in order to helpfully affect the patient.

Stephen writes that his phantom sensation is "bigger than [him]" and "beggars words". This description, I argue, parallels that of the infant in Winnicott's model, as he suggests that a baby is not originally a complete human being: it is one with the mother and psychosomatically fragmented. "There is no such thing as a baby" (Winnicott 1960, 38), Winnicott writes: the infant is part of a relationship. In addition, the baby is helpless and cannot describe its sensations as it has no cognitive ability or knowledge of language at this time, and I suggest that the baby's situation resembles Stephen's un-articulable experiences. For Winnicott, a baby is psychosomatically unintegrated, and becomes integrated as it matures. It may develop if the carer holds the baby to create a continuity of being, so that the infant can learn to cope with impingements from its environment. He writes that integration occurs when a person "com[es] together and feel[s] something" (Winnicott 1945, 150), or becomes a "unit", when they feel as though they are "seen or understood to exist by someone [... that they] have been recognised as a being" (qtd. in Jacobs 1995, 36). Indeed, Stephen feels as though his absent limb moves when he can see it in the mirror. In Winnicott's terms he can recognise himself as a being a "unit", as having a more complete ego. For Winnicott, it is when another individual recognises the baby that it feels that "I am here, I exist here and now" (qtd. in Jacobs 1995, 46). Echoing this is Stephen's statement that you "watch and monitor that movement in the mirror. It really helps to focus on the afflicted area and move it [...] you can feel that phantom foot and you can flex that phantom ankle and wiggle those phantom toes" (Sumner 2015). Stephen, like the baby, feels as though he exists, as though he can feel himself upon recognising himself. He continues (as quoted above), "I gazed into a mirror at a sound limb that was bending [...] in place of this epicentre of electrical storms I was literally suffused with a sense of calm, completion". This echoes the baby's process of integration in Winnicott's model, which can take place through a transitional object.

The transitional object can be any number of things such as a "wool cloth" or "blanket" that helps the child cope with its primary carer's temporary absence. It can also be linguistic; he states: "[a]s the infant starts to use organised sounds [...] there may appear a 'word' for the transitional object" (Winnicott 1991, 5). This symbol can also lead to a feeling of psychosomatic integration.[8] The objects allow the child to grow from a fragmented and dependent baby to a more independent and complete individual. It separates the subjective baby from the objective world, the "me" from the "not-me", and is in an intermediate state, a "potential space" between the subjective and objective senses of self. It is also, Winnicott states, the basis for language and cultural experience, and I want to suggest that thinking about the transitional object in relation to mirror therapy provides a unique way of understanding the phenomenon. Stephen explains to others on Reddit that the mirror helps him to "command" the phantom pain, that it is a "magical" solution, and that it allows him to control his muscle coordination. Indeed, Winnicott writes: "[i]n relation to the transitional object the infant passes from (magical) omnipotent control to control by manipulation (involving muscle coordination pleasure)" (1991, 10). Also, like the transitional object, the mirror image involves "[t]he existence of an intermediate area, neither inside the individual nor outside him, [... it] is therefore based on a paradox" (Clancier 1987, 90). The object embodies a contradiction between illusion and objective reality: it is part of the subject and separate from it.

Stephen's mirror image also involves a paradoxical relationship between illusion and reality, as it is an illusion that can be visualised and has a physical effect. It is part of the subject and separate from it as it is not the actual limb but a reflection of his existent one, and in this way functions as a transitional object.

> The essential feature in the concept of transitional objects and phenomena, is *the paradox, and the acceptance of the paradox*: the baby creates the object, but the object was there waiting to be created and to become a cathected object.
>
> *(Winnicott 1991, 104)*

The baby must accept that the transitional object is never completely part of itself and is part illusion. Similarly, Stephen must accept that the mirror image is not an existent limb, but an illusory one, and that, as suggested of the process of integration and psychoanalysis, the subject is never completely healed. Stephen writes that the mirror can "eradicate everything BUT the burning sensations", though these sensations are "mild", and although the transitional object may help the individual separate from dependence on the carer, "[t]he finished creation [of the self] never heals the underlying lack of sense of self" (Winnicott 1991, 64).

As noted, Winnicott believes that traumatised individuals can begin to restructure themselves through a certain kind of psychoanalytical support. Adam Phillips (2007) explains that the "analyst, like the mother, facilitates by providing opportunity for communication and its recognition" (141), and the mirror, in Stephen's case, provides the opportunity to visualise and psychically communicate to the body that the phantom is real.[9] Moreover, the therapeutic encounter echoes the ("potential") space of the transitional object, in that it "provides space to play, to create illusions, and to move through disillusionment into new perceptions of and approximations to reality" (Jacobs 1995, 61). In this way, therapy is connected to a transitional object and space, which, I argue, parallels the space in which one's phantom limb is reflected in mirror therapy. I now want to return to Stephen's statement that when he teaches others to use the mirror he tells them to "LOOK, MOVE, IMAGINE. It really helps in making a new map, which is what you are doing". Similar to the psychoanalytic process, mirror therapy involves playing with images and creating illusions through the body, mind and imagination, which enables a process of restructuring. In psychoanalysis, this works because, according to Winnicott, early relationships with the carer have shaped the individual's mind, and psychoanalysis offers the potential to alter the mind's map. However, it is not only in analysis that individuals may feel supported and grow towards psychosomatic cohesion and independence, it is through other objects and people in their life.

Christopher Bollas writes:

> The way people interact reveals implied or tacit assumptions about their relation to the self as object. Each person forms his own "culture" through the selection of friends, partners and colleagues. The totality of this object-relational field constitutes a type of holding environment and reveals important assumptions about the person's relation to the self as an object at the more existential level of self-management.
>
> (Bollas 1987, 49)

In Stephen's case it was the support of family and friends that enabled him to effectively use the mirror. He writes, "[m]y recovery was complete in virtually every way, largely thanks to the help of a phenomenal group of family and friends plus a really good rehab therapist" (Sumner 2015). It was, therefore, not only the mirror itself, but also the strength provided by others that allowed him to successfully engage in mirror therapy. He later states,

> I have a great family and dynamite friends, so I was super-duper lucky in that regard. For all of them, I would say they did the right thing: it was like, whoa! That's a big one, but he's a big strong guy and won't want a big ol' fuss [...]. So I got a huge amount of very quiet assistance.
>
> (Sumner 2015)

It was not only the familial presence and trust in Stephen that was helpful, but also their quiet assistance, a familial relationship that echoes the healthy therapeutic relationship in Winnicott's theory. Winnicott writes that it

> is not the accuracy of the interpretation so much as the willingness of the analyst to help, the analyst's capacity to identify with the patient and so to believe in what is needed and to meet the need as soon as the need is indicated verbally or in non-verbal or pre-verbal language
>
> (qtd. in Phillips 2007, 140)

It is often in silence and through gestures that the patient can begin to psychosomatically integrate, as this preverbal experience replicates that of the infant.

By recreating the infant's experience of learning to use transitional objects, the pattern of how the subject is shaped may begin to alter. As Bollas writes: "[i]ndeed, the way she [the carer] handled us [...] will influence our way of handling our self" (1987, 36). He also notes that the "search for symbolic equivalents to the transformational object, and the experience with which it is identified, continues in adult life" (1987, 17), again suggesting that in order to psychosomatically integrate throughout life, the individual seeks assistance from these kinds of symbolic (transitional) objects. For Stephen, the mirror image symbolises a phantom delusion (which is replacing a loss). Through a slow process of playing with the mirror image, and with support from others, he was able to more thoroughly connect his psyche and soma. Although Stephen emphasises the importance of supportive individuals in his life, it is ultimately his own strength that allows him to heal. He writes:

> One of the most persuasive and beautiful things about the therapy is that no one "administers" it to you. You have to take the initiative: you have to take the mirror in your own hands and take personal intimate steps to improve your own well-being. To me this forms a fundamental part of the effectiveness of the therapy. I can't give it to you; you have to give it up to yourself.
> *(Sumner 2015)*

Stephen's description of mirror therapy functions in a similar way to Winnicott's model of psychoanalysis, in which the patient should have space to find their own gestures and experiment with them in a safe place and to grow increasingly independent. As Annette Kuhn writes in *Little Madnesses* (2013), this space "involves an interrogation of the existence of a sustaining self, a self able to engage with and make use of the world, of relationships with persons and things located in 'the *potential space*' between the individual and the environment" (Kuhn 2013, xviii). It is a space for language and gestures, a space between self and other. And I suggest that Perec's text *W* also acts as a transitional object, which, through a process similar to mirror therapy, helps Perec cope with feelings of physical and psychical fragmentation.

Like both Perec and Peter, Stephen feels broken and psychosomatically dissonant in relation to a loss. However, unlike Peter, Stephen is able to repair this feeling through the use of an object that is both present and absent and illusory and real, an object that acts as a mediator between the mind and body, the "me" and the "not-me" (as Winnicott terms it).

Sumner's *Phantom Pain: A Memoire* (2015) describes his experience in the hospital after his motorbike accident. He writes, "I'm lost in loss [...]. I'm having a problem with loss" (Sumner 2015, 24–25). Shortly after the loss of his limb, it seems as though Stephen could not digest the sudden bodily loss that resulted from his motorbike accident, and that he was psychically lost in a physical loss. Similarly, throughout *W*, Perec writes about the loss of his mother in the Second World War both directly and metaphorically. At one point, he describes a scene in which he has broken his arm and is wearing it in a sling, which, I will argue, stands for the way in which he has embodied the loss of his mother.

The loss of his mother at an early age, he indicates, has been registered in the mind and transformed into a fictionalised and psychosomatic one. This embodiment is echoed in Stephen's explanation that after his accident, he attempts to understand which body parts belong to him, as he writes, "my new arm hangs above me. Hangs in a sling and from a stand" (Sumner 2015, 12). It is unclear to the reader whether this new arm is the existent, pre-amputation, arm or the amputated one, which is presumably reflective of Stephen's own confusion at the time. Both Stephen and Perec demonstrate a psychosomatic split and find it difficult to discern the "real" from the "unreal". Stephen writes: "I also know that somewhere down there I'm missing […]. It's mostly in my head" (Sumner 2015, 42). What, he seems to ask, is physically real, and what is psychically real? Perec's account of having broken his arm echoes this sentiment, as he later discovers that the accident did not, in fact, happen to him but to a friend. Like Stephen, Perec is attempting to locate psychical pain through his body. The broken arm seems to him an appropriate representation of his emotional pain, so he mistakenly attributes the accident to himself.

In order to cope with these feelings, Stephen and Perec use strategies that possess several of the characteristics of a transitional object. Winnicott (1989) explains that the transitional object assists in creating a psychosomatic "border", in separating the baby from the "not-me" as it becomes a "unit". Related to this, Stephen writes, "I'm sitting up taking stock and I find I can't affix any borders to me" (Sumner 2015, 44). As he attempts to comprehend and integrate the trauma of his accident, he struggles to separate the true from the false, the "me" from the "not-me", the phantom from reality. This difficulty with self-definition is also found in *W*, as psychoanalysis and writing help the author to create a bodily border with which to separate from feelings of incomprehensible fragmentation. For Perec, it is language that acts as a border that allows him to begin defining himself and integrating his mind and body. For Stephen, it is the mirror that forms a visible outline. These borders (shaped through the transitional object, the text of *W*, and the mirror) are not "completely" existent or "real", as they involve the imagination, body and mind. Perec plays with this illusory border in *W*, as he devises memories such as the arm in the sling, which he discovers in the process of writing *W* to be imaginary. It is the fictionalised version of the self, as is also perceptible in Stephen's case, that helps Perec undo his feelings of fragmentation and loss. By linking the mirror phenomenon to the transitional object and to *W*, it becomes clear that a certain type of object, and moreover, a certain type of exchange that involves a relationship between the self and other, and presence and absence, can begin to undo particular forms of suffering.

Conclusions

Both case studies demonstrate some of the shortcomings of medical treatments. For Peter, although those within the medical world attempted to help and had good intentions, they ultimately caused him more harm. Although Stephen's encounter with doctors was not harmful, the medications prescribed to him were unhelpful. He was, however, exposed to mirror therapy, which was invented by a neurologist, but also entails a psychosomatic cure. Like the traumatised baby in Winnicott's model, Peter and Stephen are driven to integrate their psyche and soma, and in different ways they attempt to re-form themselves. While Peter attempts to restructure himself through an act of self-destruction, it is through the support of others that he is able to experience feelings of relief. However, his desire to self-amputate does not dissipate, and his life becomes endangered. Stephen's restructuring, alternatively, is attained through a partially illusory object, which offers something similar to what language offers—a symbolic exchange. Since this kind of symbolic exchange is simultaneously illusory and physical, part of the self and the other, and fragmented and whole, I suggested that certain dialogues that involve these components might provide further insight into what can assist in repairing the psychosomatically fragmented individual. Certain psychoanalytic thought, and particular types of literature and fiction that are concerned with this kind of exchange, might illuminate ways of facilitating psychosomatic integration. This does not indicate, however, that language can cure those with BIID or PLS, but rather, that a linguistic analysis of the syndromes' central aspects is important.

Peter and Stephen share a discord between the mind and body, self and other, and illusion and material reality, which generates painful feelings. Apotemnophilia, however, is felt in the body and involves a stronger psychical experience of a felt lack. Although it is often triggered by a childhood encounter, as seen in Peter's experience with Helen, it is not necessarily attributable to a sudden accident or loss. Moreover, those with BIID pursue physical self-destruction in a desire to appease pain rather than to cause it. As conveyed in Peter's description of the pleasurable pain of tying his ligatures, then, there is a blurred boundary between the desire to remove a limb and to cause pain. There is a paradoxical desire for self-repair through self-fragmentation. Though such a drive for self-repair is also apparent in Stephen's case, he conveys the inverse, the mirror image of those with BIID. While, like Peter, Stephen wants to remove a (imaginary) limb in order to appease his pain, it is not because the limb feels as though it is absent, but because it feels as though it is present. Peter, on the other hand, attempts to repair the split between his mind and body through self-amputation, through which he hopes to transform his psychical sense of reality into a physical one. While for Peter, communicating with others is at times helpful in appeasing his feelings of alienation, it is also problematic, as he is often (dangerously) advised by others with similar difficulties. This raises the question of whether there is a particular type of communication that can be helpful. In the case of Stephen, although communication assists in providing the strength to heal, ultimately, it is the mirror illusion that offers him relief. And although the mirror is not language, it parallels language, in that it is an illusory presence that can affect the body. Since Peter and Stephen struggle with similar feelings of psychosomatic fragmentation, and Stephen's is assisted by an illusion that functions in a way similar to language, what might this relationship mean for the fractured individual? To address this question, I turn in the next chapter to an exploration of other disciplines that take an interest in the ways in which the mind and body interact through symbolic exchanges.

Notes

1 As discussed in the Introduction, the term "wannabe" refers to those with BIID who self-injure, self-amputate, or pursue black-market surgery
2 Since this book is concerned with the body, and the body is fluid, or according to Anzieu, "[t]he skin is permeable and impermeable" (qtd. in Segal 2009, 45), the divide between internal and external is blurred. As Drew Leder explains,

> the inner body is characterized primarily by its recession from awareness and control. The body surface, conversely, is lived out primarily through ecstasis. Yet this contrast does not constitute a new dualism. It only serves to highlight the limit points of a complemental series that embraces interfusion, exchanges, and intermediate modes.
>
> *(Leder 1990, 56)*

Although I differentiate internal and external at times, this is not to suggest that there is a binary, keeping Leder's explanation in mind. I use these terms at times for clarity, and in response to the use of the words by other theorists (such as Winnicott and Melanie Klein's).
3 All the quotations from Peter's story are taken directly from the text, which includes misspellings and misused words. Although this could be considered problematic in the following analysis, I am predominantly interested in what we can discover from the way in which he expresses himself more generally, rather than deciphering the exact meanings of the words he uses.
4 Although Freud's definition of disavowal changed, Jean Laplanche and J.B. Pontalis (1996) write that it is a (common) "mode of defence which consists in the subject's refusing to recognise the reality of a traumatic perception" (118).
5 Although I am drawing a parallel between Winnicott's theory and Peter's experience here, I am not claiming that it was not the removal of the entire leg (that Peter desired) that engendered Peter's feelings of relief.
6 Since Stephen uses a flat mirror rather than a mirror-box, I refer to the phenomenon as mirror therapy throughout this chapter. However, the original model by Ramachandran was a mirror-box, and therefore I also refer to it as a mirror-box elsewhere in this book.
7 As with Peter, I have not altered the grammatical errors in Stephen's statements.
8 It is this definition that I use as a template for my use of the word "symbol", as it is both illusory and concrete, and in this way reflects the mirror-box.
9 This is not to suggest that mirror therapy can replace psychoanalysis, but to provide a way of understanding more about how this type of psychosomatic integration works.

References

Aisenstein, Marilia. "Psychosomatic Solution or Somatic Outcome: The Man from Burma – *Psychotherapy of a Case of Haemorrhagic Rectolitis.*" *Reading French Psychoanalysis*. Edited by Dana Breen, Sara Flanders, and Alain Gibeault, London: Routledge, 2009, pp. 463–477.

Bollas, Christopher. *The Shadow of the Object: Psychoanalysis of the Unthought Known*. New York: Columbia UP, 1987.

Blanchot, Maurice. "Literature and the Right to Death." *The Work of Fire* [*La part du feu*, 1949]. Translated by Charlotte Mandell, Stanford: Stanford UP, 1995, pp. 300–344.

Clancier, Anne, and Jeannine Kalmanovitch. *Winnicott and Paradox: From Birth to Creation.* London: Tavistock Publications, 1987.

Critchley, Simon. *Very Little – Almost Nothing: Death, Philosophy, Literature.* London: Routledge, 2004.

Freud, Sigmund. "*The Uncanny*" [*Das Unheimliche*, 1919]. *The Standard Edition of the Complete Psychological Works of Sigmund Freud,* vol. 17, 1917–1919. Edited and translated by James Strachey, London: The Hogarth Press and The Institute of Psychoanalysis, 1955a.

Freud, Sigmund. "Studies on Hysteria" [*Studien über Hysterie*, 1895]. *The Standard Edition of the Complete Psychological Works of Sigmund Freud,* vol. 2, 1893–1895. Edited and translated by James Strachey, London: The Hogarth Press and The Institute of Psychoanalysis, 1955b.

Freud, Sigmund. *The Ego and the Id* [*Ich und das Es*, 1923]. Translated by James Strachey, New York: Norton, 1961.

Jacobs, Michael. *D.W. Winnicott.* London: Sage Publications, 1995.

Kuhn, Annette. *Little Madnesses: Winnicott, Transitional Phenomena and Cultural Experience.* London: I.B. Tauris, 2013.

Lacan, Jacques. *Écrits: a Selection.* Translated by Alan Sheridan. New York: Norton, 1977.

Laplanche, Jean and J.B. Pontalis. *The Language of Psychoanalysis.* New York: Karnac Books, 1996.

Leder, Drew. *The Absent Body.* Chicago: University of Chicago, 1990.

Mensaert, Alex. *Amputation on Request.* London: lulu.com, 2011.

Nortvedt, Finn, and Gunn Engelsrud. "'Imprisoned' in Pain: Analyzing Personal Experiences of Phantom Pain." *Medicine, Health Care and Philosophy Med Health Care and Philos,* vol. 17, no. 4, 2014, pp. 599–608.

Perec, George. *W or The Memory of Childhood* [*W ou le souvenir d'enfance*, 1975]. Translated by David Bellos. London: Collins Harvill, 1989.

Phillips, Adam. *Winnicott.* London: Penguin, 2007.

Segal, Naomi. *Consensuality: Didier Anzieu, Gender and the Sense of Touch.* Amsterdam: Rodopi, 2009.

Sumner, Stephen. *Phantom Pain: A Memoire: It's All in Your Head.* Bloomington: Archway Publishing, 2015.

Winnicott, D.W. "Primitive Emotional Development." *The International Journal of Psycho-Analysis,* vol. 26, no. 3–4, 1945, pp. 137–143.

Winnicott, D.W. "Theory of the Parent", *The International Journal of Psycho-Analysis,* vol. 41, no. 3, 1960, pp. 585–595.

Winnicott, D.W. "Fear of Breakdown." International Review of Psychoanalysis, vol. 1, 1974, pp. 103–107.

Winnicott, D.W. "Psycho-Somatic Disorder." *Psycho-Analytic Explorations.* Cambridge: Harvard UP, 1989, pp. 103–118.

Winnicott, D.W. *Playing and Reality.* London: Routledge, 1991.

3

SCIENCE, LITERATURE, AND PSYCHOANALYSIS

Nun ist die Luft von solchem Spuk so voll,
Daß niemand weiß, wie er ihn meiden soll.

Now fills the air so many a haunting shape,
That no one knows how best he may escape.

Goethe, Faust

Freud's *The Psychopathology of Everyday Life* (1960 [1901]) opens with this epigraph, illuminating not only the inextricability between literature and psychoanalysis, but also their similar concern with "haunting shapes", with the daunting unknown. One individual who suffers from apotemnophilia writes on the Internet Yahoo! Group "Fighting It:" "it is possible that the neuroscience of BIID might have very little to do with its cause, and even less to do with any potential treatment" ("Fighting It"), raising the question as to how the syndrome can be explored beyond a neurological view. In response to this question, I will be employing psychoanalysis and literary works to examine the two conditions, because they help to illuminate the complex dimensions of the limb scenarios and the mirror-box treatment. This chapter will primarily examine the difficulties with a solely neurological approach, focusing on a neurological reductivism, which can fail to distinguish how the "mind" is more than the (physical) "brain". Following this, I shall discuss the affinity between psychoanalysis and literature.

The problem with naming a problem: science and psychoanalysis

As demonstrated by Peter and Stephen, psychiatrists were unable to help relieve pain, and sometimes, in the case of Peter, they increased his feelings of alienation. For Stephen, a mechanism that treated the mind and body at once was helpful, one that involved his "looking, moving, and imagining". (https://medium.com/mosaic-science/mirror-man-2e099226a7). The most successful treatments for these conditions, researchers have found, do not involve a purely medicinal method: they treat the psyche and soma in more unconventional ways. As mentioned, these include, for BIID, the minifying lens experiment, and for PLS, the "Bear Claw" method, GMI, and the rubber hand and foot illusion (which has also been tested for BIID). These methods, although promising in some cases, have not been successful in eradicating pain, and have not been adequately tested. For those with BIID, CBT methods have, in a small minority of cases, reduced the obsessive-compulsive component and need for self-amputation. In the case of PLP, though few studies have been conducted, CBT has (at times) been helpful in allowing amputees to cope with phantom sensations, and reduce the irritation involved in having a phantom a limb. The most prominent study of CBT and phantom limbs (Sherman et al. 1984), found that only 1% of participants reported lasting benefits from CBT methods mirror therapy demonstrated a higher success rate (though more research is needed). As noted, although CBT and mirror therapy are similar in that they are both solution-focused and based on the concept that the mind can affect the body, the methods are different. In addressing conditions such as chronic pain, anxiety, mood disorders, and prevention of mental illness, CBT can help individuals cope emotionally with symptoms and stress levels, often by allowing them to adopt a more positive outlook. The mirror-box, while it can alter amputees' psychosomatic feelings through the mind, does not begin with the psyche-it is a physical mechanism. Furthermore, the mirror-box involves an illusory mirror image, a visual symbolisation of the phantom, which, unlike CBT, is helpful in altering (rather than teaching the individual to cope with) phantom sensations. The symbolisation of the mirror-box, I suggest, reflects the way in which symbols are used in psychoanalysis. psychoanalysis Although it begins in the psyche rather than through a physical object, psychoanalysis differs from CBT because it is concerned with searching for meaning by tracing symbols within the patient's unconscious. However, psychoanalysis is not often taken as seriously in the medical world, perhaps because (as with mirror therapy) illusion is central to its process. According to Perur, Stephen Sumner contends that mirror therapy is not often recognised in the medical world, " '[w]ell it's not scientific' – simply because mirror therapy looks too simple" (Perur 2014). Although the mirror-box may not conform to preconceived notions of science, it can work to treat psychosomatic conditions. Psychoanalysis, as it is also concerned with the way in which illusion is integral to treating or understanding psychosomatic conditions, can thus lend insight.

Psychiatrist Bishnu Subedi and George T. Grossberg (2011) state that for PLS, "most successful measures employ multidisciplinary approaches in the management of pain and in rehabilitation" (3). Since the syndrome is felt in the body but located in the mind, researchers must attend to not just the (physical) brain, but also the (psychical) mind. Bertram Malle (1991) states: "I maintain that, due to the current state of empirical science [...] we may have to change our concepts of physical states in order to relate them to non-physical phenomena in an intelligible way" (95). According to Malle, the "mind-body problem" cannot be sufficiently explored through an empirical system, there must also be a method that focuses on the non-physical. PLS, I suggest, not only calls for this kind of exploration, but also demonstrates its importance. As Elizabeth Grosz (1994) remarks, the "irreducibility of psychology to biology and of biology to psychology can be illustrated with [...] the phantom limb" (89). It is because psychoanalysis deals with precisely this with how the body is shaped through the psyche that it seems natural to use this discourse. More specifically, the field is concerned with exploring delusion, misplaced pain, and a fragmented and unknowable self, which are also central to the limb phenomena. Psychoanalysis, moreover, poses questions regarding imaginary concepts of wholeness. Indeed, "[t]he phantom", writes Grosz,

> is an expression of nostalgia for the unity and wholeness of the body, its completion. It is a memorial to the missing limb, a psychical delegate that stands in its place. There is thus not only a physical but also a psychical wound and scar in the amputation or surgical intervention into any part of the body.
>
> *(1994, 73)*

BIID also involves the psychical feeling of a physical wound that is related to an expression of the desire for bodily unity. In this way, PLS, BIID and psychoanalysis raise the question how the unified image of self is decentralised by a fragmented and unknowable other, and how this other shows through in symbolic forms. As Terry Eagleton writes, in psychoanalysis, "I am not actually the coherent, autonomous, self-generating subject I know myself to be in the ideological sphere, but the 'decentred' function of several social determinants" (150). Jean Laplanche and Jean-Bertrand Pontalis (1996) write that psychoanalysis is "a method of investigation which consists essentially in bringing out the unconscious meaning of the words, the actions and the products of the imagination (dreams, phantasies, delusions) of a particular subject" (367). Since both of the limb conditions raise questions about the relationship between delusions and illusions of one's coherence that cannot be understood in the medical world, analysing the syndromes from a psychoanalytic perspective is vital.

Norman Doidge (2007) writes that the mirror-box is a treatment that "uses imagination and illusion to restructure brain maps plastically without medication, needles, or electricity" (194). In this sense, it is a kind of embodiment of psychoanalysis, as psychoanalysis is interested in how symbolising elements of the imagination and illusion (dream work, for instance) can alter one's mind and actions. Doidge writes that the mirror-box can alter the brain (rather than the mind), which indicates that the mind and body are inseparable, and continually altering one another. Dreams, for instance, are central to analysis, where they are not only considered inseparable from reality, but provide clues to understanding pain. A fantasy may illuminate how and why a patient may unwillingly repeat painful experiences. Psychoanalysis then, as Doidge (2007) writes of the mirror-box, works by "fighting one illusion with another" (186). If PLP and a patient's pain can be altered through fantasy, perhaps this is because, according to Doidge,

> "pain is an illusion" and [...] "our mind is a virtual reality machine," which experiences the world indirectly and processes it at one remove, constructing a model in our head. So pain, like the body image, is a construct of our brain.
>
> *(2007, 192)*

The mirror-box and analysis, therefore, can be effective because they work in a removed space that plays with image, material reality, the psyche, and moreover, a specific form of emptiness (inside the room and inside the mirror-box, or the mirror itself).

As mentioned, although Ramachandran uses creative, imaginative, and untypically scientific tools to explore the BIID and phantom limb disorders, he also insists upon finding a biological cause. In *Tell-Tale Brain* (2011), he writes that apotemnophilia is sometimes seen as arising from a Freudian wish-fulfilment fantasy because a limb resembles a penis. However, Ramachandran finds "these psychological explanations unconvincing. The condition usually begins early in life, and it is unlikely that a ten-year-old would desire a giant penis (although an orthodox Freudian wouldn't rule it out)" (2011, 255). First, Ramachandran's reasoning is questionable here, as it would seem that, from this point of view, the child would be wanting to castrate a penis (cut off a limb), rather than desiring one. Second, orthodox Freudian or not, I think that one of the difficulties in Ramachandran's stance against psychoanalysis in this instance is his literal perspective, his failure to account for a more symbolic or abstract view. Ironically, however, in the mirror-box, it is an image or symbol of a limb that has physical results. Thus, while psychoanalysis addresses non-rational processes similar to what we see with mirror treatment, Ramachandran employs an empirical way of thinking. Empirical statements that demand answers and solutions do, however, illustrate a form of thought common to Freud's work. Freud and Ramachandran are thereby similar in this sense, as they look to cure pain through the mind, and by attending to individuals' illusions (psychological illusions for Freud and the mirror illusion for Ramachandran).

Although Ramachandran dissociates the mirror-box from psychoanalysis, I suggest that the mirror-box sets out to do what, in a different way, psychoanalysis does: to reconstitute the mind and body through an illusion. Like the psychoanalytic exchange, it may allow the individual to reintegrate her known, unknown, and imaginary notions of self through symbolic expression. Though Ramachandran largely dismisses Freud's theories, Freud, like Ramachandran, found that illusions and the imagination were vital to understanding pain. However, the mirror-illusion takes place through a physical object that can be seen, and is thus more aligned with the empirical sciences, since it involves a linguistic exchange in a private place. It is, moreover, often about self-discovery, as opposed to the swift eradication of pain.

A dialogue from the Yahoo! Group "Fighting It" exemplifies the scepticism towards psychoanalysis. In 2005, a member named Dan voiced his disbelief in psychoanalysis, stating that therapy proposes nothing new, that there is no progress. He "expect[s] [therapists] to be able to tell [him] what they propose to do and how it has helped others". However, in 2009 Dan describes a positive experience in treatment, explaining that he and his analyst developed a theory and a story (related to maternal love) as to why he may have the condition, which enabled him to live with BIID more "happily". In "Fighting It", Dan writes of the narrative he developed with his analyst:

> All of this, if it is real, happened before I could remember it. That is also a time when things we learn become a permanent part of us. It would be interesting to know if other people with BIID had similar experiences, but it would be hard to find out without some in-depth psychoanalysis. There is also the risk that an analyst could create false memories and the whole thing is just smoke and mirrors.
>
> *("Fighting It")*

A physician named Larry responds to Dan's post:

> That is pretty close to what I think about the whole of psychoanalysis. Psychoanalysis has never been shown to be effective in treating anything (more than controls, for instance). Psychoanalysis has been in pretty deep disrepute now for some years in academic and scientific medical circles. Further, what you propose is, basically, a non-testable hypothesis.
>
> *("Fighting It")*

This dialogue interests me because it addresses many of the issues we have been discussing: that a method that sets out to cure BIID does not work, that a certain kind of psychoanalytic exploration can help us to understand the condition, and that many are not open to treatment due to the importance placed on empirical science. However, it is ironic that the one comment Larry responds to, that the "whole thing is just smoke and mirrors", dramatises exactly what the mirror-box does: it makes a whole thing (a whole body) out of mirrors. Thus, although Larry is sceptical, it is precisely a mirror illusion that works to treat phantom limb pain. This link between the mirror-box and psychoanalysis, therefore, is not only metaphorical but also effective. Rather than asking how psychoanalysis helped, Larry rejects it for the false memories it is bound to create. However, if both the mirror-box and Dan's experience in psychoanalysis reduce pain, what, we may ask, is problematic about "smoke and mirrors"? I suggest that minimising the need for proof and being open to a non-immediate cure and an imaginative method can prove beneficial. And since both PLS and BIID involve a feeling of psychosomatic fragmentation, the mirror treatment in PLS can be used to learn more about, not cure, the feelings of rupture and unity experienced by those with BIID. Psychoanalysis focuses on the relationship between symbols, the body and the mind, while mirror therapy conveys that a symbol can be helpful in altering problems with bodily fragmentation and wholeness. By exploring psychoanalysis, therefore, we can understand more about the problem with bodily fragmentation experienced by those with BIID and PLS. I now want to investigate the importance of illusion and symbolism in psychoanalysis in more detail, in order to expand our understanding as to how "smoke and mirrors", and narratives in analysis, relate to textual works. How, I ask, does the theory that Dan and his analyst developed help Dan, and how does this relate to literature?

What's the story? Psychoanalysis and narrative

Dan illuminates what is at the core of BIID and PLS: that they involve physical experiences that cannot be completely understood, and that a determinate cause for their occurrence cannot be named. Psychoanalysis worked for Dan because he and his analyst developed a theory—a temporary story, rather than a specific reason for his pain. Although the story of Dan's childhood may have been devised in psychoanalysis, it is exactly this, a story, which proved beneficial.[1] Since certain kinds of psychoanalysis and literature are interested in how stories and the imagination constitute the individual, and both BIID and PLS involve an imagined and fictional version of the self, I will investigate what psychoanalysis and literature, when read together, can tell us about these two phenomena. Psychoanalysis and literature, writes Josh Cohen, share "the task of interpreting forms of expression whose meanings are slippery and ambiguous" (Cohen 2015). Perhaps, therefore, they can help us interpret the elements of BIID and PLS that the biomedical field struggles to decipher. I want to begin this exploration by discussing the links between psychoanalysis and literature through the work of theorist Peter Brooks.

Brooks' (1992) concern lies in "how narratives work on us, as readers, to create models of understanding, and with why we need and want such shaping orders" (xiii). Why, asks Brooks, do individuals need fictions to shape themselves, and how does this work? His question, then, echoes those raised by BIID and PLS—the question of why and how amputees may be driven to reshape themselves through a phantom, and why some individuals with four limbs feel disturbingly misshapen. In relation to these issues, Brooks is concerned with how psychoanalytic and literary studies are interested in how one is shaped through narratives, and why it is important to develop this relationship. He writes,

> [p]sychoanalysis matters to us as literary critics because it stands as a constant reminder that the attention to form, properly conceived, is not a sterile formalism, but rather one more attempt to draw the symbolic and fictional map of our place in existence
>
> *(Brooks 1987, 348)*

In psychoanalysis, a subject's story can be modified through the analyst's presence, which consequently psychically and somatically reshapes the individual (ostensibly).

Psychoanalytic narratives, explains Brooks, are not stable. They are open, transformative, and capable of producing change, similar to certain types of literary narratives. Brooks explains that literature and psychoanalysis can create these transformations through symbols. This sheds light on how the phantom limb is modified through the mirror-box, as the mirror illusion stands for the phantom limb, a fiction of one's completion.

Peter Brooks suggests that the human drive to make sense of oneself in the world through stories is related to a desire for wholeness. And Harold Schweizer (1997) writes that

> [t]he desire for the aesthetic seems to have its motivation in the patient's fundamental need to counteract his dismemberment with at least a symbolic form of presence—even if that presence can only be in language, the presence of an other.
>
> (52)

The psychoanalytic patient may go to analysis in order to learn about a feeling of rupture, as a "dismembered" reader might experience a symbolic form of presence through a text. Paralleling this concept, an amputee's dismemberment can be counteracted with a symbolic form of presence: the mirror illusion (which, as explained in the introduction, is a kind of symbol), and in this way, the mirror image is related to language. They can both diminish fragmentation with a symbolic presence. While the process of soothing a feeling of rupture can be productive in psychoanalysis and literature (though in different ways), the desire to "counteract dismemberment" is painful for those with BIID and PLS. Like the literary text, writes Brooks (1994), psychoanalysis "reconfirms the presence of the analysand, reveals him—in his state of dismemberment—as the subject of a story, through which telling the patient might become (temporarily) whole—as whole at least as the story itself" (17).

This concerns a kind of storytelling that can be useful in psychoanalytic and literary processes; as Brooks contends, they have the capacity to alter the analysand or reader. I will later explore how psychoanalysis and reading involve similar passive and active experiences, however, unlike reading, psychoanalysis is concerned with healing. Since they both have the capacity to transform the reader or analysand, it is important to explore what they convey about PLS and BIID. While individuals with these conditions struggle with a drive towards wholeness, psychoanalysis and literature often turn away from "completion" and towards ambiguity. Since the mirror-box breaks up an idea of unity through a symbol (of the invisible limb), it presents a different kind of "healthy narrative", albeit non-linguistic. The "story" of temporary wholeness is told through bodily symbols which, although similar to those open-ended stories in some literature and analysis, cannot be comprehended because it does not involve language. It is because certain kinds of literature and psychoanalysis use language to read how we are shaped by the imagination that these frameworks cast a different light upon the conditions.

In order to further understand the psychoanalytic and literary interest in narratives, I turn to Brook's "Fictions of the Wolf Man" in *Reading for the Plot* (1984). I shall explore how Freud's case study of the "Wolf Man", in "From the History of an Infantile Neurosis" (2006 [1918]) dramatised his switch from aiming to find the analysand's "true history" in session to admitting the inability to do so. Although I will soon examine the "Wolf Man" case study in detail, for now it is necessary to know that it chronicles the childhood of Sergei Pankejeff, a 23-year-old who consulted Freud because he had suffered from a physical collapse, a gonorrhoeal infection, and an incapacity for independence. The patient also revealed a childhood ridden with neurotic disorders that led to an anxiety dream, which became the subject of Freud's essay. In this dream, Pankejeff's bedroom window opened of its own accord, revealing an image of six or seven wolves with large tails, sitting on various branches on a tree. Frightened of being eaten, the child screamed and woke up. Brooks writes that in analysis, Freud used the dream to decipher the patient's life history. However, this process entailed a more scientific account of the imagination, which proved problematic. This analysis, I suggest, is reflective of the neurological models currently being applied to BIID and PLS. Both methods, in other words, involve a desire to grasp an original meaning. Brooks (1992) contends that Freud's case study exhibits a

> reality structured as a set of ambiguous signs which gain their meaning from a past history that must be uncovered so as to order the production of these signs as a chain of events, eventually with a clear origin, intention, and solution, and with strong causal connections between each link.
>
> (270)

Through the patient's dreams, Freud attempted to unearth a more cohesive and comprehensible history. However, explains Brooks, the "Wolf Man" case study conveys a change in direction as Freud began to realise the impossibility of defining Pankejeff's past. He admits that a biographical story cannot be proved: the "case is properly undecidable" (Brooks 1992, 277). As opposed to a specific narrative, what Freud unearths is that how "we narrate a life even our own life within an orderly narrative [...] is dictated by desire" (Brooks 1992, 281). Psychoanalysis, at this point, became less directed towards empirical science and moved towards a more ambiguous framework. For Brooks, this parallels a change in the field of literature—a movement away from formalism and towards modernism in which the "insistent past must be allowed to write its design at the same time one attempts to unravel it" (Brooks 1992, 282). I will now investigate how this concern with unravelling plays out in the analyst's room and in literature by returning to the concept of transference.

Transference is the carrying over of all dimensions of previous and especially the earliest relationships. It is when the patient sees in the analyst "the return, the reincarnation, of some important figure out of his childhood or past, and consequently transfers on to him feelings and reactions which undoubtedly applied to this prototype" (Freud 2010, 52). In psychoanalysis, this "remembering" is not an "attempt to bring a particular moment or problem into focus". The purpose is rather to "recognis[e] the resistances which appear there, and mak[e] them conscious to the patient" (Freud 1958, 147). By disclosing repressed impulses through a linguistic exchange, the analyst may reduce the likelihood of repetition. As noted in the introduction, transference both stands for and re-enacts the past, and in this way, it affects an individual's reality, just as literature and the mirror-box can involve fictions that can change the way a person feels. This kind of fictional re-enactment, suggests Brooks, is also involved in the process of reading. He writes that transference and literature present a "perpetually reversing counterpoint of self and other, closure and opening, origin and process" (Brooks 1992, 283), which counters the attempt to find a specific cause, an attempt sometimes problematic in biomedical research. While BIID and PLS demonstrate a drive towards wholeness—reflective of several scientific models—the mirror-box reflects a more open psychoanalytic and literary endeavour, as it does not aim to find a definitive reason for the phantom: it simply makes it visible. This kind of open exchange is integral to certain types of poetry. As Trilling (1950) writes, "Freudian psychology is the one which makes poetry indigenous to the very constitution of the mind. Indeed, the mind, as Freud sees it, is in this greater part of its tendency exactly a poetry-making organ" (Trilling 1950, 52). Here, Trilling is alluding to the ambiguous vicissitudes of the unconscious mind. Similar to some poetic forms, the unconscious is non-linear; its meanings cannot be "known", it does not contain objective answers or "[compress] the elements into a unity" (Trilling 1950, 53). In relation to this, while BIID and PLS also involve drives to "compress elements into a unity", mirror therapy and certain kinds of literature and psychoanalysis do not. Although the mirror-box is curative, and literature is not, we will soon develop links between the healing possibilities of literature and the mirror-box.

Although Freud created "coherent, finished enclosed, and authoritative narrative[s]" (Elliot 2002, 277) for his patients, this began to shift in the "Wolf Man" case study, also shifting the entire psychoanalytic project. Throughout the study, Freud continually returns to the (previously noted) dream in an aim "to trace memories of sexual scenes back to an original trauma, to a defining event in childhood through which seductions and symptoms could be put into an orderly structure" (Elliot 2002, 17). Freud (2006) proclaims that in "the course of the treatment we often came back to the dream but only arrived at a complete understanding of it during the last months of the therapy" (221). Here Freud expresses both a belief that he has arrived at a definite answer, and also uncertainty, as he continually returned to and altered his interpretations. Through the process of analysis, Freud came to the conclusion that Pankejeff's trauma may have occurred when "consciousness in the child has not yet developed its full range of characteristics and is not yet entirely capable of being converted into language-pictures" (Freud 2006, 292). This case study led Freud to suggest that generally, traumas may not be reproduced as memories, they are the results of reconstruction. Though children may have been too young comprehend traumatic experiences, they were affected by them and left with incoherent traumatic impressions, and thus, it is not the trauma itself, but the memory that is traumatic. Freud's recognition that we cannot accurately remember all traumas created a shift in his focus, as he began to explore the "complex, muddied way in which external events are suffused with fantasy and desire" (Elliot 2002, 17); science, here, became more ambiguous. Paralleling Freud's endeavour, the neurobiological field often attempts to find answers for BIID. However, from this Freudian perspective, the desire to self-amputate may refer to something unknown. For Freud, a wound can be repaired by analysing the psyche through a linguistic exchange, rather than by attempting to discover "true" experiences (although this wavers). As he writes, "psychical reality was of more importance than material reality" (1925–1926, 37). Psychoanalysis thus moved away from a medical exploration of neurosis and towards an analysis of the human imagination—of how early childhood fantasies shaped future realities, thoughts, and physical reactions. Since they both involve an imaginary version of completion, BIID and PLS must also be studied from a model that focuses on the importance of the human imagination. However, since the two syndromes, like the traumas and fantasies in the unconscious mind and the experiences that occurred before they could be comprehended, cannot be completely understood through language, how can we begin to understand them? I turn to André Green to explore this question because, as mentioned in the introduction, both these syndromes contain delusional elements, which are connected to Freud's concept of psychosis.[2] While Freud considered psychotic patients "unsuitable for psychoanalysis" (Green 2011, 79), Green is interested in asking how we can think differently about the psychotic mind. Thus, I now explore how Green's theories can open ways of thinking about the "delusional" elements of BIID and PLS, and moreover, what this can convey about the split between wholeness and fragmentation that is central to these two conditions.

Notes

1 This stance on psychoanalysis is closely associated with a "hermeneutic" stance in psychotherapy, most prominently outlined in Roy Schafer's *A New Language for Psychoanalysis* (1976). In short, he suggests that psychoanalysis is the most efficacious narrative in therapeutic terms. He is interested in looking toward "a new and fruitful interaction between psychoanalysis and all those intellectual disciplines concerned with the study of human beings as persons" (Schafer 1976, xi). In so doing, he attends to what he calls "action language", which includes psychological activity "that can be made public through gesture and speech … [and] has some goal-directed or symbolic properties" (Schafer 1976, 10).
2 For more on this see Freud's "The Future of an Illusion" (1927).

References

Brooks, Peter. "The Idea of a Psychoanalytic Literary Criticism." *Critical Inquiry*, vol. 13, no. 2, 1987, pp. 334–348.
Brooks, Peter. *Reading for the Plot: Design and Intention in Narrative*. Cambridge: Harvard UP, 1984.
Brooks, Peter. *Psychoanalysis and Storytelling*. Oxford: Blackwell, 1994.

Cohen, Josh. "Psychoanalytic Bodies: Psychic and 'Actual' Bodies in Literature." *The Cambridge Companion to the Body in Literature*. Edited by David Hillman and Ulrika Maude, Cambridge: Cambridge UP, 2015, pp. 214–229.

Doidge, Norman. *The Brain That Changes Itself: Stories of Personal Triumph from the Frontiers of Brain Science*. New York: Viking, 2007.

Elliott, Anthony. *Psychoanalytic Theory: an Introduction*. Durham, NC: Duke UP, 2002.

"Fighting It." *Yahoo! Groups*. http://groups.yahoo.com/group/fighting-it/.

Freud, Sigmund. "An Autobiographical Study, Inhibitions, Symptoms and Anxiety, Lay Analysis and Other Works" *The Standard Edition of the Complete Psychological Works of Sigmund Freud*, vol. 20. Edited and translated by James Strachey, London: The Hogarth Press and The Institute of Psychoanalysis, 1925–1926.

Freud, Sigmund. "The Future of an Illusion" *The Standard Edition of the Complete Psychological Works of Sigmund Freud*, vol. 21. Edited and translated by James Strachey, London: The Hogarth Press and The Institute of Psychoanalysis, 1927.

Freud, Sigmund. "Remembering, Repeating, Working-Through" ["Erinnern, Wiederholen und Durcharbeiten", 1914] *The Standard Edition of the Complete Psychological Works of Sigmund Freud*, vol. 12, 1911–1913. Edited and translated by James Strachey, London: The Hogarth Press and The Institute of Psychoanalysis, 1958.

Freud, Sigmund. "The Psychopathology of Everyday Life" [*Zur Psychopathologie des Alltagslebens*, 1901] *The Standard Edition of the Complete Psychological Works of Sigmund Freud*, vol. 6. Edited and translated by James Strachey, London: The Hogarth Press and The Institute of Psychoanalysis, 1960.

Freud, Sigmund. "From the History of an Infantile Neurosis" [*Aus der Geschichte einer infantilen Neurose*, 1918]. *The Penguin Freud Reader*. Translated by Adam Phillips, London: Penguin, 2006.

Freud, Sigmund. *An Outline of Psycho-analysis* [*Abriss der Psychoanalyse*, 1940]. Translated by James Strachey, Mansfield Centre: Martino, 2010.

Green, André. "The Work of the Negative and Hallucinatory Activity (Negative Hallucination)." *On Freud's "Negation"*. Edited by Mary Kay O'Neil and Salman Akhtar, London: Karnac, 2011, pp. 75–145.

Grosz, Elizabeth A. *Volatile Bodies: Toward a Corporeal Feminism*. Bloomington: Indiana UP, 1994.

Laplanche, Jean and J.B. Pontalis. *The Language of Psychoanalysis*. New York: Karnac Books, 1996.

Malle, Bertram F. "Phantom Limbs, the Self, and the Mind-body Problem: Comment on R. Melzack." *Canadian Psychology*, vol. 32, no. 1, 1991, pp. 94–95.

Perur, Srinath. "The Mirror Man." *Mosaic The Science of Life*, 2014. No pagination. http://mosaicscience.com/story/mirror-man.

Ramachandran, VS. *Tell-tale Brain: A Neuroscientist's Quest for What Makes Us Human*. New York: W.W. Norton, 2011.

Schafer, Roy. *A New Language for Psychoanalysis*. New Haven: Yale UP, 1976.

Sherman, Richard A., Crystal J. Sherman, and Laura Parker. "Chronic Phantom and Stump Pain among American Veterans: Results of a Survey." *Pain*, vol. 18, no. 1, 1984, pp. 83–95.

Schweizer, Harold. *Suffering and the Remedy of Art*. State Univ. of New York Press, 1997.

Subedi, Bishnu and George T. Grossberg. "Phantom Limb Pain: Mechanisms and Treatment Approaches." *Pain Research and Treatment*, 2011. www.ncbi.nlm.nih.gov/pmc/articles/PMC3198614/.

Trilling, Lionel. *The Liberal Imagination: Essays on Literature and Society*. New York: Viking, 1950.

4
NEGATIVE HALLUCINATION AND "THE MAN FROM BURMA"

André Green and negative hallucination

Some psychoanalysts after Freud returned to the concept of psychosis, arguing that, contrary to Freud's opinion, it may be analysable if perceived through a different lens, one that thinks about language in a different way. One of these theorists is Melanie Klein, who suggested that psychotic states in childhood are central to human development, and that a psychotic psychical structure correlates with how we use language. "In early infancy", she writes, "anxieties characteristic of psychosis arise which drive the ego to develop specific defence-mechanisms" (Klein 1946, 292). Although this does not suggest that all infants are psychotic, the "psychotic anxieties, mechanisms and ego-defences of infancy have a profound influence on development in all its aspects, including the development of the ego, super-ego and object relations" (1946, 99). Klein's development of object-relations theory which focuses on how symbols (linguistic and otherwise) form and inform objective and subjective notions of self provides a different view of language. For Klein, language derives from unconscious fantasies, which "have both psychic and bodily effects […]. They even determine the minutiae of the body language" (Isaacs 2018, 112). This perspective allowed Klein to return to Freud's "disinclination for tackling psychotics" (Green 2011, 124), and thus, provides a way for us to understand more about apotemnophilia and the phantom limb condition. Although these conditions are not labelled psychotic, of course, they do consist of psychotic mechanisms.

According to Klein, psychotics face an intolerably painful "reality" or an over-intensity of instincts, which are echoed in the BIID and phantom limb syndromes: both phenomena involve an intolerable feeling and painful "realness". Klein theorises that infants develop psychoses based on the ego's introjection and projection of good and bad objects. The blueprint for this is the mother's breast, which is a good object when it is available, and bad when absent. This bad object both encapsulates a projection of the baby's own aggression and is also seen as being dangerous. She writes:

> [o]ne of the earliest methods of defence against the dread of persecutors, whether conceived of as existing in the external world or internalised, is that of scotomization, the *denial of psychic reality*; this may result in a considerable restriction of the mechanisms of introjection and projection and in the denial of external reality, and it forms the basis of the most severe psychoses.
>
> *(Klein 1987, 117)*

For Klein, it is essential for the baby to develop good objects in order to integrate her ego. This concept of projecting and introjecting objects that parts of oneself can be directed onto others through fantasy is what founds object relations theory. The theory hinges upon the way in which an infant develops its psyche in relation to others and the environment. Wilfred Bion followed Klein here, adding "the innovation of a theory of thinking [...] at the basis of psychosis" (Green 2011, 125), his focus centring upon Klein's model of the fragmented self.

As Birksted-Breen and Flanders write, "[t]he emphasis on the destruction of psychic links in the mind has been one of the central contributions of Bion and has been studied as a characteristic of psychotic functioning" (2010, 39). Again we are reminded of the delusions and rupture involved in BIID and PLS, lending yet another perspective on the syndromes' relation to a psychotic psychic structure. Bion also writes about the mind's split as, for him, splitting can lead to further fragmentation, a concept that is central to object relations theory. Specifically, object relations theorists are predominantly concerned with how a psychical split relates to subjectivity/objectivity, how an individual creates her own personal borders, and how she is shaped through somatic and pre-linguistic experiences. In relation to this, both BIID and PLS concern shaping oneself within the environment, as those with BIID wish to physically reshape their bodies, and those with PLS react to a change or difference in bodily form and can be healed by visualising a physical shape of bodily unity. These reactions cannot be thoroughly understood through language, and thus, here, I turn to theorists interested in the way in which linguistic and bodily absences are intertwined.

I begin with psychoanalyst André Green, because he focuses on how language is connected to the split described in Freud's "Wolf Man" case study, the split reflective of that in BIID and PLS. For Green, this split is not only central to the mind, but to language itself. To provide a little context, Green is aligned with object relations theorists, and developed a concept that is fundamental to studying psychosis, called "negative hallucination". Though Freud introduced the term in 1890 (to refer to a lack in perception), negative hallucination for Green is "the *representation of the absence of representation*" (Green 2010, 363), a specific and indefinable lack. Since those with BIID feel as though their bodies represent their own absence, and the phantom limb is a subjective representation of an absent limb, it is helpful to look at the conditions from Green's perspective.

Negation is a term central to Green's work, which is connected to Bion's and Winnicott's ideas about how containment and holding found "the symbolic matrices of thought" (Green 1986, 139), but different in that he emphasises the "silent, invisible, and 'imperceptible'" (Green 1986, 139). Negation, for him, is "the theoretical concept which is the precondition for any theory of representation, whether it is dreams or hallucination which is concerned" (Green 2010, 363). Negation frames and enables representation, laying the groundwork for thought. Negative hallucination thereby has both a negative side (linked to destruction and absence) and a positive side (central to one's ability to think and represent). "Periodically, then, everyone may resort to the mechanism of negative hallucination without there being any serious consequences for their psychic functioning" (Green 1986, 111). For Green, this double (positive and negative) can be seen in the "Wolf Man's" acknowledgement and denial of castration. To explore negative hallucination, Green analyses Pankejeff's three hallucinations of the severed finger, which I suggest are also reflective of BIID and PLS.

In "The Work of the Negative and Hallucinatory Activity", Green reminds us of the three hallucinations and memories the "Wolf Man" recalled in his Freudian analysis: in the first the patient hallucinated having cut his finger but could not look at or experience the pain. In the second he claims that this was false, that actually in the hallucination a tree shed blood when he cut it with a knife. Finally, Pankejeff remembers having a relative with six toes, whose extra toe was amputated. To analyse this, Green gathers traces of specific absences within Pankejeff's story: the "void which separates the finger from the hand, the absence of pain, the silence, the state of collapse and above all the inability to look" (Green 2010, 362). By directing attention to absences, and ultimately the extra toe memory, Green begins to unpack the more abstract negation that underlies the specific absences in Pankejeff's hallucination. This is clear in the patient's immediate rejection of the first hallucination (in which his finger was cut), because he negates the hallucination as immediately as it is described. Pankejeff denies his pain and claims that the memory was false. If the cut is analogous to castration, suggests Green, Pankejeff is identifying with his mother (as Freud believes that the child thinks the mother is castrated).

In the second hallucination, when the patient cuts the tree, Green suggests that he identifies with his father because, as Freud believes, the child who witnessed his parents' *coitus a tergo* thought that the father was cutting off the mother's penis (again, a problematic theory). Interestingly, he explains, the third memory of the extra toe discloses a dual logic—both "[r]ecognition and denial: there is indeed a cut connected with a violent bodily amputation, but it leaves bodily integrity intact and even makes it more 'normal'" (Green 2011, 97). There is an obvious similarity with apotemnophiles who also feel more intact and normal when amputated. For Green, a similar paradoxical split is central to all human thought. He writes: "[i]nstead of bringing about a union, the work of the negative separates and obstructs all choice and positive investment" (2010, 360); the removal of the extra toe and the desire to remove a limb in BIID both aim towards an idea of unity through destruction. The concept of wholeness in both scenarios is predicated upon amputating an excess (as Peter removed his "excessive" body parts in the desire for unity).

The "Wolf Man" and Peter, therefore, both deny and accept fracture, which they have no choice but to sustain by creating a specific form of absence. They are constituted through a split from which they cannot escape and which they must maintain through a delusion, one that enacts both destruction and completion. In Green's words, those who cannot accept a "yes" or "no" "have preferred to play the role of a prosthesis upholding the disavowal of castration, right to the end" (2010, 361). Green (1986) sometimes refers to this position as a borderline (a more psychotic) case: to "be a borderline implies that a border protects one's self from crossing over or from being crossed over, from being invaded, and thus becoming a *moving border* (not *having*, but *being* such a border)" (63). It protects against identifying with the "castrated mother" and the "castrating father", and from the environment. Pankejeff exemplifies this because, as depicted by the hallucination, he embodies a split. From this perspective, those with BIID and PLS are manifestations of this borderline state because they *are* moving borders. They both obscure and suspend a loss, carving themselves out either through (from this perspective) self-castration or an imaginary bodily frame.

Though Green (1986) links Pankejeff's borderline example to psychosis here, he does not believe the patient to be unanalysable or psychotic because the subject's concept of objective reality "coexists with his psychic reality" (230). Thus, rather than attempting to reach a specific answer, as we saw Freud struggle to do and as demonstrated in neurologists' struggles to define BIID and PLS, Green's viewpoint is helpful in forming an alternative concept about the psychotic mind-set. Since Green contends that a fissured state is common not only to psychosis but also to other forms of thought, this acts as a starting point to explore the two syndromes. He writes: "I would simply point out that structured thought is only established in discontinuity and that this structuring discontinuity involves, in the spaces, the blank which constitutes any chain of thought" (Green 2010, 363). However, in a person with psychosis, the blank pre-representational state persists, leaving the individual in a primitive state that hinders the ability to represent. Many people with psychosis have difficulty representing and thus, communicating. Green contends that since language is structured through representations, it is a problematic tool for exploring psychosis. Perhaps by learning more about how language is connected to negative hallucination to that fragmentation and abstraction that precedes representation we can more adequately approach the psychotic rationale. Green writes that negative hallucination "carries out its informative function by making us aware of how its object is 'blanked out' and leaves a mark by the very manner in which it disappears" (Green 1986, 138).

Green found that psychotic patients tend to show linguistic difficulties and must therefore embody an unusually prominent form of negative hallucination. Although in analysis, psychotic patients do not recognise and use words in a "normal" manner, he argues that psychosis is analysable, but calls for a different form of analysis. If the analyst listens to the "blanks" in a patient's speech, he suggests, meaning can be disclosed. To do this, the analyst must "arrange things [language] in such a way that it reveals itself spontaneously" (Green 1986, 78). The analyst and patient in this scenario use "the negative in their own way; the delirious patient positivises it, the analyst negativises it a second time in order to represent not thought but meaning. A bridge thrown between the two allows them to meet mid-way" (Green 2010, 366). For example, if the "Wolf Man" positivises a negative through the hallucination of a cut finger, the analyst may speak in a certain way that brings forth other thoughts, like the memory of the extra toe. Here, patient and analyst can gather images in a therapeutic setting without promising a cure or explanation and, through this dialogue, meaning may be revealed and used to learn about the patient, and perhaps even decrease the need for psychotic/borderline defences. This process may shed light on how the mirror-box works to comfort the patient because it, like the analyst in this model, negativises the phantom limb delusion a second time. The mirror-box shows the individual's underlying negation through a representation to help her cope with destruction. It allows the amputee to see herself through a symbol, which also provides a different way of viewing how the analyst in Green's theory discloses a patient's hidden representations. I now want to provide an alternative understanding of these ideas by turning to a case study that ties these strands of thought together. The study exemplifies how the body acts as a carrier for the psyche, how listening to blanks within language (in order to symbolise hidden fantasies) can help to decrease bodily wounds.

Interrupting nothing: psychosomatics and "The Man from Burma"

In Marilia Aisenstein's case study, "Psychosomatic Solution or Somatic Outcome: The Man from Burma – *Psychotherapy of a Case of Haemorrhagic Rectocolitis*" (2010 [1993]), she writes about her experience with a patient, "Mr L", who had a life-threatening haemorrhagic rectocolitis (a disease of the colon). Through analysis, she began to discover that his body had registered repressed mental wounds, that his "thought-activity was split-off" (Aisenstein 2010, 463) and as she began to unearth "symbolic meaning" (Aisenstein 2010, 468) through a certain kind of psychoanalytic dialogue, the patient's illness subsided. In order to find meaning, she listened, not to the words that he was saying (as his language was unusually factual and unemotional), but to the deficiencies in his speech. At one point, by asking a question about a dream, she discovered that he had repressed a trauma, and he began to reveal the split-off part of himself concerning his wife. He was able to access his unconscious fantasies and the somatic illness dissipated. Although this method is similar to Freud's, it differs in that Aisenstein attempts to avoid the "cohesive" narratives that Freud struggled with. She believed that interpretations might only re-traumatise the patient and increase his somatic symptoms, so she communicated with him in a fragmented manner.[1] Aisenstein's study also differs from Freud in that it takes an interest in the psychotic mind-set, which Freud believed to be unanalysable.

Although there is a difference between those with BIID and Mr L (because Mr. L's wound shows up on his body and those with BIID have *more* choice, as they are driven to destroy their body), Mr L acts as an example of the way in which the soma can register a psychical wound, and how this can be worked-through by listening to language in a certain way. While examining this relationship, my reading will also explore the way in which the mirror-box is a both a metaphor for the process in this analytic case and an embodiment of it. Marilia Aisenstein has "been very influenced in [her] research by the work of André Green, on narcissism, destructiveness, and what he calls the work of the negative" (Aisenstein 2006, 678). However, her research focuses on patients' physical reactions to psychological distress. She writes: the "psychoanalytic treatment of patients suffering from somatic disorders is a return to the very sources of the psychoanalytic quest" (Aisenstein 2006, 668). In "The Indissociable Unity of Psyche and Soma" (2006), Aisenstein explains that in practice, she has "been confronted with patients who treat their bodies 'like a foreign land'. The body thus becomes the site of enactments that may be explosive" (678). The link to the BIID sufferer here is obvious: the individual feels that her (whole) body is alien, and subjects it to violent acts.

To return to the question of how to think about BIID and PLS from beyond a medical outlook, Aisenstein explains that in most psychosomatic situations "[i]t is unusual for patients suffering from a somatic illness to be treated by psycho-analysis rather than by a strictly medical intervention. This means that the suffering body was excluded from the field of psychoanalysis" (Aisenstein 2006, 668). Hence, not only has a strictly scientific viewpoint restricted psychoanalytic endeavours in the medical field, but it has also stifled studies of the body within psychoanalysis. Psychosomatic theory speaks to this lack in the field, as Aisenstein conveys in looking for a non-scientific and open-ended "solution" to bodily symptoms. In so doing, she alludes to a problem with scientific logic, because, like Larry (the physician with BIID whom we saw in the earlier "Fighting It" conversation though to a lesser degree), Mr L epitomises a scientific way of thinking: he is uninterested in any deviation from fact. Closed off to abstract ideas, the patient, Aisenstein explains, had difficulties speaking about anything non-factual. He read no literature or fiction, indicating his fear of absorbing the non-concrete, and was very diligent at performing tasks, indicating a preference for physical action over thought. In analysis, Aisenstein initially echoed his linguistic patterns. She writes,

> I gave him a very 'scientific' explanation of the mechanisms of nightmare and of the sleep-dream system. I was thereby trying to enable him to take an interest, as a scientist, in his mental apparatus, and hence in its functioning – a phase which might precede familiarisation with his own mental productions.
>
> *(Aisenstein 2010, 468)*

By engaging in the patient's form of thinking, she felt as though she could both understand him more effectively and also engender a more comfortable setting.

She believed that this would create a safe space that could enable the subject to break down his defences.

Mr L's life-threatening haemorrhagic rectocolitis (which he was about to treat through a dangerous surgical removal of a colon and artificial opening in the stomach) came about just after he suddenly decided to give up smoking, which Aisenstein suggested could be seen as "self-castration". She alludes to this "castration" perhaps because it illustrates the link between the psychical and the physical: in this instance he attempts to control a lack. The subject also had difficulty withstanding silences, which she believed gestured towards a desire to control empty spaces. This desire, Aisenstein suggests, may have shown up on the body in his stomach and colon (the surgical removal). The silences that had been erased from Mr L's speech, in other words, may have needed a place to go, thereby manifesting upon the body.

Mr L's "concrete" form of speaking finally slipped when he said Burma instead of Bulgaria (when discussing something mundane), a mistake that opened a previously disavowed traumatic history. The more questions the analyst asked in relation to this slip, the more she learned about his past, dreams, and less logical mental processes. What was primarily revealed was that Mr L had divorced his first wife, after which she went to Burma and was stabbed to death in the stomach. He did not want to discuss this however, because it might "reopen old wounds" (Aisenstein 2010, 468). However, the case study suggests that disavowing this memory had painful effects: it caused the closed-off wounds to open themselves upon his body. Since he ignored them psychically, the wounds manifested themselves physically. However, they also saved him, in a way, by bringing him to analysis where he was given the space to formulate a more robust identity. Thus, Mr L's mental lack was counteracted with a bodily wound, which turns our attention to something central to the two syndromes—how the body and mind counteract one another. While the phantom limb is more clearly a psychical account of physical pain, BIID (especially in light of this case study) suggests a physical record of a mental rupture. In the case of Mr L, Aisenstein was able to engender a more illogical conversation by resurrecting these wounds in analysis, and together, they formed a healing factual and fictional history. Mr L proceeded to reveal problems with his current wife concerning building a house and having a child. These problems were also suggestive of his desire to control emptiness, perhaps alluding to a hidden trauma. However, Aisenstein continually acknowledged her inability to confirm any of these histories, memories, or theories.

This admission is dramatised in her writing, as she refers to other psychoanalysts' theories throughout the study, often hinting at how they may have influenced her own interpretations. In so doing, Aisenstein is attempting to avoid the trap that Freud fell into: of allowing a theory to dictate a case, rather than creating an open interpretation. For example, in discussing the traumatic death of Mr L's first wife, Aisenstein speculated that lacks in speech were the most significant parts of the dialogue, that the more something had been disavowed, the more painful it must have been. She wondered: does this result from the patient's attempt to "reactivate the primal fantasy of *seduction of the child by the adult* and, with it, one of the forms of the threat of castration?" (Aisenstein 2010, 469). Aisenstein acknowledges that Freud's "seduction theory"[2] may be applicable, while also recognising that it may not. These questions, she suggests, can never be answered. This method of ambiguous writing may also confront the reader with her own tendency to draw conclusions, because there is room to question Aisenstein's references. We are thus reminded of the phantom limb sufferer, because the amputee fills a lack with a completion that feels true. This notion of filling a lack with unity is ruptured in Aisenstein's study, as she conveys the reader's, the patient's, and her own proclivity to complete the story. She acknowledges that she will borrow from other analysts' theories to connect Mr L's language, body, and fantasies.

One case study Aisenstein discusses in her essay "The Indissociable Unity of Psyche and Soma" (2006) exemplifies Green's influence, because it reveals how affects are "turned into sensory impressions or, rather, into signs in the body" (Aisenstein 2006, 671). Since the phantom limb and apotemnophilia call for exactly this type of exploration (because they are physical problems that words cannot fully explain or cure), Aisenstein's ideas help us think about them differently. Furthermore, she is interested in the most beneficial ways of using language to trace the latent stories behind wounds, which is also conveyed in her style of writing. Her case study refers to literature and philosophy, thereby exemplifying the importance of using literature and psychoanalysis together. Accordingly, in "The Man from Burma" (2010) she uses the first line (which is also the title) of Mallarmé's poem, which reads, "*'Un coup de dés jamais n'abolira le hasard'* ['A cast of dice never will abolish chance']". It is implied that the poem, like the patient, can be interpreted ad infinitum: "*'Toute pensée émet un coup de dés'* ['Every thought produces a cast of dice']" (Aisenstein 2010, 476). By using Mallarmé's language, which, as Maurice Blanchot writes, "does not imply anyone who expresses it, or anyone who hears it: it speaks *itself* and writes *itself*" (1995, 41), Aisenstein foregrounds the importance of subjective language, echoing her own experience with Mr L. It can be interpreted in many ways but cannot be completely explained through language, reflective of Mallarmé's message and writing. In relation to this, Mr L's body carries a loss and is in this sense a symbol of loss itself, a symbol that cannot be completely explained through language, thus illuminating PLS and BIID. Rather than attempting to explain (as Freud found problematic in the "Wolf Man"), Aisenstein subdues the patient's physical wounds by unveiling his dreams and fantasies, a process that is materialised in the mirror-box, which erases pain through an illusion. She suggests that it is not the analyst or the patient who has the authority, but the expression itself.

In the analytic exchange, she states,

> while the intention was to open the way to chains of representations, there was a risk of blocking the process by interpretations which, although correct, might be premature and might stoke up the instinctual side before the establishment of a representational system.

(Aisenstein 2010, 473)

She is careful not to re-traumatise the patient by confronting him with too many interpretations or breaking down his defences too quickly. Aisenstein explains that she and Mr L are both (re)creating the story of his past, and that since it is formed through fantasies and dreams, it is partially fictive. They are devising a story together through the fantasies and thoughts that emerge from their conversation, in order to help the patient to, in a sense, fill in his blanks without closing them off. This raises the question of how split-off traumas can be traced through fantasies, which can be visualised in the mirror-box (as it presents an illusion of a foreign part of oneself). Aisenstein was able to shift Mr L's trauma away from body and towards his psyche through a fantasy. By discussing dreams and creating memories of an unknowable past, they were able to access a split-off part of the self, a split that resembles a psychotic mind-set that Freud deemed un-analysable. Aisenstein writes,

> I am now convinced that it is no longer possible to neglect the concept of splitting in the field of psychosomatics" because it involves "a form of antithought which is concrete and cut off from the roots of its drives and disembodied.
>
> *(Aisenstein 2006, 678)*

In "The Man from Burma", (Aisenstein 2010) that cut-off anti-thought is incarnated as a wound. This reading provides a perspective on why BIID and PLS both involve feelings of disturbing bodily alienation, and reactions to bodily loss and presence that cannot be sufficiently explained or comprehended. In BIID, a psychical wound is made manifest on the body; in the phantom limb syndrome, a physical wound is carried to the mind. Similarly, in the mirror-box, the somatic wound is carried towards the psyche through a fantasy version of self. However, she notes that this process of carrying the wound to the mind puts the patient at risk of creating a psychically delusional solution in place of the previous somatic one, of carrying it too far. Although the work was still in progress when she wrote the essay, by shifting the traumatic lesion towards the mind, Mr L's body felt less pressure and the wound was contained. The mirror-box, I suggest, materialises how a psychosomatic split can be dispelled through an illusion.

Thus, Aisenstein's study, Green's theory, and mirror-box therapy suggest that conjuring illusions from negative spaces (Mr L's gaps in speech, negative hallucination, and the mirror-box itself) may remove some of a wound's pressure, whether orientated in the body, as seen in PLS, or the mind, as with BIID. Rather than attempting to find the meaning of delusion, Aisenstein works, as Green suggests of the analyst's role, to "arrange things in such a way that it reveals itself spontaneously" (Green 1986, 78). In this way, the analysand's unknown, unconscious self will, ostensibly, begin to show through—that "internal stranger at once disturbingly unlike you and infinitely more like you than you want to acknowledge" (Cohen 2013, 20). I will now take a deeper look at this concept of the "internal stranger" by exploring literary and psychoanalytic writings that centralise the notion of the foreign self.

Notes

1 Aisenstein's study is also related to a concept developed by Pierre Marty and Michel de M'Uzan, called "operational thinking", in which "drive-related excitation that fails to find an outlet in the mind through ideational representations and affects is discharged by means of behaviour and/or somatisation" (Birksted-Breen and Flanders 2010, 439). The concept echoes what Freud called "actual neuroses", which he deemed unsuitable for psychoanalytic treatment due to a difficulty in identifying patients' emotions. Those in the School of Psychosomatics, to which Aisenstein was affiliated, believed that it was possible.
2 Between 1895 and 1897, Freud developed a theory that neuroses stem from childhood experiences of sexual seduction. However, he later began to believe in the seduction as an oedipal fantasy of the child rather than an action of seduction on the part of an adult, which, as famously argued by Jeffrey Masson, is problematic in situations that involved actual sexual seduction.

References

Aisenstein, Marilia. "Psychosomatic Solution or Somatic Outcome: The Man from Burma – *Psychotherapy of a Case of Haemorrhagic Rectolitis.*" *Reading French Psychoanalysis*. Edited by Dana Breen, Sara Flanders, and Alain Gibeault, London: Routledge, 2010, pp. 463–477.

Aisenstein, Marilia. "The Indissociable Unity of Psyche and Soma: A View From the Paris Psychosomatic School." *International Journal of Psycho-Analysis*, vol. 87, 2006, pp. 667–680.

Birksted-Breen, Dana, and Sara Flanders. "General Introduction." *Reading French Psychoanalysis*. Edited by Dana Birksted-Breen, Sara Flanders, and Alain Gibeault, London: Routledge, 2010, pp. 1–51.

Blanchot, Maurice. *The Work of Fire* [*La part du feu*, 1949]. Translated by Charlotte Mandell, Stanford: Stanford UP, 1995.

Cohen, Josh. *The Private Life: Why We Remain in the Dark*. London: Granta, 2013.

Green, André. "The Death Drive: Meaning, Objections, Substitutes." *Reading French Psychoanalysis*. Edited by Dana Breen, Sara Flanders, and Alain Gibeault, London: Routledge, 2010, pp. 496–516.

Green, André. *On Private Madness*. Madison: International Universities, 1986.

Green, André. *Psychoanalysis: A Paradigm for Clinical Thinking*. London: Free Association, 2005.

Green, André. "The Work of the Negative." *Reading French Psychoanalysis*. Edited by Dana Breen, Sara Flanders, and Alain Gibeault, London: Routledge, 2010, pp. 355–367.

Green, André. "The Work of the Negative and Hallucinatory Activity (negative hallucination)." *On Freud's "Negation."* Edited by Mary Kay O'Neil and Salman Akhtar, London: Karnac, 2011, pp. 75–145.

Isaacs, Susan. "The Nature and Function of Phantasy." *Developments in Psychoanalysis*, 2018, pp. 67–121.

Klein, Melanie. "A Contribution to the Psychogenesis." *The Selected Melanie Klein*. Edited by Juliet Mitchell, New York: The Free Press, 1987. No pagination.

Klein, Melanie. "Notes on Some Schizoid Mechanisms." *International Journal of Psychoanalysis*, vol. 27, 1946, pp. 99–110.

PART II
Symbolic exchanges and reconstitutions

5

THE MIRROR-STAGE, BLANCHOT, AND "ORPHEUS'S GAZE"

*Nur weil dich reißend zuletzt die Feindschaft verteilte
sind wir die Hörenden jetzt und ein Mund der Natur.*

Only because enmity tore you in two at last
Can we now hear and act as Nature's mouth.

Rilke, Sonnets to Orpheus (XXVI)

These lines of poetry from Rilke's *Sonnets to Orpheus* (1922) might suggest that the artist must be torn in order to create her work: that it is in a state of fragmentation that the individual is open to expression. In this poem, Rilke is specifically referring to the myth of Orpheus, in which Orpheus's art condemns him to rupture. When he defies the gods by looking into the Underworld, Orpheus's body is torn to pieces. However, he continues to sing through his broken body; he sings when he is not one but many different parts. I turn to Rilke here, because the poem draws our attention to the trajectory of this chapter, which looks at physical, linguistic, and symbolic rupture. It starts with Jacques Lacan's concept of the mirror stage and then moves on to Maurice Blanchot's thoughts on literature and fractured language, as discussed through his essay "Orpheus's Gaze" (1982a).

Both Peter and Stephen explained that their conditions felt "strange": for Peter, a "strange inner feeling" that he was meant to be disabled, and for Stephen, a "strange" and "uncanny" feeling that "your arm or your leg […] is GONE. Yet it's still agonizing you" (Sumner 2015). These feelings resonate with Freud's concept of the uncanny, which involves a feeling produced from a paradoxical hominess and hiddenness, a simultaneous discomfort and a home-like comfort,[1] where "'hidden forces' within me destine me to be forever other to myself, to an indelible strangeness within" (Cohen 2005, 70). The feeling is also echoed in a man's description of BIID in the documentary *Complete Obsession* (2000), which he describes as being "in the wrong body". The uncanny body is, in this way, conscious for those with BIID and PLS. It is at once the most familiar and the most foreign place.

Moreover, the "uncanny is an experience of being *after oneself*, in various senses of that phrase. It is the experience of something duplicitous, diplopic, being double" (Royle 2003, 16), and indeed, those with BIID and PLS struggle with a division between wholeness and unity. They are tortured by an alternate version of self that differs from their physical realities. While individuals with phantom limbs feel that their amputated body is whole, those with BIID feel that their physically whole body is ruptured. These experiences of double-ness parallel what Jacques Lacan calls the mirror stage, where a child is set up with a split—a feeling of fragmentation that contrasts the mirror image, an image which is "an imaginary anatomy or body phantom" (Grosz 1994, 42). The child experiences something similar to what those with PLS and BIID experience: a split between physical and imaginary, wholeness and fragmentation. Since, as Grosz (1994) writes, "Lacan suggests that this desire for a solid, stable identity may help explain our fascination with images of the human form" (43), Lacan's model may provide insight into the desire for wholeness in those with BIID and PLS.

The mirror stage

Lacan discusses how a baby's sense of self is initially ruptured and helpless: it can feel parts of its body that it cannot visualise, and it does not have a sense of proprioception. In "The Mirror Stage as Formative of the *I* Function" (1949), Lacan suggests that we are born into the world with a "primordial Discord betrayed by the signs of uneasiness and motor unco-ordination of the neo-natal months" (3); we are dependent upon the support of others, which he calls the *infans* stage. According to Vicky Lebeau (2008), in "the state of infancy, or *infans* (literally, without language), the small child tends to be discovered at the limit of what words can be called upon to tell, or to mean" (16): the baby is unable to comprehend itself and its environment. However, Lacan theorises that when the baby is between the ages of six and 18 months, it recognises its own image in the mirror, usually when another individual is holding it, and it will identify with that framed image. This self-recognition involves a feeling of enjoyment, and from this point on, the child forms itself through a split—between the fragmented self, and the image of unity with which it identifies. This is where the child is introduced into what Lacan calls the Imaginary order. Lacan's theory can be used to reflect on Freud's and Otto Rank's notion of the uncanny, which also introduces an idea of the double as related to the mirror reflection. Freud writes in "The Uncanny" that Rank "has gone into the connections the 'double' has with reflections in mirrors" (1955, 234). These perspectives suggest that each human being has one image of wholeness and one of rupture. From Lacan's point of view, this mirror double creates an "alienating identity, which will mark [… its] entire mental development" (Lacan 1977, 5).

The *infans* self is set up in relation to its ideal image because it desires to be the impossible (the mirror image). Hidden behind this ideal mirror image is the fragmented, subjective self, which lurks in the background. The *infans*, which aims towards the illusion of a coherent ego, quietly haunts the individual (often through dreams), which in the psychotic structure leaks into reality. The psychotic element is the fantasy of the self's integrity and wholeness, a structure reflective of BIID and PLS. It is the ego that "helps protect the individual against the threat of incoherence and impotence and provides a fictitious coherence" (Bailly 2009, 40). The mirror image, moreover, becomes "the threshold of the visible world" (Lacan 1977, 3) that assembles the ego, and forms "the social dialectic that structures human knowledge" (Lacan 1997, 4). Individuals unconsciously strive for a false wholeness that is linked to the way in which they interact with the environment.

Throughout life, therefore, the mirror stage unconsciously remains a part of the individual, and I suggest that those with PLS and BIID dramatise this stage. Although the sufferers did not, presumably, go through the stage (between the ages of six to 18 months) differently from others, the kind of split between the fragmented body and illusory cohesion that is outlined in the mirror stage is a conscious and painful experience for those with BIID and PLS. Phantom limb sufferers often experience physical feelings of rupture and helplessness that contrast with a feeling of wholeness, which is reflective of Lacanian mirror "body phantom" (Grosz 1994, 42). As Stephen Sumner explained, the phantom sensation was "bigger than me", the burnings and electrical shocks "totally beggar words". The description here parallels the *infans*, the fragmented baby who is "at the limit of what words can be called upon to tell, or to mean" (Lebeau 2008, 16). Stephen states, "[t]he first instant that I gazed into a mirror at a sound limb that was bending and waggling and all, in place of this epicentre of electrical storms […] I was literally suffused with a sense of calm, completion". Here, Stephen appears to be experiencing something similar to the baby in Lacan's model—a split between an obscure sensation of fragmentation and helplessness, and a whole mirror image that causes a sense of relief and jubilation. In Peter's case, the mirror stage is in a sense reversed: rather than idealising a whole mirror image, his ideal wholeness is associated with a fragmented sensation reflective of the *infans*. Although reversed, the apotemnophile suffers from a feeling of rupture that stands in relation to a fantasy of unity. It would seem, from this perspective, that those with phantom limbs and BIID are stuck with an exaggerated state of being which remains undigested "within". They are confronted with bodily fragmentation that reaches for ungraspable unity, which for most people remains hidden in the unconscious. Their imaginary wholeness, in other words, is recognised through rupture.

Consequently, based on this Lacanian paradigm, the ego cannot provide an illusory coherence to protect the subject against incoherence in the same way, thereby leaving those with the conditions vulnerable. For Lacan, the ego works to protect the individual by conjuring phantoms to fill the gaps in between the *infans* and the illusory completion. One's mirror-image, writes Lacan,

> is still pregnant with the correspondences that unite the I with the statue in which man projects himself, with the phantoms that dominate him, or with

> the automaton in which, in an ambiguous relation, the world of his own making tends to find completion.
>
> *(1977, 2)*

The absences experienced by those with BIID and PLS, it would seem, are too apparent to be hidden by phantoms, and are instead shown through them. Those with BIID feel helplessly ruptured, a feeling related to a phantom concept of wholeness. And PLS involves a conscious experience and image of bodily fracture that is, rather than being hidden by a phantom wholeness, exacerbated by one. The phantom limb and BIID drives towards unity thus display the ruptured self's aim to become its illusory mirror image. What is at issue, therefore, is that while for everyone, "this fragmented body [… can appear] in the form of disjointed limbs, or of those organs represented in exoscopy [it …] usually manifests itself in dreams" (Lacan 1977, 3), for those with PLS and BIID, it seems to have escaped the realm of fantasy and seeped into reality. The subjective other that quietly haunts most individuals comes to life. This is exemplified by one member of "Fighting It" who explains that her father was a "monster". When she broke her arm at the age of eight, he was temporarily caring, causing her to have dreams about becoming disabled. Then, she writes, "[w]hen I was 12, I recognized that the dreams became a compulsion […]. My thoughts became so intense I nearly couldn't stand it. I wanted to take an machete and cut off my hand". It seems as though dreams of a "fragmented body" and "disjointed limbs", reflective of Lacan's concept, have spilled over into a reality. For those with BIID, moreover, this fragmented body is not visible to others, at times causing them to feel increasingly isolated. Those with PLS, alternatively, are visibly fractured, and recognisably "different". However, the mirror illusion allows those with phantom limbs to look momentarily "complete" (through a symbol of the phantom), thereby causing a feeling of, as Stephen describes it, "deep comfort".

For Lacan, this *infans* and mirror ideal make up the "social dialectic that structures human knowledge" (Lacan 1977, 3). This social structure forms the Symbolic order, where language, signs, and perceptions are organised. The Symbolic contrasts the Imaginary order's illusory wholeness, fragmentation, and loss. Part of this loss involves the child's ultimate desire to be the mother's "Phallus", which is "a penis plus the idea of its absence" (Leader et al. 2000, 89), that seems to complete the mother (again, the mother is defined through a lack). The idea is that the baby is always searching for what the mother desires so that it can be the Phallus for her. However, since it is impossible to completely understand her, the baby interprets the mother with false meaning, leaving it to search for what is always beyond itself. The infant's interpretations are being formed through yet another double: that the baby can complete the mother, and that this is futile. The realisation of this futility—that the baby cannot be everything to the mother (the Phallus)—is what Lacan calls "castration", which occurs when an object obstructs the possibility of pleasing the mother. This object is called the Name of the Father, which takes the Phallus's place and destroys the infant's illusion. Castration, then, creates the necessary symbolic gap between the mother and baby that allows the latter to develop a sense of independence. The Name of the Father can take many different (symbolic) forms throughout life: it is the blueprint for symbols and language that structure the unconscious. Thus, language can always be traced back to the Phallus, to a specific and ungraspable absence. Lacan's theory of the linguistic system correlates with structuralist linguistics, which proposes that "a word is a word because it is different from other words" (Leader et al. 2000, 49): the linguistic system is founded upon a lack (a concept soon examined through Blanchot's thoughts on literature). The key here is that symbols and language are inseparable from the body and the environment.

For Lacan, therefore, language is primarily "other" to the individual: a person's sense of place in the world is achieved through entry into the Symbolic order. It is what the world "says" about its image that causes the *infans* to disappear behind social ideals or "norms". The failure of this process results in psychosis. Lacan theorises that this may occur if there is no Name of the Father, and the baby is left unable to experience castration and form independence from the mother. Here there is no platform with which to symbolise and to enter the linguistic world, leaving the baby structured by a false image of being one with the mother. Furthermore, explains Lionel Bailly (2009), the baby "cling[s] to its fantasy that it may have the Phallus, or even be the Phallus for the mother" (84). Without a sufficient symbolic foundation, using metaphors is difficult, causing the individual to create meaning through delusions that give order to the world. The psychotic individual may then act out or hallucinate the desire to be the Phallus or to be "castrated".

This scenario can be visualised in BIID, which does not suggest that those with BIID are wholly "psychotic". However, Lacan's concept of the psychotic structure may tell us more about the phenomenon,[2] especially taking into account the limb's resemblance to the Phallus. If Lacan believes that the inability to castrate can cause a child to cling to the fantasy of being or having the mother's Phallus (of being complete), the phantom limb condition enacts this. It involves a person who clings to the fantasy of an appendage that is both there and not there. Those with BIID reflect something similar, as most believe that they will attain wholeness. However, just as the baby in Lacan's theory is unable to appease and complete the mother, amputation often fails to appease an individual's desire for wholeness.[3] Some sufferers seem to actualise the loss instead of symbolising it.

Both conditions also enact a predominantly physical, as opposed to linguistic, manifestation of felt rupture. It would seem, then, that those with PLS and BIID are stuck with a pain resulting from a crisis in psychical functioning at the level of the Imaginary, which they cannot return to or make sense of. The mirror-box phenomenon demonstrates how an individual may symbolically regress to this stage in the present, because by reinserting her whole mirror image along with her fracture, the individual repeats the mirror stage. In this scenario, one can see one's whole image, decreasing the ego's compensation for the *infans'* lack through a fantasy (the phantom limb). Does this reveal an entrance through illusion to the Symbolic order, wherein a person may reinsert the name of Name of the Father?

Perhaps the mirror-box limb presents the individual's image of having a Phallus (an illusory appendage that is both present and absent), which both appeases a desire to be complete and also shows that this is impossible. If so, can the mirror-box enable an amputee to visualise and embody the illusion of symbolic castration (making up for what she was unable to do in her infancy at the level of the Imaginary), and thus symbolically reduce the need to cling to a delusional one? If in Lacanian thought, a psychotic structure prevents an understanding of metaphoric self and world, the attempt to simultaneously sever and hold on to one's body (through the mirror-box symbolic castration and BIID amputation) suggests an unconscious attempt to alter a sense of objectivity as it was formed through the entry into the Symbolic. A desire for castration may be connected to a desire for social and symbolic integration. Furthermore, as briefly noted, if a word is defined by its differences (it is separated or cut away from something in order to be understood),[4] the wish to remove one's appendage demonstrates an embodied form of symbolisation from yet another angle. This connection illustrates how a person may attain meaning from a certain demarcation. In order to understand more about how BIID and PLS relate to symbolism and language, I turn to Maurice Blanchot, whose writings reflect upon linguistic rupture, and the relationship between the imaginary and the material.

The words of Blanchot

Like Lacan, Blanchot conceives of language as being structured through a lack. Blanchot suggests that this lack lurks behind the linguistic system, similar to the way in which the ruptured *infans* ("without language") haunts the individual in Lacanian thought. In discussing Blanchot, Paul de Man (1971) writes, we "try to protect ourselves against this negative power by inventing stratagems, ruses of language and of thought that hide an irrevocable fall" (73). Echoing amputees who develop a phantom in place of their fracture, language involves the non-material, which works to hide an underlying void. Literature, for Blanchot, turns towards this void or, as Leslie Hill (2001) puts it, "[l]iterature [...] deals in phantoms" (17). Similarly, those with BIID paradoxically hide a lack: although they desire to experience and visualise fracture, they are also driven to contain it. I argue that since the linguistic and the somatic are permeable (or, to return to Naomi Segal's statement, texts "invoke the movement of eye or hand towards something one ought to be able to caress" [2009, 120]), Blanchot's literary theory is not only abstract but corporeal, and can lend insight as to how the body is conceived of in BIID and PLS. I am interested in what Blanchot's thoughts on literature can reveal about the desire to contain, perceive, and hide a lack, as exemplified in the BIID and phantom limb conditions. What is central to these links is that like a phantom, language carries traces of the past, of what is not exactly there. Although it is composed of signs and expressed through the body (whether read, written, spoken or heard), a word's meaning cannot be fully understood. Language parallels the phantom limb at a structural level, because it is a physical and psychical experience that cannot be captured or shared, a feeling involving a loss. For de Man (1971), "[l]anguage, with its sensory attributes of sound and texture, partakes of the world of natural objects and introduces a positive element in the sheer void" (69), just as the phantom limb, though unseen, is a feeling, a positive component, that replaces a lack.

To expand upon these ideas and provide a little context as to how Blanchot's writing relates to the two syndromes, I shall begin by exploring his thoughts on literature. For Blanchot, literature is not confined to a certain philosophy or literary group, "it is not a matter of developing a unified theory or encompassing a body of knowledge" (Blanchot 1992, xxv). A unified discourse closes off knowledge by attempting to answer questions instead of opening knowledge by asking them. He aims instead to answer questions with more questions, because the "question inaugurates a type of relation characterised by openness and free movement, and what it must be satisfied with closes and arrests it" (Blanchot 1992, 13–14). The exemplary question that concerns Blanchot is the question of literature which, for him, is outside any discipline that attempts to define it. Leslie Hill (2001) explains: "any literature that knows itself to be literature, Blanchot implies, is by that token no longer literature" (19), and this is because literature's very nature is to illuminate what language cannot know. What cannot be known about language is its meaning and comprehensive definitions, partially because it is formed through subjective and ambiguous psychical images and perceptions. Instead of attempting to define literature through ordinary language, therefore, Blanchot "steadily borders on the inexpressible and approaches the extreme of ambiguity, but always recognises [words] for what they are" (de Man 1971, 62). He does not attempt to clarify language but to bring out its ambiguous nature. Thus, Blanchot's writings are difficult to define and interpret: he is "fundamentally opaque at the level of comprehension" (Critchley 2004, 31).

His writing dramatises an interest in a reader's failure ever to capture authorial meaning. Moreover, he, following Barthes' "The Death of the Author" (1982 [1967]), suggests that in some literature, the work is separate from the author and takes on a life of its own: words are exposed as having already been formed and coming from outside the individual. As Barthes writes, "literature is that neuter, that composite, that oblique into which every subject escapes, the trap where all identity is lost, beginning with the very identity of the body that writes" (Barthes 1975, 2); as language takes over, the author is, in a sense, erased. We are reminded here of the Lacanian ego, which, as explained, is formed through an image of self as other in the mirror, and of one's identity having been structured through others. Just as, for Lacan, one does not have complete control of one's identity, for Blanchot, once the book has been written, the author cannot control the way it is read, or how time and context informs its readings. The work thus exists "only by and for itself" (de Man 1971, 68), and yet does not exist at all. Hill (2001) writes that "[l]anguage becomes perpetually and irreducibly double: it affirms the need for discourse, but it also bears witness to that which, within words themselves, remains unspoken, unspeakable, and absolutely other" (15). Here Hill refers to the two slopes of literature.[5]

The first slope (which is sometimes referred to as *everyday language*) is "that meaningful *prose*, which attempts to express things in a transparent language that designates them according to a human order of meaning" (Critchley 2004, 60). It is the word and book which can be read, theorised, and which is part of culture. The second slope is that which can never be completely communicated, understood, or grasped through the word or text, "a form of art that leaves things to themselves in some way" (Critchley 2012, 100). "In some way", because things cannot be completely left to themselves: any representation of a thing transforms it to some extent. The first slope of literature that aims to represent is, according to Simon Critchley (2012), "that Sadistic-dialectical labour of negation that defines the Subject itself, whereby things are killed in order to enter the daylight of language and cognition" (60). When something is named, it is inscribed with preconceived notions that erase its particularity: in attempting to represent an idea, the thing itself is erased.[6] Those with BIID manifest this in the need to erase part of themselves to be complete. They must cut into their felt ruptured body to be seen as unified, just as the word must be cut away from its ambiguous origins to form a fictional sense of cohesion. In this way, one can only be seen through a certain kind of annihilation, which BIID individuals seem both drawn towards and away from. This, I propose, reflects the literary writer's plight as Blanchot conceives it.

Moreover, it is a well-known idea that writers desire immortality through their words, which continue to create meaning posthumously. Ulrich Haase (2001) writes that "the dread of death is expressed in the dream of writing the definitive book, the most outstanding novel which might bestow immortality on its author" (51). Here again, we see a bodily and textual double, as the text both can and cannot bestow immortality (though the author's words remain, the author herself is separate from them). Something similar is perceptible in the BIID condition, as exemplified by the German man (discussed in Chapter 2) who froze his toes: perhaps an attempt to immortalise the body while simultaneously proving its mortality. Though the toes might remain, they represent his death, an absent part of himself. Haase (2001) continues, but "death cannot be overcome, and the book, once written, always disappears in the face of the demand of the work" (51–52). The text both bestows immortality upon the author and reveals the author's absence, and the frozen toes both immortalise the man's presence (as they are preserved) and reveal his absence (as they represent and are formed through a loss). Similarly, the phantom limb bestows immortality upon the once present (in most cases) limb, while also acting as a constant reminder that the limb is not there. In relation to this concept, Blanchot (1982b) postulates that we have "two relations with death, one which we like to call authentic and the other inauthentic" (155): while death can be grasped (the physical body), it cannot be comprehended. Hill (2001) writes, "[o]n the one hand, death is negation, separation, language [...] it founds the order of human possibility". However, death also "escapes negation [...] it is an obscure constraint that can never be experienced for itself by any living human self". Thus, the only way that it can be addressed is "indirectly, through ritual, myth or fiction" (182). Death is both what makes us human and keeps us from being "complete" (as it cannot be fully comprehended), and our only way of attempting to understand it is through perception, images, and language. In death then, the body can only be comprehended through signs or symbols. While most may unconsciously experience their mythical or fictional nature, it is painfully conscious for those with BIID and PLS. Returning to Lacan, those with BIID and PLS echo the psychotic structure: in psychosis "the unconscious is at the surface, conscious. This is why articulating it doesn't seem to have much effect" (Lacan 1993, 11). However, I ask, is there a way of articulating the soma that may have an effect? To explore this question, I will examine Blanchot's thoughts on how a body of text can or cannot be articulated. If the body can only be deciphered through a sign, the text holds an interesting place because it is both physical and metaphorical: it is a body composed of signs. BIID and phantom limbs thus mirror the text, because they are physical (felt) and symbolic extensions of self.

Blanchot's discussions of literature often play with the questions raised here. He is interested in the silence within words, the pre-linguistic, fragmentary, and dream-like images. "If madness has a language", he writes, "and if it is even nothing but language, would this language not send us back (as does literature although at another level) to [...] a non-dialectical experience of language?" (Blamchot 1992, 201). This raises the question as to whether "madness" can be related to what preceded language before the word is cut away. Can a person momentarily break the Lacanian Symbolic order of social dialectics and feel their "discordant" images and gestures? Can we get in touch with what precedes the confines of fantasy wholes? Blanchot touches on these questions by interrupting literary tradition. In attending to the false idea that language signifies its referent, he discloses the negation within it, to let that *infans* seep through the cracks. This negation is what Blanchot calls the *space of literature*. Huffer (1998) explains that this space

> exposes the trap of truth: the closer we get to it, the more we lose it, because the only way we can say it is by holding up the reflective screen of language, the mirror in which all we see is ourselves.
>
> *(187)*

This description of the space of literature cannot help but remind us of the mirror-box. It holds up a reflection of the phantom that shows its absence (the image is not the phantom) through a reflection of the self (the existent appendage), and the closer we get to the phantom, the more we see its erasure. And it is the space of literature that, for Blanchot, also brings out its negation.

Thus far, we have explored how in attempting to reach cohesion to avoid facing fracture, a sufferer of BIID or PLS and a writer can face a false dialectic: the disturbing double similar to that outlined in Lacan's theory. By writing in a fragmented manner, Blanchot illuminates the way in which a text simultaneously contains the known and the unknown body of work (the known words and their incomprehensible rupture). The mirror-box also shows the image of one's wholeness and simultaneous un-wholeness. Instead of aiming to resolve absence as seen in everyday language, the phantom limb, and self-amputation the mirror-box, like Blanchot's literature, exposes the inability to do so: "literature is literature *because* it lays bare its self-recognition as untruth" (Huffer 1998, 187). The mirror-box exposes the phantom's untruth through a symbol of itself. In light of this, the struggles of those with both conditions are related to a wider discussion of fragmentation upon which Blanchot's writings hinge. Thomas Carl Wall (1999) explains:

> [h]e writes fragments, and even writes about fragmentary writing [...]. Anamorphic, the fragment's only life is its separation from any whole, any narrative, and any history. It cannot be put in place and therefore demands from the writer something other than form. It demands destruction.
>
> *(84–85)*

The mirror-box, anamorphic, distorts one's body to make it look whole from one point of view, and fragmented from another. Unlike the phantom limb an illusion that can be based upon a historical memory of pain or a narrative of normality the mirror-box stands alone in a moving present. While it shows the appeasing image of unity, it simultaneously demands something other than form: that the individual glance at her destruction.

It is in the process of writing, according to Blanchot, that a moving hand may also reveal one's annihilation. As he discusses in "Literature and the Right to Death" (1947), language only represents its object through its destruction. Blanchot (1995) writes: "[w]hen [literature] names something, whatever it designates is abolished; but whatever is abolished is also sustained, and the thing has found a refuge (in the being which is the word) rather than a threat" (329). Though a writer may visualise a part of herself on paper when the words she uses shape her thoughts, the words also disclose her own erasure: a non-threatening experience, or perhaps a desire. Blanchot (1995) continues, "literature's ideal has been the following: to say nothing, to speak in order to say nothing" (324). As suggested in our earlier discussion, from a Lacanian perspective, those with apotemnophilia and PLS echo unconscious attempts to return to an infant's fragmented state in the present moment and (unsuccessfully) reform themselves as symbols—to be "castrated" and free of the mirror image's critical gaze. If the mirror-box offers an alternative way to see oneself as a symbol and break up one's preconceived notions of self, fragmentary writing may offer a similar refuge from the desire "to grasp in its entirety the infinite movement of comprehension" (Blanchot 1995, 325).

De Man (1971) explains,

> [i]n his interpretive quest, the writer frees himself from empirical concerns, but he remains a self that must reflect on its own situation. He can only do this by "reading" himself, by turning his conscious attention toward himself, and not toward a forever unreachable form of being
>
> *(77)*

This idea is embodied in the amputees who reflect on their own fracture in the mirror-box. Here, the amputee, like the writer may begin to free herself of "empirical concerns" (of the drive to be physically complete) when she literally reflects upon her own fissure with the mirror-box: she may integrate her rupture through a fictional self-image. Thus, fiction seems the best place to further explore these connections, which I now set out to do through Blanchot's essay "Orpheus's Gaze" (1982a).

Orpheus's Gaze

"Orpheus's Gaze", Blanchot proposes, is central to *The Space of Literature* (1982), because it hinges upon what cannot be grasped, which is an essential component to the question of literature. Anne Smock (1982) explains in the introduction that this space "is like the place where someone dies: a nowhere, Blanchot says, which is *here*" ("Introduction" 10). This, as I have sought to show, can be elaborated in terms of BIID and PLS because they involve feelings based in a lack. Individuals with BIID feel an absence within a presence, and those with PLS feel a presence that is objectively absent: sufferers with both conditions, therefore, embody a "nowhere, which is here"—a theme central to Blanchot's essay "Orpheus's Gaze". First, in content, the story of Orpheus reflects these conditions because Orpheus struggles with the dichotomy between unity and fracture: he lives forever in a broken body that is simultaneously alive and dead. Moreover, in form, Blanchot presents a fragmented language that, like Orpheus's body, holds up a simultaneous presence and absence and thus can illuminate the struggles experienced by those with BIID and PLS.

"Orpheus's Gaze" is based on the Greek myth of Orpheus the artist (musician and poet), who due to his singing is granted the right to descend into the Underworld to bring his wife, Eurydice, back to life on the condition that he does not turn to look at her. However, unable to resist, Orpheus glances back. As punishment, he is dismembered and thrown into a river where he continues to sing (although Blanchot does not mention this part of the myth in his essay). Orpheus's need to see Eurydice is often used as an allegory for the desire for completion, thus reflecting the BIID and PLS drives towards impossible wholeness. The attempt to bring Eurydice back, moreover, is comparable to the writer's attempts to bring understanding to what cannot be known. "His [Orpheus's] *work*", writes Blanchot (1982b), "is to bring it back to the light of day and to give it form, shape, and reality in the day" (171)—this shape, for the writer, is the word. Orpheus's desire to see Eurydice, however, leaves him at a loss, which stands for Blanchot's belief that when something is named, its singularity vanishes. Here, his glance back allegorises the literary writer who uses language to "tell finite things in an accomplished fashion that excludes the infinite" (Blanchot 1982b, 144): the writer cannot completely convey thought. Through a Lacanian lens, the *infans* is hidden behind the mirror image and, as those with apotemnophilia and PLS show, attempts to be complete remain futile. However, it is this loss that defines Orpheus, the writer, and those with BIID and PLS.

Orpheus's desire to see Eurydice in the light of day and to represent her is what makes language and the story of Orpheus possible, yet it is also what renders it impossible (because it is founded upon the paradoxical impossibility of representation). Without a physical loss (for those with PLS) or feeling of loss (for the BIID sufferer) the sufferers would, presumably, not form an (consciously) ungraspable form of unity. Therefore, the Orpheus myth and the two conditions are consecrated through their erasure; as Blanchot (1982) states, the "work is Orpheus but it is also the adverse power which tears it and divides Orpheus" (226). The two conditions thus reflect Orpheus's gaze and the text, in that they involve a need to materialise one's existence by making one feel complete, while destroying it to reveal one's rupture. Again, we are faced with an absence, which, for Orpheus, is represented by Eurydice.[7] Eurydice, moreover, is a specific absence, which parallels the BIID and PLS suffers, because they are tortured by a specific void. Those with BIID want the limb cut in a specific place, while amputees' phantoms are often frozen in place. As a member of "Fighting It" writes, "many of us have a line of demarcation—a specific point where the body image map ends". For phantom limb sufferers, "about half of them" writes Norman Doidge (2007), "have the unpleasant feeling that their phantom limbs are frozen" (184). It is implicit that while an ambiguous absence can be hidden in the unconscious (as seen in Freud's work), a specific one may cause discomfort, and in these situations, enough discomfort to create a kind of delusion. This reminds us of Lacan's take on the psychotic structure, in which one is stuck with an incomplete Castration (a specific absence) that results in a difficulty structuring oneself through language. Orpheus and those with BIID and PLS parallel this in their struggle to represent a specific negation.

Hassan (1971) writes that in Blanchot's essay this specific loss (of Eurydice) "represents the silence that Orpheus must, and can not attain" (19). By glancing back, Orpheus illustrates a desire to see "the dissimulation that appears", to see "Eurydice in her shadowy absence" (Blanchot 1982, 172). However, this glance ruptures the possibility of perceiving the unknown. Thus, she "is the instant when the essence of night approaches as the other night" (Blanchot 1982, 170). This "other night" differs from "the night" because while the night is the opposite of the day (Blanchot 1982, 167–168), the other night is part of it, like the unconscious that always resides silently in consciousness. The other night is that fragmentation that rests within the individual's comprehensible wholes, similar to that *infans* which precedes the mirror image. We see this embodied in those with BIID, as rupture is not the opposite of wholeness, wholeness can only be achieved through rupture. In this way, rupture and unity are inseparable, and thus fictional concepts. Similarly, the phantom limb is only (subjectively) present because the individual is amputated; rupture and wholeness are intertwined, though they are still at odds—only rupture is visible. The mirror image in the mirror-box, alternatively, visually presents the inextricability of rupture and wholeness: though an amputee may appear to be whole, she is still lacking a limb, it is her phantom that can be erased. Similarly, the other night "is always the other, and he who senses it becomes other" (Blanchot 1982, 169). In the other night, "the void is [...] coming toward him [he who approaches the other night]" (Blanchot 1982, 169). By glancing back at Eurydice, Orpheus turns towards the void within the day, and senses his simultaneous absence and presence: he, echoing amputee who sees herself as four-limbed in the mirror and releases her phantom, is other to himself. In this moment, he wants to see nothingness, that side that is other, and this, for Blanchot, defines the artist. Orpheus, then, stands for the literary writer in Blanchot's thought who is concerned with what language veils, with what cannot be grasped. The literary work confirms the irreducibility of lack and ambiguity. The mirror-box, I propose, materialises these thoughts because like the word, it shows the amputated individual what is barely there: a space in which the individual exists only through images. By glancing into this other (whole) image of oneself to see nothingness as it is (the absence behind the mirror image), the individual echoes Orpheus's glance into the Underworld.

Furthermore, Orpheus's glance comes from an unknown part of himself, and the BIID and PLS sufferers' aim to resolve finitude stems unknowable origins. Orpheus is, writes Blanchot (1982), "seduced by a desire that comes to him from the night" (174), which relates to the writer's calling. "No one begins to write, Blanchot says, who is not already somehow on the verge of this ruinous look back, and yet the sole approach to that turning point is writing" (Blanchot 1982, 15). Here, art stems from a desire to perceive the night or "madness" veiled within "day": the artist is haunted by a void. When Orpheus glances back to see Eurydice, she disappears. If a certain kind of literature allegorises this impossibility, so does the mirror-box: in glancing at one's phantom, it disappears. Thus, in writing (as Blanchot conceives it), Orpheus's glance, and the mirror-box, the desire to see a specific absence negates that absence, and this is partially due to a movement (whether it be writing, reading, glancing back, or fictively moving a phantom). Wall (1999) explains that Blanchot's writing involves "movements, or spaces [that] are precise and anamorphic insofar as they cannot be interrogated, or even properly experienced or narrated" (101). Since the act of writing or reading involves a continual movement, its meaning cannot be completely grasped, so like Orpheus, the writer (or in this case reader) "himself is absent" (Blanchot 1982, 172). In a similar way, the moving image in mirror therapy can erase one's phantom, and expose the absent limb, revealing that "death without end, the ordeal of the end's absence" (Blanchot 1982, 172). What, I ask, does this connection illuminate about the mirror-box? To begin, Blanchot believes that an individual can be exposed to her fracture in the movement of reading, because she is also being affected by the words at hand—in reading, one's more cohesive thoughts are broken up by new thoughts. Thus, as the mirror-box alters the phantom feeling, the text affects the reader; one's cohesive version of self is altered by a new image. Here, the reader and the amputee become other. Kevin Hart (2004) writes that the "'I', "becomes a 'he' or a 'one'; and [...] enters the realm of the fragmentary which is also the space of community" (17): if a reader loses part of her self in the act of reading, she, in a sense, becomes language (and the symbols within language).

In this textual interaction, "there is no exact moment at which one would pass from night to the *other* night" (Blanchot 1982, 169) because one is always a symbol, one's identity always an illusion, the imaginary is always within. In this way, the text does not literally transform the reader into a symbol, but rather, reminds her that she is, in part, composed of them. This can be clarified through Lacan's theory that the individual has been inscribed by others, that the *infans* disappears as her identity is formed through others' definitions. It is in the movement of reading that, from a Blanchotian point of view, the individual may be able to glimpse beyond those imaginary and symbolic formations from which she has been constructed. If literature, for Blanchot, brings this to light, so too does the mirror-box. By moving a limb in the mirror by, as Stephen wrote, "looking, moving, and imagining", you can "touch the pain", and "eradicate [almost] everything". Wall (1999) explains (referring to the reader), if "I can 'imagine the hand that writes them,' I will only find myself face-to-face with a gaze that does not regard me, that dispenses with me" (103). In being dispensed of in this way, Blanchot suggests, one may be free of oneself, "outside oneself, ecstatic, in a manner that cannot leave the 'oneself,' the proper, the essence, intact" (Sallis 1995, 97). In facing one's erasure, the intrusion of one's (falsely) whole self can perhaps be partially lifted.

Orpheus's gaze, explains Blanchot,

> is thus the extreme moment of liberty, the moment when he frees himself from himself and, still more important, frees the work from his concern, frees the sacred contained in the work, *gives* the sacred to itself, to the freedom of its essence, to its essence which is freedom.
>
> *(Blanchot 1982, 175)*

Freedom is approached partially because Orpheus defies the authoritative gods who told him not to look. He transgresses the law, and in so doing takes authority. It is this action, however, that also causes Orpheus's death, indicating that in order to take authority of the text in the act of reading, and to approach this freedom, one must "die" (in relation to, for instance, Barthes' "The Death of the Author"). However, instead of falling into the Underworld and dying completely, Orpheus remains in a space between life and death: he is forever broken. Orpheus's glance backwards, therefore, only reiterates his (to return to Blanchot's statement), "death without end, the ordeal of end's absence" (Blanchot 1982, 172). In a similar, yet concrete sense, the mirror-box presents an amputee's endless fragmentation: the phantom movement effaces the felt limb. Here, the amputee may be able to experience a feeling of completion in being torn (as Stephen described it: a "sense of calm, completion"). The mirror limb, like the literary work, allows the absence to exist as absence, contrasting those with PLS, those with BIID, and, as Blanchot calls it, everyday language. "Orpheus's Gaze", and the gaze into the mirror-box thus convey how seeing one's fracture through a symbol of one's simultaneous absence and presence may engender a release wherein one has "no self-identity to obey" (Hassan 1971, 19).

A literary writer, explains Haase and Large (2001), "must advance into this impersonal language and allow it to speak in her place" (64). By embodying a symbol of one's phantom in the mirror-box, the felt weight (or excess) of one's phantom decreases, just as the "weightless gaze of Orpheus" (Blanchot 1982, 176) frees his desire to see Eurydice. The mirror-box thus reflects Foucault's description of Blanchot's concept of literature, which is:

> no longer [...] a power that tirelessly produces images and makes them shine, but, rather, a power that undoes them, that lessens their overload, that infuses them with an inner transparency that illuminates them little by little until they burst and scatter in the lightness of the unimaginable.
> (Foucault 1998, 152–153)

This kind of writing is, for Blanchot and Foucault, associated with "madness", as it is concerned with representing and turning towards madness through a certain kind of (fragmentary) literature. Thinking about language in this way may open avenues to understanding apotemnophilia and PLS. The mirror-box, moreover, presents to the individual what she was unable to perceive, as literature, according to Blanchot, opens new thoughts. Instead of tirelessly shaping absence to a false whole, both the mirror-box and literature can show one's "inner transparency" to unravel the "weight" of pain, so that an individual can "unti[e] himself with his own hands" (Foucault 1998, 162). Reading and writing literature in this way is allegorised in Orpheus's eternal position between life and death, love and loss, fragmentation and wholeness, which the mirror-box concretises. One may "look, move, and imagine" one's phantom to approach an alleviating sense of absence. I now want to turn to the question: what happens if a person cannot enter this space? What if the individual who sees an absence she is drawn to embody is consumed by the impossibility to do so? I will explore these questions through an analysis of Powell and Pressburger's *The Red Shoes* (1948).

Notes

1 This derives from Freud's etymological analysis in "The Uncanny", wherein he emphasises that the meaning of the word *unheimlich* overlaps with its opposite, *heimlich*. In this way, the word itself is uncanny, it reveals a hidden other. "The *unheimlich*", writes Freud, "is what was once *heimlich*, homelike, familiar; the prefix 'un' is the token of repression" (1995, 15).
2 Having a psychotic structure differs from being a psychotic because a psychotic structure connotes an incomplete castration. Though one may have "been able to gain some degree of 'access to the metaphor' and to understand the existence of a symbolic level of functioning, he has accepted neither that he has not got the Phallus" (Bailly 2009, 85).
3 Though many individuals with BIID feel as though they are cured upon amputation, others continually feel the need to amputate other body parts, face difficulty and danger in the amputation process, and still feel misunderstood post-operation. I am not stating that people who want to amputate should not, I am looking at why they may want to, and how experiences involved in BIID are explored in other ways.

4 I am generally referring to the idea that words obtain meaning in their relation to other words; they must be removed from ambiguity to be apprehended.
5 Blanchot's essay "Literature and the Right to Death" (1947) focuses on these ideas. Here Blanchot suggests that communication negates the "other", the thing written negates what it represents. In Blanchot's words, "when I speak, death speaks in me. [Speech …] is there between us as the distance that separates us, but this distance is also what prevents us from being separated, because it contains the condition for all understanding" (Blanchot 1995, 324).
6 Blanchot follows Hegel here, who writes that language "immediately overturns what it names in order to transform it into something else" (Hegel qtd. in Blanchot 1992, 35).
7 This analysis of the Orpheus myth reads Eurydice as a metaphorical absence, rather than a "female" lack.

References

Bailly, Lionel. *Lacan: A Beginner's Guide*. Oxford: Oneworld, 2009.
Barthes, Roland. *The Pleasure of the Text* [*Plaisir du texte*, 1973]. Translated by Richard Miller, New York: Hill and Wang, 1975.
Barthes, Roland. "The Death of the Author" in *Image-Music-Text*, New York: Hill and Wang, 1967.
Blanchot, Maurice. "Literature and the Right to Death" 1947.
Blanchot, Maurice. "Orpheus's Gaze" in *The Space of Literature*, trans. Ann Smock, Lincoln: U of Nebraska Press, 1982a.
Blanchot, Maurice. *The Space of Literature* [*L'espace littéraire*, 1955]. Translated by Ann Smock, Lincoln: U of Nebraska, 1982b.
Blanchot, Maurice. *Infinite Conversation* [*L'entretien infini*, 1969]. Translated by Susan Hanson, Minneapolis: U of Minnesota, 1992.
Blanchot, Maurice. *The Work of Fire* [*La part du feu*, 1949]. Translated by Charlotte Mandell, Stanford: Stanford UP, 1995.
Cohen, Josh. *How to Read Freud*. New York: W.W. Norton, 2005.
Complete Obsession. Performance by Nikki Stockley and Aden Gillett. BBC, Horizon, 2000. Television Documentary.
Critchley, Simon, Carl Cederström, and Todd Kesselman. *Impossible Objects: Interviews*. Cambridge, UK: Polity, 2012.
Critchley, Simon. *Very Little – Almost Nothing: Death, Philosophy, Literature*. London: Routledge, 2004.
De Man, Paul. *Blindness & Insight: Essays in the Rhetoric of Contemporary Criticism*. New York: Oxford UP, 1971.
De Man, Paul. *The Resistance to Theory*. Minneapolis: U of Minnesota, 1997.
Doidge, Norman. *The Brain That Changes Itself: Stories of Personal Triumph from the Frontiers of Brain Science*. New York: Viking, 2007.
"Fighting It." *Yahoo! Groups*. http://groups.yahoo.com/group/fighting-it/.
Foucault, Michel. *Aesthetics, Method, and Epistemology*. Edited by James D. Faubion, translated by Jonathan Murphy, New York: New Press, 1998.
Freud, Sigmund. "The Uncanny" [*Das Unheimliche*, 1919]. *The Standard Edition of the Complete Psychological Works of Sigmund Freud*, vol. 17, 1917–1919. Edited and translated by James Strachey, London: The Hogarth Press and The Institute of Psychoanalysis, 1955.
Grosz, Elizabeth A. *Volatile Bodies: Toward a Corporeal Feminism*. Bloomington: Indiana UP, 1994.
Haase, Ulrich M., and William Large. *Maurice Blanchot*. London: Routledge, 2001.

Hart, Kevin. *The Dark Gaze: Maurice Blanchot and the Sacred*. Chicago: U of Chicago, 2004.
Hassan, Ihab. *The Dismemberment of Orpheus: Toward a Postmodern Literature*. New York: Oxford UP, 1971.
Hill, Leslie. *Bataille, Klossowski, Blanchot: Writing at the Limit*. Oxford: Oxford UP, 2001.
Huffer, Lynne. "Blanchot's Mother." *Yale French Studies*, no. 93, 1998.
Lacan, Jacques. *Écrits: a Selection*. Translated by Alan Sheridan. New York: Norton, 1977.
Lacan, Jacques. "The Mirror Stage as Formative of the *I* Function" (1949)
Lacan, Jacques. *The Psychoses* [*Les psychoses*, 1956]. Translated by Russell Grigg, New York: W.W. Norton, 1993.
Leader, Darian, Judy Groves, and Richard Appignanesi. *Introducing Lacan*. Oxford: Icon, 2000.
Lebeau, Vicky. *Childhood and Cinema*. London: Reaktion, 2008.
Rilke, Rainer Maria. *Sonnets to Orpheus*. New York: Norton & Co. Ltd., 1922. Epigraph Translation by Naomi Segal.
Royle, Nicholas. *The Uncanny*. New York: Manchester UP, 2003.
Sallis, John. *Double Truth*. Albany: State U of New York, 1995.
Segal, Naomi. *Consensuality: Didier Anzieu, Gender and the Sense of Touch*. Amsterdam: Rodopi, 2009.
Smock, Ann. "Introduction." *The Space of Literature* [*L'espace littéraire*, 1955]. By Maurice Blanchot, translated by Ann Smock, Lincoln: University of Nebraska, 1982.
Sumner, Stephen. *Phantom Pain: A Memoire: It's All in Your Head*. Bloomington: Archway Publishing, 2015.
Wall, Thomas Carl. *Radical Passivity: Lévinas, Blanchot, and Agamben*. New York: State U of New York, 1999.

6
THE RED SHOES

Powell and Pressburger's film follows the life of ballerina Vicky Page, who, haunted by her desire for love/art and life/death, retreats into an illusion, which is represented by Vicky's role as Karen in *The Red Shoes* ballet. In the ballet, the red slippers control Karen's body, a theme that resonates with those with BIID and PLS, whose bodies are alienated. Discussing this theme through the film raises questions about rupture, illusion, and freedom in rupture. Vicky's opening dialogue with the ballet impresario Boris Lermontov sets the tone for the film when he asks her why she wants to dance, and she replies, "why do you want to live?" He states, "I don't know but I must". "That's my answer too" (*The Red Shoes* 1948). Impressed by her vigour, Lermontov casts Vicky as the prima ballerina in *The Red Shoes*, after which she becomes famous and marries composer Julian Craster. When Lermontov discovers their affair, he forces her to choose between the comforts of human love and being the greatest dancer that the world has ever known (*The Red Shoes* 1948), which causes her to leave Julian for the ballet, and consolidates her choice of art over life. Shortly thereafter, a force strikes, as the red shoes overpower her body and carry her off a balcony, echoing the *Red Shoes* ballet that made her famous. It is Julian who finds her, gathers her in his arms, takes off her red shoes, and she dies.

The initial frame story is based on the Hans Christian Andersen (1869) fairy tale of the same name, which is about a little girl (Karen) who is given red shoes that will not stop dancing until she finally has her legs cut off by an angel. While the shoes continue to dance without her, Karen is sent to heaven. *The Red Shoes* ballet within the film—a 17-minute segment—proceeds from this original tale, where Vicky plays Karen, yet the ballet takes on a surreal effect in which Vicky's performance coalesces with her fantasies. The segment begins with an evil shoemaker who sells a pair of red ballet slippers to Karen—who is accompanied by her male partner. The shoes progressively carry her away from her partner, as he is transformed into cellophane. Left lost, alone, and haunted by the shoemaker's shadow, Karen attempts to return home to her mother, only to be stopped by the shoes. At this point, the shoemaker's shadow returns and is refigured into the apparitions of Lermontov and Julian. Karen then falls to the Underworld and dances with a sheet of newspaper, which temporarily takes the shape of her partner. When the shoemaker reappears, he guides her through the Underworld until, finally, a priest removes her red shoes and she dies.

The ballet is portrayed as being a hallucinatory rendition of what takes place in Vicky's mind, gesturing towards her psychological decline and disappearance into Karen, her "other self". This descent, I suggest, is triggered by Vicky's erasure in life, because throughout the film, her role as a dancer shadows her identity. I now want to read this portrayal of the other self with Blanchot's idea of literature (focusing on the word that is always haunted by its double), the mirror stage (the mirror image that is preceded by its *infans*), and Orpheus's loss of Eurydice. Throughout the film, Vicky is often relegated to be an "object:" she is passive to the men's' demands. Although she asserts herself at times, and her psychological processes are foregrounded, Powell and Pressburger also allude to her progressive erasure. Her initial choice of art over life foreshadows this, as she is pressured to conform to predominantly patriarchal roles (of a "housewife", Lermontov's protégée, and a famous dancer). As her fame increases, she progressively fades behind these roles. We see this in a scene in which Vicky first discovers that she will be the prima ballerina, and Julian wonders what it feels like to find oneself famous. She responds, "you're not likely to know if you stay here talking much longer" (*The Red Shoes* 1948): a statement indicative of one's effacement behind a public name (reflective of Lacan's Symbolic). At this moment, a newspaper that features an interview about *The Red Shoes* ballet brushes Vicky, foreshadowing the newspaper dance in the performance in which she is visibly obscured by language: she is lost behind an image (which I will soon discuss).

Vicky's personal relationships with both Julian and Lermontov cement this loss of identity. When Julian and Vicky have their only intimate moment, he tells her that one day, when he's old, he would like for someone to ask when he was most happy. He tells her that his response would be to say that he was with Victoria Page. The other person would ask if he was referring to the famous dancer, and he would say yes, but then we were in love. Here, Vicky is again defined though her absence (her death), their love only structured by art. Definitively, Lermontov tells her: "great superiority is only achieved by agony of body and spirit. What do you want from life? To live?" and she replies, "to dance" (*The Red Shoes* 1948); she is only free within art. Like Orpheus, she turns away from life. She does not choose death, but the agony of the body and spirit, the decay and darkness within life, and also work, discipline and performance.

This parallel between Orpheus and Vicky gives way to a variety of others, which I will now draw out to demonstrate how they both illuminate and are illuminated by the BIID and PLS. First, the film and essay (Blanchot 1982) feature artists who are driven to pursue art and death over life and love, and who are consequently left in a state of physical rupture. Second, both pursue the impossible task of relinquishing their desire for completion in the "other". Thus, they reflect the state of those with PLP and BIID, who strive for an impossible sense of completion through a state of physical rupture. Furthermore, as Orpheus "unknowingly [...] moves toward the work" (Blanchot 1982, 174), Vicky moves towards art's darkness by continually choosing death over life, as allegorised in the ballet. Ultimately, both characters are haunted by a double that stands for their fragmented self (Orpheus by Eurydice, and Vicky by Karen), as the PLP and BIID sufferers are haunted by their double (the body image they desire).

Just as Karen (Vicky's other) is only released when her shoes are removed (she can finally die to escape the tortures of her body), and Vicky's pain only ceases when she dies, the BIID sufferer's "mind is at peace" (Mensaert 2011, 19) when the limb is amputated. One individual explains: "I was given my amputation not because I wanted it, but because that was the only way to stop me from wanting it" (Mensaert 2011, 19). Moreover, in the Hans Christian Andersen story, although the community warns Karen not to wear them, "Karen thought only of her red shoes" (Andersen 1869, 4). Despite the community's condemnation, the protagonist is not portrayed as being mentally ill but confused and alone, a sentiment echoed in both the film and the ballet within. Similarly, although BIID sufferers, as Peter demonstrated, may be perceived (or are afraid of being perceived) as mentally ill, their dialogues often convey that they feel misunderstood. Indeed, for Lacan, everyone is formed through a lack (a desire for "the Other") and lives through an illusion. However, if the lack is too large, so is the illusion, thereby forming the hub of psychosis (delusion). Although Vicky is not psychotic, she enters a delusional state in the dance, exemplifying a loss that in Lacanian theory relates to a desire for an other.

Accordingly, in *The Red Shoes* ballet, it is the male shoemaker who seduces Karen into wearing the shoes, and who shadows her throughout the segment. Remaining indistinct and anamorphic throughout, the shadow resembles Lacan's concept of the hommelette[1] that is silently part of the individual.[2] Moreover, the shadow in the ballet morphs into Julian and Lermontov, again calling up Lacan's concept of the psychotic structure, in which the individual is haunted by a missing Name of the Father. As Lacan's theory suggests, it is the desire for an ungraspable other that consumes Vicky, as it is Eurydice's allure that calls Orpheus into the "other night". Lacan (1998) writes: "we have, in Eurydice twice lost, the most potent image we can find of the relation between Orpheus the analyst and the unconscious [...] the unconscious finds itself, strictly speaking, on the opposite side of love" (25). Eurydice depicts how the unconscious is present as a discontinuity: it always leaves the individual with a loss. "To flee it [the other night]" Blanchot (1982) writes, "is to be pursued by it. It becomes the shadow which always follows you and always precedes you" (169). The unconscious cannot be outrun because it exists within, which Vicky illustrates in her endless flight away from life's pressures and towards death, and Karen, from her shoes/shadow.[3] This indicates that although many have shadows from which they cannot escape, some individuals' desires for the "other" may cause them to conjure up illusions. Apotemnophilia and PLS demonstrate that, while this may engender creativity for some, for others it may take over reality. Their shadows transgress the objective and seep into a psychical and physical experience. The limbs, like embodied shadows, present an absence of reflection (as counterbalanced by the mirror-box reflection).

If the ballet segment provides insight into Vicky's psychological state, it suggests that Vicky's desire for the "other" has caused her to create a fictional whole. This is particularly illustrated in a scene in the ballet when, just after Karen's partner disappears, she descends to the Underworld. Here, she first appears translucent, only to become opaque when she is encircled by a sheet of newspaper. The scene's opening seems to suggest that she is only resurrected through words, through her representation. Once opaque, she leaps towards the newspaper, which is transformed into the image of her partner, as her white dress becomes obscured by indecipherable words. Although the words resurrect her, therefore, they also veil her, thus dramatising the paradoxical nature of language we have explored through Blanchot's work. Blanchot (1995) writes, "Speech has a function that is not only representative but also destructive. It causes to vanish, it renders the object absent" (30).

Vicky's delusion reflects the writer's desire to bring forth the unknown, an inclination to communicate through a "phantom [which] is meant to hide, to appease the phantom night […] we dress it up as a kind of being; we enclose it, if possible, in a name, a story and a resemblance" (Blanchot 1982, 163). Dressed in words and dancing with a phantom of language, Vicky hides behind her illusion of Karen in the Underworld. Thus, Vicky and Karen, like those with phantom and BIID appendages, are chased by a trauma that drives them into the arms of fiction, suggesting that here, illusion is fundamental to expressing feelings of rupture. Similarly, a text shapes fiction from absence. As Blanchot argues, however, language cannot completely communicate fracture. The desire to capture wholeness through illusion is rendered impossible. Literature that exposes this ruse of completion parallels Vicky's illusion, because it too reveals a sense of underlying fracture. These links suggest that by creating an illusion to escape from reality, an individual may only be faced with its impossibility.

When she dances with her partner in the Underworld, Karen illustrates how linguistic expression may not be enough. She attempts to bring life to absence through language to (in Blanchot's words) "gain control over things with satisfying ease. I say, '[t]his woman', and she is immediately available to me, I push her away, I bring her close, she is everything I want her to be'" (Blanchot 1995, 322). The partner in the ballet hidden behind indecipherable words is Vicky's creation, suggesting that language can be used to control the other. However, the blanketed partner is not real and cannot be grasped, for he fades away at her touch: the Other cannot be understood through words. Although Vicky and the man embody language, it is not language, paradoxically, but the body and dance through which they communicate. The scene thus illustrates those themes central to the first slope of literature: that language is created to withstand absence, yet it is not capable of establishing complete communication. If the movement shows that Karen is only able to dance with her partner when covered in an indecipherable language in the

Underworld, Powell and Pressburger allude to an existence beyond words, a communication that takes place through the body and imagination.

Beyond everyday language, their dance, like Blanchot's notion of literature, brings out

> the trembling, pre-linguistic darkness of things [...] this second slope is not satisfied with [sic] bringing Eurydice into the daylight, negating the night, but rather by [sic] wanting to gaze at her in the night, as the heart of the essential night.
>
> (Critchley 2004, 63–64)

The dance, therefore, like the second slope of literature "becomes concerned with the presence of things before consciousness and the writer exist; it seeks to retrieve the reality and anonymity of existence prior to the dialectico-Sadistic death drive of the writer" (Critchley 2004, 54–55). If Karen is haunted by death, this non-linguistic (yet not without language) scene offers a moment of relief, a retreat from pain, where rather than helplessly dancing away from her absence, she dances with it. It is through an image of language (words), rather than the meaning of words, that Karen is able to let go.

Put another way, might this image not demonstrate Lacan's notion of the mirror stage, that pre-linguistic state of the *infans*? When Karen's fall away from the light of day into the Underworld erases her public presence, and Vicky's art erases her identity, both characters hide in an imaginary world. Karen's dance with an imaginary double thus resembles the moving, ruptured, and non-linguistic *infans*: although Karen moves through a ruptured body, she does so through an illusion of being with the other within language.[4] If the individual unconsciously desires to function at the level of the Imaginary, Vicky's dance as Karen illustrates this desire. Her fall to the Underworld may connote a lapse into a pre-linguistic state, also resembling Blanchot's space of literature. If we return to Leslie Hill's statement that the space of literature is a "nowhere that is here", and apply it to the film, we see how Karen is in the Underworld (a visible nowhere), and only exists in the imagination of Vicky (who is also a figure of absence). Orpheus, too, is in the Underworld through a fragmented body, and the *infans* always exists just beyond grasp. These links convey a different view of those themes perceptible in both limb conditions the BIID appendage that belongs nowhere, and the imagined phantom limb. If, as earlier discussed, this nowhere that is here may offer a feeling of freedom, how, I shall now ask, can this be seen in *The Red Shoes*, and what can this reveal about the mirror-box?

The newspaper scene ends when Karen falls towards her partner's arms, he returns to a sheet of paper, her dress returns to white, and she peacefully drifts to the floor: the only moment of rest. This movement, for me, resembles the writer who, to return to de Man (1971), "frees himself from empirical concerns" (77). Karen's gestures and movements arise more naturally and freely when she sheds her linguistic veil. Here, something within words, not words themselves, allows for a mutual dialogue where (as Hart stated) "'I' becomes a 'he' or a 'one'" (2004, 17), where the individual becomes (in a way) a symbol. Powell and Pressburger allude to the idea when Julian tells Vicky, and when you're lifted by the dancers, "my music will transform you!" To which she asks, into what? A flower? A cloud drifting? A white bird flying? "Nothing matters but the music" (*The Red Shoes* 1948). In forgetting representation, Vicky is free of herself. Nietzsche's *The Birth of Tragedy* (2008 [1872]) may provide more insight here because it discusses another double: the Dionysian, which is associated with music, disordered and undifferentiated reality and death; and the Apollonian, which is associated with art, order and a differentiation. In becoming other to herself through music (a white bird flying), Vicky falls into the Dionysian, and because she gives herself to "this noble illusion, tragedy may now move its limbs to dithyrambic dance and surrender itself without a thought to an orgiastic feeling of freedom, which it is allowed to flourish as music in itself, thanks alone to this illusion" (Nietzsche 2008, 113–114). In dancing, Vicky moves away from the Apollonian realm of order, and enters the Dionysian "dissolution of the individual and [her] unification with primordial existence" (Nietzsche 2008, 27). The ballet lures her towards a Dionysian state in which she, as Blanchot (1982) writes of Orpheus, "loses [her]self" in the "song" where she is "infinitely dead" (173). For Orpheus, this leap towards erasure "lifts concern, interrupts the incessant by discovering it" (Blanchot 1982, 175), analogous to a writer who may also express her own notions of self. In dancing, Vicky is free of Julian and Lermontov; she can rest when her shoes overtake her, falling into an image of herself, which produces a kind of freedom. In the mirror-box, this idea becomes actual and more immediate: becoming a symbol engenders a physical freedom from a false sense of unity. One individual with a phantom limb writes: "at the point the 'effect' occurs with the mirror, there is usually an overwhelming release of emotion that is not unpleasant. After this initial effect, the person feels pleasantly different" ("Phantom Limb Pain" n.d.). Here, part of the individual is erased through the mirror symbol, which has physical results; the more abstract ideas take on a different kind of reality in apotemnophilia and the phantom limb phenomenon.

The Red Shoes blurs the lines between fact and fiction, between Vicky and Karen. Towards the end of the film, Karen overshadows Vicky's actions, as portrayed most clearly when Vicky's shoes possess her by carrying her body off the balcony's edge. Although "the exceptionally sanguinary nature of Vicky's demise upset many critics" (McLean 1988, 42), perhaps Powell and Pressburger gesture towards a release, as foreshadowed by Karen's dance. Ian Christie's analysis of the film, which focuses on the "explicit and veiled" nature of Vicky's death, suggests that, as quoted earlier, in Vicky's final leap to suicide,

> Powell illustrates death not only by an ellipsis but also by an eclipse of the body [...]. Her body [is] in free fall, her flesh and the tulle of her dress cross the frame, merging together, out of focus and disordered. A strange suspension gives the illusion of weightlessness.
>
> *(Christie 2005, 235)*

The image here is not of pain, but of freedom to return to Julian's remark "of a white bird flying". If Karen's fall into the Underworld involved a dance with her own absence, which indicated a self-release and moment of rest, does Vicky's death not also depict a similar kind of freedom? And if so, how does this illuminate the death of the phantom limb in the mirror-box? How does her death resemble the mirror image that simultaneously animates and annihilates the phantom limb?

First, by submitting to her rupture through dance, Vicky, like the individuals using the mirror-box, releases a painful pressure of being caught between life and death (she becomes Karen). And just as Karen's fall to the Underworld is not precisely death, Vicky's fall in the film's closing scene is not precisely suicide, but an ambiguous death (which Michael Powell confirms in his autobiography, *A Life in Movies* [1986]). In dying, then, Vicky submits to her own absence, which, I want to suggest, is what allows her dance to live on (like the feet that move without Karen in the Andersen tale). We see something similar in Orpheus, whose song exists through his infinite fissure, as Vicky's dance lives on after her death, as allegorised in the film's final moment when the ballet continues without her. To clarify, Vicky's death occurs just before the performance, leading to a chilling scene in which Lermontov decides to continue the play with a spotlight in her place, clinching her role as being a figure of her own negation. Paradoxically, however, this scene also finalises the impossibility of her absence: because she is an artist, her death is unending. Analogous to language, as Blanchot conceives it, Vicky is only a figure of her negation. And it is this last scene that, reflective of (Blanchot's concept of) literature, acknowledges this underlying void. The spotlight, paralleling Orpheus's gaze, "consecrates the song", because in order to produce art, "one has to possess the power of art already [… to] write, one has to write already. In this contradiction are situated the essence of writing, the snag in experience, and inspiration's leap" (Blanchot 1982, 176). Thus, Orpheus and Vicky are driven from elsewhere to sacrifice life and leap into the darkness, to fall into a kind of existence suspended between life and death. When read alongside BIID and PLS, the drive to perceive and experience life/death derives from a feeling of rupture that is linked to a desire for unity. However, in submitting to a simultaneous existence and non-existence, a re-dying, by becoming a symbol in the mirror-box, one is momentarily free of oneself. I now want to turn our attention towards how Vicky's rupture can be linked to film's viewer, and the medium of the film itself, and how this connects to PLS and mirror therapy.

To approach this, I will analyse three ideas in conjunction: that the cinematic experience reflects the experiences conveyed within the film, that the spotlight in Vicky's place echoes the phantom limb and mirror-box, and that the film itself allegorises the mirror-box. I contend that in observing her struggle with fragmentation, the audience may unconsciously identify with her, albeit from a safe distance. Ian Christie (2005) writes that in *The Red Shoes*, "death is foreseen, that is to say articulated as a possibility, for the spectator it nevertheless remains unthinkable […]. The character on whose presence the story is based, and in whom they [the viewers] invest their emotions, cannot die" (234–235). This suggests a disavowal of annihilation,[5] which echoes that of the phantom limb sufferer, whose body denies an absence. The final scene, where Vicky is represented by a spotlight, continues Christie, challenges the viewer with the "violence [...] of a confrontation between the presence of the body and its absence in the place it should occupy" (Christie 2005, 236). The spotlight reflects her phantom, in other words, and in watching it, the viewer sees her presence and absence at once. Thus, those within the film who are viewing the ballet, particularly Lermontov, cope with Vicky's absence through a phantom of her presence, another fetishistic disavowal reflective of the phantom limb and the mirror-box (as they both involve a simultaneous denial and recognition of a lack). This scene spills over into the cinematic experience, as it too may act as a coping mechanism in the wake of the Second World War. It may cause observers to disavow (Vicky's) annihilation, while allowing them to visualise it. It is the mirror limb that conveys a similarly simultaneous presence and absence through an image, which echoes the film itself—a reflection of images which, in this case, may appease spectators' fears without denying them. Thus, the ballet, film, and the mirror-box all demonstrate forms of relieving and attempting to relieve absence. And although the cinematic experience may not be seemingly physical, as the mirror-box demonstrates, a particular kind of image can have a psychosomatic effect. In sum, then, the phantom limb and mirror-box phenomena are reflected in Vicky's character, which the spectators (both in the film and those viewing the film) might identify with, albeit, at a removal. The pain of lack may be alleviated through artistic depictions of absence. Reflective of psychoanalysis from Freud's point of view, a particular kind of art or the mirror-box can allow the amputee or spectator to look into the "internal world of our thought and [... enable] us to 'understand' something in the external world, to foresee it and possibly alter it" (Freud 2010, 53).

Literature can have a similar effect. Peter Brooks (1993) explains that literature aims to discover, but not resolve uncanny feelings and experiences: "[i]f the motive of poetry is an attempted recuperation of an otherness, often that otherness is our own body" (2). The mirror-box shows the body as a sign with which the individual can perceive her rupture and reduce the urge to physically re-experience it. Furthermore, a particular kind of literature, like the mirror-box, may engender a reincorporation of the unknown. As Blanchot (1982) states, "language's power consists in making the immediate appear to us not as the most terrible thing, which ought to overwhelm us [...] but as the pleasant reassurance of natural harmonies or the familiarity of a narrative habitat" (41). Here, the "power" of literature (and implicitly art) is to bring forth that unfamiliar "other" that engenders tormenting feelings. Blanchot indicates that in so doing, the narrative can help reshape the foreign body into a home-like one: it can make the uncanny more familiar. This chapter's discussions of literature, film, and psychoanalysis have in its examples of how an individual who is plagued by fragmentation may retreat to delusion provided insight into an alternative route. If, as stated in the introduction, "we constitute ourselves as human subjects in part through our fictions" (Brooks 1987, 341), the mirror-box concretises this, as it demonstrates how fictional images of self and self-as-other can change realities. The possibility of causing the unfamiliar to become more pleasantly familiar is also central to the process of a psychoanalytic working-through, which I shall now explore through the work of D.W. Winnicott.

Notes

1 According to Slavoj Žižek:

> Lacan imagines lamella [hommelette] as a version of what Freud called 'partial object': a weird organ which is magically autonomized, surviving without a body whose organ it should have been, like a hand that wanders around alone in early Surrealist films.
>
> *(Žižek, How to Read 62)*

2 Although both the shadow and the shoes haunt Vicky, the shoes represent that physical torture we have been discussing in relation to the two syndromes, while the shadow, as Naomi Segal (2007) writes, "privileges a visual relation to the object" (262). We are reminded of the inseparability between the visual, psychic and physical, and how this is represented in the film.
3 Powell and Pressburger exhibit their own experience with this, as Powell's autobiography *A Life in Movies* (1986) reveals, "The ballet demands body and soul from its practitioners" (656). However, Powell and Pressburger, unlike Vicky, are not consumed by the illusion: "The movies were purely representational" (1986, 656).
4 If for Lacan, psychoanalysis "is about accompanying the patient towards his/her subjective truth" (Bailly 2009, 35), this reunion between Karen and her partner may also signify a reunion between the objective self and the subjective hidden other, that shows through in analysis.
5 It is worth noting that the film was made just after the Second World War. Powell explains:

> we had all been told for ten years to go out and die for freedom and democracy, for this and for that, and now that the war was over, *The Red Shoes* told us to go and die for art.
>
> *(Powell 1986, 653)*

Thus, the audience's possible suppression can also be related to a general post-war trauma. Though I will not expand on this here, it is connected to the foundations of this book and the discussion of Georges Perec.

References

Andersen, Hans Christian. *The Red Shoes*. London: Routledge, 1869.
Bailly, Lionel. *Lacan: A Beginner's Guide*. Oxford: Oneworld, 2009.
Blanchot, Maurice. *The Space of Literature* [*L'espace littéraire*, 1955]. Translated by Ann Smock, Lincoln: U of Nebraska, 1982.
Blanchot, Maurice. *The Work of Fire* [*La part du feu*, 1949]. Translated by Charlotte Mandell, Stanford: Stanford UP, 1995.
Brooks, Peter. *Body Work: Objects of Desire in Modern Narrative*. Cambridge: Harvard UP, 1993.
Brooks, Peter. "The Idea of a Psychoanalytic Literary Criticism." *Critical Inquiry*, vol. 13, no. 2, 1987, pp. 334–348.
Christie, Ian, and Andrew Moor. *Michael Powell/International Perspectives on an English Filmmaker*. London: BFI, 2005.

Critchley, Simon. *Very Little – Almost Nothing: Death, Philosophy, Literature*. London: Routledge, 2004.
De Man, Paul. *Blindness & Insight; Essays in the Rhetoric of Contemporary Criticism*. New York: Oxford UP, 1971.
Freud, Sigmund. *An Outline of Psycho-analysis* [*Abriss der Psychoanalyse*, 1940]. Translated by James Strachey, Mansfield Centre: Martino, 2010.
Hart, Kevin. *The Dark Gaze: Maurice Blanchot and the Sacred*. Chicago: U of Chicago, 2004.
Lacan, Jacques. *The Four Fundamental Concepts of Psychoanalysis* [*Les quatre concepts fondamentaux de la psychoanalyse*, 1973]. *The Seminar of Jacques Lacan, Book 11*. Translated by Bruce Fink, Boston: W.W. Norton & Company, 1998.
Mensaert, Alex. *Amputation on Request*. London: lulu.com, 2011.
McLean, Adrienne. "The Red Shoes." *Dance Chronicle*, vol. 11, no. 1, 1988, pp. 31–83.
Nietzsche, Friedrich Wilhelm. *The Birth of Tragedy* [*Geburt der Tragödie*, 1872]. Translated by Douglas Smith, Oxford: Oxford UP, 2008.
"Phantom Limb Pain, Ramachandran and the Mirror Box." *NL People*. No date, no pagination. www.23nlpeople.com/brain/Phantom_limb_pain.php.
Powell, Michael. *A Life in Movies: An Autobiography*. London: Faber, 1986.
The Red Shoes. Directed by Michael Powell and Emeric Pressburger. Performance by Moira Shearer, Anton Walbrook, Marius Goring. Eagle-Lion Films, 1948. DVD.
Segal, Naomi. "Living the Body Metaphors: Is the Lost Object an Imaginary Friend, a Phantom Limb or a Second Skin?" *The Flesh in the Text*. Edited by Thomas Baldwin, James Fowler and Shane Weller, Bern: Peter Lang, 2007, pp. 261–281.
Žižek, Slavoj. *How to Read Lacan*. New York: W.W. Norton, 2007.

7
BREAKDOWN
D.W. Winnicott

> Hi, I attempted to amputate my left hand in 2005 and it was reconstructed […]. Now that time has passed I am ready to definitively amputate the hand. I am open to traveling within N. America to stage the accident and am looking for someone to corroborate the "story line." Having been there once before I kind of know what I'm getting into and what to expect and "not do again." […] anyone interested in sharing my journey?
>
> *("Fighting It" n.d.)*

This man with BIID reflects the struggle of a certain kind of traumatised individual outlined in Winnicott's "Fear of Breakdown" (1974). The writer of this email expresses a desire to (re)experience fracture, create a fictional story to do so, and to be supported in this endeavour. In Winnicott's model, traumatised individuals might experience something similar, albeit in different forms: in order to control a feeling of loss, they may attempt to relive a certain type of accident or rupture. They may do so, he suggests, through dangerous and destructive acts. Winnicott suggests, however, that there may be a healthier and more productive way to experience fracture, which takes place through a particular kind of relationship.

D.W. Winnicott was a psychoanalyst and paediatrician trained by Melanie Klein, one of the cofounders of object relations theory. Many of her ideas, including those about play, pre-oedipal developments, "internal" and "external" objects, and babies' subjective experiences of their bodies, were integral to his work. His theories centre upon how individuals form subjective and objective notions of self, how they develop in relation to others, and how patterns of growth are formed through the early environment. These patterns, he suggests, are developed in connection with maternal care and psychosomatic integration, which is essential to his essay "Fear of Breakdown" (1974) The essay is one of his most famous partially due to his belief that the fear of breakdown (and implicitly psychosis) is universal. He writes: "there must be expected a common denominator of the same fear, indicating the existence of universal phenomena" (Winnicott 1974, 103). Since "Fear of Breakdown" outlines what Winnicott calls "a reversal of the individual's maturational process" (Winnicott 1974, 88), I shall begin by summarising his theories of human development.

For Winnicott, a baby comes into the world dependent on and inseparable from its mother,[1] and continually learns to exist as a separate individual. This occurs as the mother adapts to the baby and slowly removes her support, allowing it to cope with absences and mend the gap between itself and her, until the child becomes less dependent on others for survival. If, however, the mother "fails" (for example, by causing the child to wait too long for her return), the continuity of the mother/child relationship will be compromised, and the child will feel psychically and physically "dropped".[2] The resulting blank (which involves a feeling of falling) becomes part of the child's physical and psychical makeup, obstructing its development, and causing any number of problems including: a fear of feeling dropped again, pain related to this fear, and the possibility of forming psychotic tendencies to defend against this pain. He writes that traumatised babies are those

> who have been significantly "let down" once or in a pattern of environmental failures [...]. These babies carry with them the experience of unthinkable or archaic anxiety. They know what it is to be in a state of acute confusion or the agony of disintegration. They know what it is like to be dropped, to fall forever, or to become split into psycho-somatic disunion.
>
> (Winnicott 1989a, 260)

Dropping, therefore (both in reality and symbolically), is part of what constitutes a trauma, and to avoid causing the baby to suffer from trauma, the carer must hold, handle, and present the child with objects at the right frequency. Winnicott writes: if "the mother is away more than x minutes [...] [t]he baby is distressed, but this distress is soon *mended* because the mother returns in $x+y$ minutes. [...] But in $x+y+z$ minutes the baby has become *traumatised*" (Winnicott 1991b, 131). Winnicott suggests that this separation between mother and infant involves a dialogue with the body and the mind, because the baby is shown how to physically grasp objects and survive through the mother's example and must form mental links to do so. The infant's independence and health, therefore, depends upon psycho-somatic integration, because it ostensibly allows the infant to "feel real" and "live creatively" (Abram 2007, 45). Winnicott writes: "[f]eeling real is more than existing; it is finding a way to exist as oneself, and to relate to objects as oneself" (Winnicott 1991b, 158). In a traumatic occurrence, however, the subject may feel a dissonance between her mind and body and feel less unified. Though Winnicott believes that independence is never completely reached, a person becomes increasingly defined as she uses objects in the environment to represent and express her feelings, so that they can be shared and more thoroughly understood by herself and the outside world. Since this covers a large scope, I will expand upon some of the specifics to ground the connections that follow.

Childhood development and breakdown

When a baby enters the world, dependent upon the environment, it is only a bundle of fragmented senses with no psychical understanding of itself and what is around it. In this state, there is "not yet a conscious and an unconscious [...]. What is there is an armful of anatomy and physiology, and added to this a potential for development into a human personality" (Winnicott 2002, 70). The infant feels the sensations that accompany the needs necessary to survival, such as hunger. Due to its disordered fragmentation and underdeveloped comprehension, however, the baby cannot satisfy those bodily needs and must rely on another human being to stay alive. It is only "a belly joined on to a chest and has loose limbs and particularly a loose head: all these parts are gathered together by the mother who is holding the child, and in her hands they add up to one" (Winnicott 1989b, 568). This stage is called "absolute dependence", where the baby believes it is one with the mother, and that the objects given to it are its own creation, this is what Winnicott calls the "illusion of omnipotence". It is through this fantasy that the baby begins to build its security, confidence, and sense of self in the world. It can only feel like a "whole and mature human being" (Winnicott 1991a, 88) through those who hold and satisfy its bodily needs. As Winnicott states, "there is no such thing as a baby" (1991a, 88). A baby cannot exist independently of the other, because there is only a relationship, as opposed to a complete individual.

This relationship sets the stage for the ego, which develops later. The ego is the individual's physical and psychical sense of self in the world.[3] Alessandra Lemma (2010) explains that "it is in part through identifying with the image the m(other) has of him that the child develops a sense of himself" (755). Moreover, explains Jan Abram, "at the *very* beginning she [the mother] *is* the baby's ego" (2007, 158). The ego is what allows the child to defend against environmental impingements, which remains strong if the baby is "sufficiently" cared for. This part in their life is registered, however, since they were not yet individuals at the time, this part of them cannot be accessed, remembered or understood. This silent (pre-linguistic) stage, he writes, "belongs to being alive. And in health, it is out of this that communication naturally arises" (Winnicott 1965, 192). Though it can never be comprehended, the fragmented self remains within, and founds the structure upon which the individual will grow. This early state, he contends, is the place where spontaneous gestures are primitively felt, it leads to one's future creativity. Although it "forms an intermediate space through which the individual and the world communicate" (Jacobs 1995, 40), it can never be completely expressed and creates a core that comprises what Winnicott refers to as the "True Self". The True Self "is the beginning of a feeling of existing and feeling real, and depends upon what he refers to elsewhere as 'a basic relation to the experience of omnipotence'" (Phillips 2007, 133). in order for the illusion of omnipotence that founds the baby's "core" self to be secured, the mother must provide a facilitating environment by adapting to the baby and satisfying its needs. By bringing it desired objects, a "good-enough mother" gives "the infant the *illusion* that there is an external reality that corresponds to the infant's own capacity to create" (Winnicott 1991b, 12). She does so through the way she "in the fullest sense, 'holds' the child, which includes the way the child is held in the mother's mind as well as in her arms" (Phillips 2007, 30), so that it does not feel traumatically dropped. However, if the baby is left too long, or the mother/carer imposes her own needs and gestures upon the baby, it will form a "False Self". In response, the child will have trouble finding, expressing and appeasing its needs. As the baby proceeds from absolute dependence towards "relative dependence", it must learn to separate from the illusion of omnipotence, which occurs slowly, as it does not continually receive the objects of its desire. Over time, the baby learns to trust that the environment will not leave its needs unmet, allowing it to withstand absences and learn to obtain objects independently.

This movement involves what Winnicott refers to as transitional objects. These objects mediate between the baby's physical desire and its correlative object in the world. It stands in for the lack when the desired object is not immediately present and occupies a space between the subjective and objective ("me" and "not-me"). Since they take up the space between an indescribable desire and its satisfaction, transitional objects stand for a paradoxically simultaneous presence and absence of subject/mother unity and the baby's body, they are "not part of the infant's body yet are not fully recognised as belonging to external reality" (Winnicott 1991b, 3). When the baby is not being held, transitional objects help the infant to cope with absence; in place of the carer, the baby can hold, for example, a "bit of cloth", "wool", or engage in linguistic "babble" (Winnicott 1991b, 5). These objects act as a bridge between the body, the psyche and the environment; they hold up the void between the baby's felt desires and its connection to the physical world. Thus, the more adequately the child learns to use transitional objects, the stronger and more unified her psychosomatic integration (ego) will become. If an infant is not sufficiently supported and cannot learn to use transitional objects, however, a split will remain between the child's mind and body, her sense of unity and separation, subjectivity and objectivity. By integrating the mind and body through transitional objects, the child is always gathering together the world around her to build her own support system, handle environmental losses, and separate from her dependence on the environment.

In this process, suggests Winnicott, she may act aggressively towards the environment to ensure that it survives her destruction. He describes this through the game "I'm the king of the castle—you're the dirty rascal" (Winnicott 1989d 112), a playful illustration of how the child separates from the environment. "With good-enough mothering and a facilitating environment", explains Abram (2007), "aggression in the growing child becomes integrated. If the environment is not good enough, aggression may manifest itself in a (self)-destructive and/or antisocial way" (89). In a "not good enough" environment, the child may become inappropriately aggressive towards herself or others, reflective of those with BIID. As one sufferer explains in "Fighting It:" "I find it very difficult to cope. Honestly— it's on my mind all day and it sucks. I'm getting real close to having a shotgun party in the desert. Accidents do happen" ("Fighting It"). Here, a desire for bodily fragmentation invades the individual's mind: there is an invasive feeling of loss. In light of Winnicott's concept of physically registering a trauma, perhaps this individual's drive to suicide indicates that the only way to destroy the mental imprint of a felt absence is by killing the body. Linguistically, the email's ironic tone indicates a simultaneity of seriousness and humour: the reference to suicide as a "shotgun party" makes light of a serious situation, just as the word "accident" makes light of the drive to suicide. This humour could be read as a psychological distancing from a physical reality. By joking about death, this BIID sufferer may be protectively separating from torment. In addition, the use of the word "accident" is paradoxical, because it is not an accident if they take it into their own hands. Perhaps they unconsciously wonder if they *are* the accident. Have they mistakenly been left in a position that causes them to feel fragmented, as though they want to kill themselves?

When read with Winnicott's model, the accident here may refer to having been "dropped" by a neglectful carer. As we will soon see in "Fear of Breakdown", Winnicott (1974) believes that early traumatic experiences that are not remembered or understood, but which are unconsciously registered throughout life, are deathlike. The traumatised individual thus grows with an inexplicable felt emptiness and unintegrated ego. He contends that the individual left in this state may desire to return to the deathlike moment of being dropped in infancy in order to re-experience, survive, and decrease its impact, which may lead to suicide. "The patient who compulsively looks for death", writes Adam Phillips, "is reaching in this way to a memory of a previous death" (2007, 20–21). Left with an indefinite feeling of physical rupture, the aforementioned BIID sufferer may, in this light, be attempting to pursue his or her accident of feeling dropped in order to control and make sense of the past. They may be driven to self-amputate or commit suicide in order to experience and survive their continually felt primitive trauma, they may be drawn to recreate the accident that happened before they could remember.[4] This may also account for his pluralisation of the word "accident", which suggests that they constantly feels the accidental, traumatising "fall", and that this imposing feeling of annihilation may be driving them to recreate it. Winnicott's "Fear of Breakdown" hinges upon this type of traumatic occurrence, which thus resonates with PLS and BIID.

As illustrated above, individuals with BIID demonstrate feelings of psychosomatic dissonance: though they appear whole, they feel incomplete. Similarly, those with PLS may feel physically whole though they are amputated. In "Fear of Breakdown", Winnicott outlines a similar state of splitting. For him, it is in the pre-linguistic state of absolute dependence in which the blueprint for further development is most distinctly drawn, rendering it most integral to one's ego construction. The essay centres upon this stage, because he believes that if something traumatic happens to an infant, it will develop throughout life without a strong "ego root", with a gap between the body and the mind. If something goes wrong in the carer's ability to hold, handle, and present the infant with objects, the child ostensibly feels "annihilated, dropped and falls forever" (Newman 1995, 342): the infant is self-defined through a lack. Due to a traumatic drop (which can occur over a long period of time), the infant cannot learn to develop independence through the use of transitional objects and is structured through a void that comprises what Winnicott refers to as a primitive agony. Though he lists these agonies in various ways (to include everything from feelings of falling to not feeling "real"), they represent the bodily loss that stems from the carer's failure to hold the child. Due to the nature of the trauma, therefore, these agonies relate to feelings of fragmentation, annihilation and fusion with the environment/other. This structural emptiness leaves the individual "all the time on the brink of unthinkable anxieties" (Newman 1995, 60), which brings us to the crux of Winnicott's theory. The "fear of breakdown", he writes, "is *the fear of a breakdown that has already been experienced*" (Winnicott 1974, 90). The subject is left perpetually afraid that her falsely constructed ego will break down and send her into the state of primitive agony that she was too young to comprehend.

Like the traumatised subject in Winnicott's model, those with BIID and PLS embody a painful and incomprehensible lack. While the BIID sufferer illustrates this through a desire to physically express a feeling of fragmentation, those with PLS cannot come to terms with it. Individuals with a phantom limb or BIID are, echoing the traumatised subject, defined by an illusory bodily ego and unable to represent certain feelings of rupture. In all three examples (BIID, the phantom limb and Winnicottian trauma), this pain can be attributed to a split between wholeness and rupture, psyche and soma. There is a metaphorical and lived element to Winnicott's theory, because while he discusses specific patients, he also considers breakdown to be more ambiguous and universal. The parallel I draw here is not exact (particularly for those with PLS who have a physical lack). It provides a useful way to examine what might be involved in apotemnophilia and PLS—a certain experience of fracture. As discussed in relation to Peter, Winnicott's viewpoint raises the question whether those with BIID are aiming to re-experience an embodied feeling of "death".

Nothing is happening

I have suggested that for Winnicott, an individual may be driven to re-experience or "remember" agony or death, to survive it and restructure herself. The subject, in other words, is unconsciously driven to go back and learn how to use transitional objects in order to build a stronger ego. She could then, ostensibly, relearn how to hold herself up, integrate her body and mind, and release the pain of emptiness. Problematically however, since "the original experience of primitive agony cannot get into the past tense" (Winnicott 1974, 91), the patient is unable to re-integrate. Although "the experience has happened", she was only a fragmented bundle, and thus, "the patient could not experience it" (Caldwell and Joyce 2011, 199). She is helplessly trapped between the fear of experiencing and the desire to experience annihilation, just as those with BIID and phantom limbs reveal a fear of experiencing and desire to experience the fragmentation by which they feel they are structured. Those with PLP generally wish to remove the phantom and experience a physical absence, but also (non-intentionally) veil the loss with a delusion. Those with BIID pursue feelings of fragmentation in the hope of feeling complete.

Thus, those who are driven to sever their limbs reflect Winnicott's theory that one may unconsciously desire to return to the primitive agony (the lack of holding) to re-experience and survive loss. Perhaps they unconsciously desire to identify with their carer in being unable to hold themselves, in order to have control of the experience. BIID also conveys a protection from the world, because one takes the loss into one's own hands. Winnicott refers to something similar as a "defence organisation relative to a primitive agony" (1974, 90). Though these defences may take many forms, he proposes that they all hinge upon the organisation of "a controlled emptiness" (1974, 94). It is the act of controlling loss, he suggests, through which traumatised individuals feel they can survive. Grasping control of their own erasure may allow them to hold up the false identity that keeps them together. This empty ego, suggests Winnicott, is organised through an illusion of whole omnipotence. Recall that in the phase of omnipotence the infant feels that it is one with the world. The function of the transitional object is to "give shape", which will "start each human being off with what will always be important for them, i.e. a neutral area of experience which will not be challenged" (Winnicott 1991b, 14). Interestingly, the phantom limb and BIID conditions reflect this kind of organisation, because their subjectively felt losses correlate with a specific part of the body. The majority of BIID sufferers know exactly where they feel that their limb is "absent". "Many of us have a line of demarcation", explains one sufferer, "a specific point where the body image map ends" ("Fighting It"). The phantom limb is also specific to a place on the individual's body: the sufferer often feels pain in the exact place her appendage should be. When read in this light, the specificity of the illusory limbs in both conditions indicates a desire to create a transitional object: a specific area that cannot be challenged.

Winnicott's essay focuses on two forms that this defensive reaction may take—one positive and one negative. The positive form is reflective of the phantom limb delusion of a presence that satiates the lack, while the negative echoes the BIID sufferer's desire for removal. Winnicott refers to the positive version as a "concept of one-ness" (1974, 95), which he compares to the notion of an afterlife. The idea is that the traumatised individual attempts to control her emptiness by explaining it, by intellectualising the way her death will take place. This individual's fragmentation is contained through a non-material version of self, paralleling the phantom limb sufferer. By envisioning an image of absence as a part of her whole being, the individual may be attempting to control her unknowable death to save it from taking over. An example of this positive one-ness, states Winnicott, is of those who "ruthlessly fill up by a greediness which is compulsive and which feels mad" (1974, 94). If the previous example is a psychological aim to substantiate one's absence, this example reveals the physical aspect of the same project. To keep from falling into chaotic agony, one's ruptured body is kept intact, its nothingness solidified and materially controlled. Reflective of the phantom limb phenomenon, both physical and psychical narratives work to repair the traumatised person's mind/body gap. Though the defence may work to keep traumatised individuals' fracture in place, their brittle self-images may remain dissonant from the environment, causing them to feel unintegrated and dissatisfied.

Winnicott describes another form of controlled emptiness that has been "negated" in "an attempt to counter the personal tendency towards a non-existence" (Winnicott 1974, 95), which, I contend, takes shape in those with BIID. If the positive one-ness covers an ambiguous lack by filling it with a specific and ungraspable defence, the negative also counteracts non-existence, albeit through an emptying out rather than a filling in. The "negated" reaction also aims to control the lack. Winnicott connects this process to the existentialist who definitively decides that there is no afterlife. Here, the individual contains her annihilation by taking it into her own hands. Similar to the previously discussed narrative of greed, this negative form may also become physical. For instance, an individual may organise her emptiness by "not eating or not learning" (Winnicott 1974, 94), causing a felt void to be projected onto the world to make it to feel real. If not eating (for example in anorexia) or not learning can be visualised by others through social interaction or bodily weight, others may notice and verbalise the loss, thus reflecting back one's empty identity to validate its existence. The BIID subject's attempt to control rupture by bringing it towards the world (through the body) exemplifies this theory. However, as stated in the introduction, unlike most people with anorexia, individuals with BIID acknowledge that their bodies are healthy: they convey a different form of defining and controlling absence. And, as Winnicott's paradigm can take several forms, I do not suggest that PLS or BIID are exact parallels of his model. Winnicott's theory brings out a core relationship between BIID and PLS (psychosomatic integration in relation to bodily rupture, and how individuals may react to a felt loss).

One form that Winnicott also discusses in the essay is suicide. He asks if this attempt to physically realise one's excessive rupture can take a more extreme form, if one will "find a solution by suicide" (1974, 93). Trauma sufferers may, destroy their bodies in order/in the effort to control their emptiness and release the agony of their painful state. However, since the felt trauma has been stored indecipherably in the mind, Winnicott suggests that the subject is "sending the body to death which has already happened to the psyche" (1974, 93). The solution of bodily rupture, for Winnicott, does not successfully repair the psyche/soma split because it does not allow the traumatised individual to experience, survive, and mentally integrate the trauma to express the pain and feel better. What is at issue, then, is that "negated" wholeness and suicide may reflect an unsuccessful desire to physically experience fragmentation in order to subdue the mental need to do so.[5] From this standpoint, BIID sufferers' attempts to experience and integrate their felt rupture are not completely successful (although they do not usually attempt suicide, as seen in Peter's case, Winnicott's theory illuminates the drive towards self-destruction). Although they may keep the subject safe from "environmental vagaries" and protect the ego, those with BIID and PLS remain divided from the world: though phantom limb sufferers may feel "whole", others see their amputated body. The BIID subject's perception of self as fragmented also remains dissonant from others' perceptions of her completion. They literally cut themselves off from the world, in some circumstances causing others to think them mentally ill or psychotic (as revealed in Peter's case).

Winnicott's definition of psychosis is a "defence organisation relative to a primitive agony" (1974, 90), in which the subject is "shown to be disintegrated, unreal, or out of touch with his or her own body, or with what we observers call external reality" (Winnicott 1989c, 64). Although the sufferers of BIID and PLS are not clinically psychotic, they do involve some psychotic mechanisms as outlined by Winnicott: they are preoccupied with an imaginary wholeness and also remain distanced from "external" reality and feel partially unreal. The question raised here is how Winnicott's suggestion as to how the psychotic patient's pain may be alleviated links to BIID and PLS, and mirror therapy. I want to examine this question by turning to an email written by a BIID sufferer responding to a woman's attempt to self-amputate:

> God, can I relate to that! I know your agony; I've been there many times. I don't mean to encourage you, but be prepared. Have a tourniquet (your belt?) and a cell phone with you- preferably with GPS for them to find you. And don't be too far from a road for access. Your femoral artery is about the same diameter of your fifth finger, you could bleed to death, so the tourniquet is very important. Know your risks, study your anatomy. LIVE as an amputee, don't die in the attempt. Be careful!
>
> *("Fighting It")*

It seems that this individual is stuck with a repetitive agony ("I've been there many times") similar to the traumatised individual in Winnicott's model. Rather than deny the torment, the individual in this email shares his pain, acknowledging that the recipient is not alone. The author of this post helps the recipient find physical protections including a tourniquet, a phone, and an accessible road: there must be a possibility that the recipient can be found, in order to ensure survival. Furthermore, the email, encourages the recipient to study her risks and her anatomy, to know herself. How, I ask, might this connect to the traumatised individual's desire to "go back" and learn how to use a transitional object to reintegrate, decrease the pain of the unknowable trauma, and feel more real? One BIID sufferer expresses the concern: "can we", he asks, "find a way to live with this simple, but important and good feeling of being ourselves also when we keep our limbs 'intact'?" ("Fighting It").

Winnicott suggests in his essay that this may be approached through psychoanalysis. He asks if one can be saved from physically annihilating what has been registered in the psyche by re-experiencing psychical death to alleviate the pressure of its threat and temptation. Can a person, he wonders, "commit suicide" "for the right reason" (Winnicott 1974, 93)? Can the analytic exchange provide a space for someone to re-experience primitive agony in a safe way, so that it can be psychically and physically integrated, thus reducing the drive to self-harm? To approach this in psychoanalysis, the patient must

> experience this past thing for the first time in the present, that is to say in the transference. This past and future thing then becomes a matter of the here and now and becomes experienced by the patient for the first time.
>
> *(Winnicott 1974, 92)*

Since the patient cannot remember the trauma, the analyst must recreate it by acting as the carer who supports and fails her, though this time slowly, re-teaching the patient to hold herself up. The patient learns to build transitional objects by "[gathering] the original failure of the facilitating environment into the area of his or her omnipotence" (Winnicott 1974, 91). This, Winnicott explains, "is the equivalent of remembering, and this outcome is the equivalent of the lifting of repression that occurs in the analysis of the psycho-neurotic patient (classical Freudian analysis)" (1974, 92).

As one BIID sufferer explains, she fears "fall[ing] in the trap where [she questions her] own feelings and desires instead of accepting them, welcoming them" ("Fighting It"). Winnicott wonders if in the traumatised patient, this kind of a welcoming may be approached in analysis: if

> the patient is ready for some kind of acceptance of this queer kind of truth, that what is not yet experienced did nevertheless happen in the past, then the way is open for the agony to be experienced in the transference, in reaction to the analyst's failures and mistakes.
>
> *(Winnicott 1974, 91)*

He suggests that the analyst who stands in for the carer must create a secure environment for the patient, to enable her to "return" to the trauma, to break down. To do so, the analyst and patient must create a new memory together, a reconstruction of the ego based on transitional objects that do not aim towards a false sense of unity and truth.

In this way, the psychoanalytic exchange is a kind of transitional object: it is a space for the patient to rebuild herself through another's help. I suggest that the mirror-box also acts as a transitional object standing in for carer who holds the baby. More specifically, the mirror-box and this kind of psychoanalytic exchange, like the transitional object, paradoxically symbolises mother/subject unity and its lack, create a space that is both illusory and real, and are simultaneously part of the body and not. In psychoanalysis, the analyst/patient relationship can shatter the illusion of omnipotence (and mother/baby unity) to allow the patient to begin accepting loss. The mirror-box, I contend, also conveys the impossibility of unity: an individual appears to be concurrently whole and missing, both held and dropped by arms that belong both to herself and the (physically whole) self she is not. Although psychoanalysis ostensibly allows the patient to "go back" to an infantile trauma, this is also an illusion because the trauma was never fully experienced (as the baby was not cognitively aware) and thus it cannot be re-experienced. Analysis is a kind of fictional re-enactment. However, it is also composed of lived moments and things: the patient and analyst's previous experiences, the dialogue being created between the two, and the room itself, thus echoing the simultaneously illusory and material composition of the mirror-box. Both processes, moreover, involve a sense of release through physical movements.

Winnicott's method of psychoanalysis focuses on this particular aspect, because he believes that the patient's bodily movements in analysis may reveal some primitive gestures that were lost when she was traumatised. He proposes that the psychoanalyst must also work with the patient's actions or, as Adam Phillips states, a "characteristic of the analytic setting for Winnicott was not exclusively verbal exchange" (2007, 138). By supporting the patient both psychically and somatically, the analyst can allow the individual to integrate her mind and her body. The mirror-box, similarly, exists between the mind and the body, links somatic fragmentation to the psyche, and can alleviate pain. In this way, it is a concrete demonstration of the transitional object. It suspends a physical loss long enough to allow for a feeling of psychosomatic integration by mediating the loss through an illusion of its presence. Thus, the analytic exchange and the mirror-box can be conceived of as a kind of transitional object that creates a space for individuals to experience fragmentation without feeling "dropped" or "annihilated", allowing them to begin accepting the reality of their fracture through the illusion of its lack. Since the transitional object is also foundational to cultural experience and artistic creativity, I shall now turn to a cultural object, a film, in order to trace its relation to "Fear of Breakdown".

Notes

1 Although the role may apply to other carers, Winnicott typically refers to the mother.
2 This idea of a "failing" or "good/not good-enough" mother is problematic, as, first, the mother is not the only person responsible for the baby. Second, the demarcation for being "good enough" is imprecise: for Winnicott, a mother can be too present or too absent.
3 The psychosomatic ego put forward here is not unique to Winnicott's thinking. Freud (1961) famously stated that "[t]he ego is first and foremost a body ego" (26). Melanie Klein (1946) suggests, "[i]ntrojection and projection [of the breast] are from the beginning of life also used in the service of this primary aim of the ego" (101). The ego for her, as for Winnicott, is physical, as the first object the baby projects and introjects is the mother's breast. Jacques Lacan also believed the ego to be physically composed, though for him, the baby "has no experience of corporeal or psychic unity" (Lemma 2009, 756). Didier Anzieu's concept of the ego correlates more closely with Winnicott's. He suggests that "the ego is primarily structured as a 'skin ego,'" so the baby's experience of its body is "mediated by what he experiences as the mother's relationship to his body" (Lemma 2009, 756).
4 To clarify, although Winnicott refers here to a specific loss in infancy, trauma can occur in different gradations throughout life, as "holding" is not specific: it applies to a variety of gradual environmental experiences. As he writes in "The Theory of the Parent-Infant

Relationship" (1960): "[t]he term 'holding' is used here to denote not only the actual physical holding of the infant. [...] [I]t refers to a three-dimensional or space relationship with time gradually added" (589). I do not suggest that those with BIID have necessarily suffered from a specific trauma; perhaps they have, whether concretely or metaphorically, been unable to digest an experience of loss or trauma and may be thus driven to re-experience it.

5 Alessandra Lemma's view of this physical removal or erasure is similar. She suggests that an individual with a difficult childhood, often characterized by a maternal deficit aims to extract a body part to be saved from further rejection. The individual, she suggests, may seek out "'surgery' a literal cutting off as the alternative to thinking and so integrating painful, 'ugly' feelings towards the self and object" (Lemma 2010, 760).

References

Abram, Jan. *The Language of Winnicott: A Dictionary of Winnicott's Use of Words.* New York: Karnac Books, 2007.
Caldwell, Lesley and Angela Joyce. *Reading Winnicott.* London: Routledge, 2011.
"Fighting It." *Yahoo! Groups.* http://groups.yahoo.com/group/fighting-it/.
Freud, Sigmund. *The Ego and the Id* [*Ich und das Es*, 1923]. Translated by James Strachey, New York: Norton, 1961.
Jacobs, Michael. *D.W. Winnicott.* London: Sage Publications, 1995.
Klein, Melanie. "Notes on Some Schizoid Mechanisms." *International Journal of Psycho-analysis*, vol. 27, 1946, pp. 99–110.
Lemma, Alessandra. "Being Seen or Being Watched? A psychoanalytic perspective on body dysmorphia." *International Journal of Psycho-Analysis*, vol. 90, 2009, pp. 753–771.
Lemma, Alessandra. *Under the Skin: A Psychoanalytic Study of Body Modification.* London: Routledge, 2010.
Phillips, Adam. *Winnicott.* London: Penguin, 2007.
Winnicott, D.W. "The Theory of the Parent–Infant Relationship" *The International Journal of Psycho Analysis*, vol. 41, no. 3, 1960, pp. 585–595.
Winnicott, Donald. "Communicating and Not Communicating Leading to a Study of Certain Opposites." *The Maturational Processes and the Facilitating Environment: Studies in the Theory of Emotional Development.* New York: International Universities, 1965, pp. 179–192.
Winnicott, D.W. "Fear of Breakdown." *Psycho-Analytic Explorations.* Cambridge: Harvard UP, 1974, pp. 87–95.
Winnicott, D.W. "Psycho-Analysis: Theory and Practice." *Psycho-Analytic Explorations.* Cambridge: Harvard UP, 1989a.
Winnicott, D.W. "Physiotherapy and Human Relations." *Psycho-Analytic Explorations.* Cambridge: Harvard UP, 1989b.
Winnicott, D.W. "Psycho-Neurosis in Childhood." *Psycho-Analytic Explorations.* Cambridge: Harvard UP, 1989c, pp. 64–72.
Winnicott, D.W. "Psycho-Somatic Disorder." *Psycho-Analytic Explorations.* Cambridge: Harvard UP, 1989d, pp. 103–118.
Winnicott, D.W., *The Child, the Family, and the Outside World.* London: Penguin, 1991a.
Winnicott, D.W. *Playing and Reality.* London: Routledge, 1991b.
Winnicott, D.W. "Communication Between Infant and Mother, and Mother and Infant, Compared and Contrasted." *Winnicott on the Child.* Cambridge: Perseus Pub., 2002, pp. 70–83.

8
DEATH PROOF

Quentin Tarantino's film *Death Proof* (2007) deals with themes similar to those seen in Winnicott's theory of trauma and, accordingly, apotemnophilia and PLS. I will consider how the protagonist—Stuntman Mike—represents the primitive agony and fracture that haunts the traumatised subject in Winnicott's model, and how the women in the first half of the film represent the traumatised subject. I consider how the car accident in the middle of the film parallels Winnicott's concept of the breakdown that occurs in therapy, and how the second half of the film exemplifies his notion of healthy independence which is sought out through psychoanalysis. The characters in the film reflect the struggle of psychosomatic rupture, and this cinematic analysis will open pathways towards understanding how the ruptured subject copes with feelings through a particular form of fiction. I also explore how the film represents and embodies a transitional space, reflective of the mirror-box.

Death Proof was released as part of a double feature that revisits American exploitation films. It chronicles the story of a "psycho" serial killer named Stuntman Mike, who chases down women and kills them in staged car accidents. I want to discuss how he exemplifies the traumatised subject, because he appears to be physically and psychically structured through fragmentation, he clings to a false and empty identity, and he seeks both to experience and to remain safe from death by staging controlled and deadly car accidents. Furthermore, like the fracture that pursues the traumatised individual, Stuntman Mike pursues the women in the film. Recall that in "Fear of Breakdown" (Winnicott 1974) the subject reacts to a lack of support by creating a falsely whole (and thus brittle) ego and identity to hold themselves up, and consequently embodies a split between emptiness and cohesion. Stuntman Mike characterises this figure because he too embodies fragmentation: his face is divided in two by a scar and he clings to a false identity, as indicated by his name being synonymous with his stage name. If by definition, a stuntman takes an actor's place and constantly faces possible death, Stuntman Mike, like the traumatised individual, embodies a ruptured identity that stands in for his "true" self.

If this falsely integrated ego replaces the lack of a mother, it is physically manifested in his death-proof car, as suggested by the car's connectedness to female desire and to his mother. Since the car is riddled with photographs of the girls he stalks, it can be seen as a replacement for a missing female figure. Moreover, Mike refers to the car as his mother's car when convincing a victim of its safety: "do I frighten you?" he asks, "is it my scar?" "It's your car", the girl answers, "sorry", he replies, "it's my mom's car" (*Death Proof* 2007). This perhaps indicates that Mike's mother has left him *driven* to cause fear and pain, reflective of Winnicott's theory that an infant who has been "dropped" is driven to psychotic tendencies. Just as the traumatised individual replaces her feeling of loss with a form of controlled nothingness, Mike's car encloses him, acting as a figure of false unity that stands in for the wound left by a missing figure of support. The traumatised sufferer's false unity leaves her feeling ruptured and thus fearing and desiring to experience her fracture physically, and Mike's actions illustrate similar desires. As visualised by the phantom limb sufferer who hides her fragmentation, Mike avoids death. His identity is paired with a "death proof" vehicle—a body that encloses, protects, and makes him feel falsely supported. Like the two limb delusions, it keeps him safely cut off from the world and environmental impingements. However, it is also within this protected defence against rupture that Mike attempts to experience and have proof of his death, as a BIID sufferer may survive her own fragmentation. Accordingly, Mike explains to his first victim that he owns a "death proof" stunt car he can drive into a brick wall, just for the experience. But, he explains, to get the benefit of it, she needs to be in his seat (*Death Proof* 2007).

Reminiscent of the BIID sufferer's statement that "accidents do happen" in reference to his own suicide, Mike attempts to control and experience death by making "accidents" happen: by preplanning the car crashes that kill his victims. Stuntman Mike's actions thus characterise those of the BIID and traumatised sufferer, who may be, to return to Winnicott, "sending the body to death which has already happened to the psyche" (1974, 93) and must continue to kill in order to survive a rupture that may not be in the body but in the mind. This does not mean, of course, that those with BIID have murderous instincts, it is just a way of exploring how and why individuals desire rupture and how it is portrayed. Just as this fragmentation haunts traumatised subject, Stuntman Mike lingers unknown and unseen in the women's environments in the first half of the film. From this perspective, Mike represents the trauma that haunts these women because he magnifies their hollowness, which is emphasised by their false identities, problematic father figures, and deceitful relationships. Reflecting the state of dependency outlined in Winnicott's model of trauma, these women are removed from their "core" identities and cling to false ones, referring to one another by fake names such as "Butterfly" and "Jungle Jane".

If these identities indicate a felt void, it takes shape in the emptiness of their relationships, for which they compensate through physical interaction. "Fear of Breakdown" states that the traumatised subject's ego "organises defences against breakdown of the ego organisation", a defence that the women illustrate by avoiding intimacy, a brittle "ego organisation that is threatened" by Stuntman Mike (Winnicott 1974, 88). Butterfly exemplifies this when she kisses someone she just met under strict conditions: that the two cannot show physical intimacy such as cuddling, or kiss for more than six minutes. Stuntman Mike recognises her vulnerability and lures her to give him a lap dance by threatening her identity in two ways. First, he tells her that she looks "wounded" because men have not pestered her, and he offers to repair that wound with his affection, standing in for her missing support. However, she is not completely persuaded to give him a lap dance until he threatens her identity by claiming that if she refuses, he will write her name down in his book as a "chicken shit" (*Death Proof* 2007). This suggests that her identity is so bereft of meaning that she must make it meaningful by appeasing his wish for physical affection. Like those with BIID and PLS, Butterfly is driven to take physical action in order to make her identity feel more whole.

If a lack of care in Winnicott's model is responsible for this empty ego, the girls' difficulties with paternal figures[1] and with their friendships, gesture towards a similar scenario. In one scene, Shanna explains that her father is attracted to her friends, including Jungle Jane, who flirts with him. To this, Jungle Jane responds that Shanna is jealous of their flirtatious relationship because it does not include Shanna. Though it seems obvious that Tarantino is playfully referencing Freud's Oedipus complex, the interaction also relates to Winnicott's model. It reveals a lack of parental support, as manifested both in the women's friendships with one another, and their dependence upon meaningless male attention to keep their identities intact. This dependence is further alluded to by Jungle Jane's comment that she calls Shanna's father by his first name, because she is not a child, and the statement that she does not want to be dependent upon their male friends. Here Jungle Jane depicts a struggle with dependency, which she unsuccessfully handles by continually vying for male attention. Since one of the girls later refers to Stuntman Mike as a father figure, he again resembles a ruptured stand-in for the wound left by a lack of care. The women, in this light, are driven to repeat the actions that leave them broken, as represented by the scene in which the psychotic stuntman murders them.

The girls and Stuntman Mike, therefore, protectively cut themselves off from others both to pursue and to hide from their rupture, reflective of the kind of self-protection described in relation to the traumatised individual and those with BIID and PLS. Interestingly, moreover, both Tarantino's film and Winnicott's essay reference poems about death. In the film, Mike recites a stanza from Robert Frost's *Stopping by the Woods on a Snowy Evening* (1923) to Butterfly, however, rather than reciting the original ending, Mike whispers, "did you hear me, Butterfly? And miles to go before you sleep" (*Death Proof* 2007). What interests me about this poem is that it involves a desire for death (of self or other) or, according to literary critic William H. Shurr (1974), "a major tradition of interpretation" is to see Frost's poem as a "deathwish, however momentary, i.e., that hunger for final rest and surrender that a man may feel" (585). In "Fear of Breakdown", Winnicott also references a poetic death wish, this time quoting John Keats:

> [w]hen Keats was half in love with easeful death, he was, according to the idea that I am putting forward here, longing for the ease that would come if he could "remember" having died; but to remember he must experience death now
>
> (Winnicott 1974, 93)

Both Winnicott and Tarantino illuminate the significance that poetry can bear in relation to expressing a desire for death. Poetry, and particularly Romantic poetry (with which both Frost and Keats are commonly identified) is concerned with the experience of death, emotion, and movement. In this way, poetry reflects the transitional space that bridges the gap between self and other, between their subjective feelings of annihilation and their ability to communicate and feel integrated with the environment. Moreover, the Romantic poetry featured in the film and in "Fear of Breakdown" signals a transition between Romantic writing that aims towards meaning and unity and fragmented Romantic writing. Thomas McFarland (1981) states: "[i]ncompleteness, fragmentation, and ruin [...] not only receive social emphasis in Romanticism but also in a certain perspective seem actually to define that phenomenon" (7). Christopher Strathman emphasises Romantic poetry's influence in the transition from writing with an aim for cohesion towards an acceptance of rupture. He explains that it

> is as though, for Blanchot, writing, in order to be what he calls fragmentary writing, must be purified of the excessive self-awareness of consciousness that inhibits romantic poetry; the subject of the ego must be obliterated or burned off so that the writing of the fragment, as fragmentary writing, can begin.
>
> (Strathman 2006, 23)

Winnicott and Tarantino's use of Romantic poetry highlights these inhibitions, as well as those changes brought forth in the discourses that followed (such as poststructuralism).

A poetic or literary lack of cohesion may provide a partially fictional space for a reader to experience a sense of rupture, thereby reflective of the transitional object or maternal holding. According to the psychoanalyst Christopher Bollas, the

> uncanny pleasure of being held by a poem, a composition, a painting, or, for that matter, any object, rests on those moments when the infant's internal world is partly given form by the mother since he cannot shape them or link them together without her coverage.
>
> (Bollas 1987, 32)

I suggest that a film can also act as a transitional object that can "hold" an individual through an absence. Like the analytic exchange put forth by Winnicott, a certain kind of art form that lacks answers can ostensibly create a space for an individual to regress towards fracture in the present and experience some of the feelings involved, without "falling". While this kind of experience can be healing in psychoanalysis and mirror therapy, these forms of art do not cure pain; however, they may allow the individual to withstand a feeling of fragmentation, and even be, as Bollas writes, "pleasurable". In viewing a film, moreover, the spectator "may identify with the characters on screen as transitional objects, already invested with a part of himself and a part of the spectator's own story" (Konigsberg qtd. in Kuhn 2013, 43). In *Death Proof*, then, the spectator may identify with the psychotically inclined and traumatised subjects, and in this way, the film may allow for the viewer to experience safely a rupture that might otherwise be disavowed (reflective of BIID and PLS).

The film may have this effect due in part to its fractured content and form. While its content depicts a pained subject, the film also structurally leaves the individual with feelings of fracture, because it switches suddenly from black and white to colour, cuts out reels, and ends scenes midway through. Though I am not claiming that Tarantino's movie replaces an analyst's role, he explains, "the audience is there to be tortured" (Tarantino 2011). The spaces between the cut reels like those between the words of a poem and the patient/analyst exchange momentarily confront the individual with a lack of cohesive meaning, with "that 'nothing': the image not seen, the look that does not happen" (Lebeau 2009, 37). Here, perhaps "[s]omething troubles, something agitates; sometimes 'in' the image, sometimes in the space that opens up between one image and another" (Lebeau 2009, 39). Through these cut reels, a space is opened for disturbing reactions (thoughts, images, physical feelings) to arise. Rather than using some figure of illusory unity to stand in for a loss (as the girls use men, Stuntman Mike uses his car, and the BIID and PLS sufferers have delusions), perhaps the viewer can be, in a sense, suspended within the medium's ambiguity. Therefore, viewers may experience feelings of fragmentation through a psychical return to trauma, an idea magnified in the scene that divides and connects the first and second halves of the film.

If the first half of the film represents Winnicottian trauma and psychosis, the middle scene represents the breakdown that can occur in therapy. Here, Stuntman Mike abruptly drives his vehicle into the girls, causing their gruesome bodily rupture. Though the scene is initially presented too quickly to comprehend, the crash is repeated more slowly from different angles, allowing the viewers time and space to integrate the accident. First, the cars collide in just an instant, as Shanna's body flies into the air and falls to death—a visualisation of Winnicott's model of the infant's bodily fall that happened too quickly and ambiguously to comprehend. The scene is immediately followed by a slower replay of the crash, this time focused on shattered windows and an empty shoe, bodies remaining indecipherable in the chaos. This version calls forth the traumatised subject's remaining pain, the helpless emptiness with which she has been left due to a fall. The scene is then shown from a different view, focusing in on the victims' expressions of shock and fear as the stuntman approaches. Suddenly, the window dismembers a leg and it falls onto the road, with Butterfly's open eyes, from this perspective, indicative of a transition into acknowledging rupture. In this scene, we can visualise the physical feelings of fracture that may stem from an environmental lack, a return to the infant's annihilation. Since, in our reading, this fracture illuminates that of the BIID and phantom limb individuals, the crash illustrates a sense of fragmentation similar to what we have been discussing—an uncontrollable feeling of bodily rupture. Moreover, the scene itself reflects the mirror-box and, accordingly, Winnicott's model of psychoanalysis (and hence, a transitional object), because it presents a traumatic rupture from several different angles, so the viewer may begin to digest the loss. This is not to say, again, that the cinematic experience can heal a traumatised subject, but rather, that the film, like mirror therapy and a certain kind of literature, can suspend a loss that may allow the observer to withstand disturbing thoughts of (in this case) physical fracture and annihilation.

Since, in Winnicott's theory, breakdown leads to a (partially fictional) reconstruction of an individual's identity by fracturing her previously structured ego, it can also be linked to the second half of the film, in which another group of women survive the Mike's intent to kill. The viewers are presented with a different fiction to repair the loss of the other characters. Contrary to those in the earlier half, these women demonstrate a movement away from dependence because they support one another, while also establishing their own independence. This is illustrated, primarily, in how their identities appear to correlate more closely with their "core" selves, the most courageous character being a stuntwoman named Zoë Bell both in the film and in life. Also differing from the other girls' more meaningless physical interactions, these characters have relationships that may lack physical contact but carry a more meaningful core. For example, a girl named Abernathy explains that she refuses to kiss someone she likes, but she allows him to massage her feet and give her a mixtape, which as opposed to a burned CD, is the test of "true love" (*Death Proof* 2007). Abernathy appears closer to her ego's primitive actions through a lack of compensatory physical contact. Instead, "true love" is approached through gestures, partially made meaningful because they are a return to the old (a tape instead of a CD). This is also reflective of Winnicott's model, where the subject's sense of being real is brought forth as they and the therapist return to the past to repair a loss, when the patient "experience[s] this past thing for the first time in the present" (Winnicott 1974, 92). Interestingly, a return to the past also drives the entire narrative of the film's latter half. First, it revisits the accident from the beginning of the movie in a different form. Second, the accident is shaped by Zoë's desire to relive an old movie—to drive the car featured in the 1971 film *Vanishing Point*. The girls set out to test-drive the car oblivious to Mike's existence, and Mike sees his opportunity to annihilate them. This time, the car is not driven to their deaths but towards a vanishing point. The women drive just for the experience of it, as Mike did; however, they do not experience a sudden trauma, as the other women did in the first half of the film. These women are equipped to withstand the threat of trauma, as they chase Stuntman Mike in order to assert their own independence and to survive. Winnicott's idea of regressing in therapy towards the baby's state aims to break down false notions of wholeness and recreate a new identity by restructuring the past. And these characters break down

Mike's protected position and restructure the past by which they have been built.

Another scene representative of this encounter with primitive agony is when (prior to the car chase) Abernathy explains that she and Zoë were at a party that was blindingly dark. When Zoë wanted to take a photo of her, states Abernathy, she instructed her to step back, until Abernathy ended up at the edge of a seven-foot ditch (*Death Proof* 2007). Though Abernathy stepped away from it, Zoë fell in and survived. If she had fallen in instead, exclaims Abernathy, she would have broken her neck. Zoë is consequently called "agile" like a "cat", and talented in this regard, to which she strangely responds, "I resemble that remark" (*Death Proof* 2007). She "resembles" strength because she is strong, and her character resembles the actress, who is a stuntwoman actually named Zoë Bell. This scene can be related to Winnicott's model, in which an individual who is afraid of falling to her death is able to survive this fall and thus have more robust resources to enable her survival. If Zoë exemplifies this independent figure, her strength later enables Abernathy to drive more safely towards her own possible death with the Abernathy's support.

This scenario unfolds as (before the women take the car on a test-drive) Zoë persuades her friend Kim to drive "Ship's Mast" with her, meaning sit on top of the moving car. Though Kim initially refuses, Zoë convinces her by promising to crack her back, give her foot massages, and "put moisturizer on her butt" (*Death Proof* 2007). Reminiscent of the way a carer may treat a child, these women only agree to face their possible deaths because they have promised to support one another both physically and psychically. They even refer to Abernathy as the mother of the "posse" who lends her belt to strap Zoë to the car, and silently sits in the back seat as they drive. The image here is reminiscent of the BIID email that advises the correspondent to have a belt with him when he self-amputates. In both examples, one individual offers a way to physically and psychically help the other survive. These mechanisms of support are also seen in psychoanalysis, as the analyst, in Winnicott's thought, must allow the patient to feel supported enough to carry her through a catastrophe, as demonstrated in the way these women support one another enough to do the same. Just as the traumatised subject gathers the "original experience of primitive agony [...] into its own present time experience and into omnipotent control now (assuming the auxiliary ego-supporting function of the mother [analyst])" (Winnicott 1974, 91), these women experience rupture while supported by one another, as they chase the psychotic stuntman and slowly break his car and body. Thus, these characters reflect traumatised patients in Winnicottian analysis because they face fragmentation and reconstruct the past with a new awareness, thereby becoming more independent. I will soon look at how the mirror-box mechanism brings out an alternative way of seeing this process because, like the film, it projects an image of surviving bodily fragmentation (when the box is removed, the limb is re-amputated through an illusion, which is this time less painful because it does not leave the individual with a lingering phantom).

The film may allow the viewer to undergo a similar process for several reasons. First, the poems in Winnicott's essay and Tarantino's movie, as well as the film's structure itself (through its cut reels and sudden deaths), may have the effect of confronting the viewer with a sense of loss. *Death Proof* also represents a return to the past, because the second half of the movie reconstructs the first or, in Tarantino's words, "the film reaches its conclusion in the middle, and then just, starts over again. And you actually see the same film again ... but now you have different information" (Tarantino 2011). If, according to "Fear of Breakdown", "it can be said that *only out of non-existence can existence start*" (Winnicott 1974, 95), perhaps the first part of the film had to end in non-existence in order for the other women's independence in the second half to begin (a metaphorical rebirth). Therefore, the film provides the audience with an opportunity to see the characters with a new awareness. It is also a return, because it reconfigures American exploitation films and allows the viewer to revisit preconceived views of film. The movie also reflects the traumatised ego's therapeutic reconstruction, because it combines fact and fiction (most prominently seen in Zoë Bell), as we also see in the narratives formed in analysis and in the mirror-box (where the phantom limb is based on the existent one). Finally, the audience is always in suspense, reminiscent of the suspension between words in psychoanalysis. For Winnicott, it is this suspension that may help someone slowly fall through primitive agony.

It is the deadly car accident that particularly magnifies the viewer's experience of breakdown, I suggest, as it echoes the healthy, albeit painful, breakdown in Winnicottian analysis. Just as the infant's primitive trauma could not be comprehended, the first visualisation of this disturbing scene occurs too quickly to digest. However, as it is repeated slowly, though it may be disturbing, the spectator must acknowledge the details of this annihilation. Similarly, in the mirror-box, the feeling of moving the phantom may be disturbing (as some with phantom limbs have reported); but with practice, they are able to integrate the loss. The viewer may also begin to integrate the emotions involved, and piece together what happened through her own thoughts, or "identify with the characters on screen as transitional objects" (Kuhn 2013, 43). Although this repetition may force the viewer to acknowledge the gruesome details of bodily fragmentation, it may ultimately decrease the shock. Similarly, in Winnicott's concept of analysis, a reconstruction of one's unknowable trauma is "very difficult, time-consuming and painful" (Winnicott 1974, 91), because the analyst must help the patient acknowledge her felt rupture in a safe place. If, however, as Tarantino's title suggests, the subject must have proof of her death to accept and survive it and proof against its impact, how can an analyst support the individual through a fall? If the subject is structured by a brittle ego, and in the painful and defensive position of both desiring and fearing death, how can the analyst avoid sending her to agony?

Winnicott proposes that in order to break the ego without recreating the trauma, an analyst must be aware of the patient's defences. Though the proposed methods of how to do so remain ambiguous and multifarious, they hinge upon the analyst's need to acknowledge that she does not know, so as not to impose a specific narrative upon the patient that threatens to re-traumatise her. The analyst must not be "a seductive imposter of the omniscient mother", but rather an "attentive but unimpinging object" (Phillips 2007, 142), and must avoid "colluding" with the subject. The analyst and patient form a dialogue that breaks up the patient's known history and reality, to leave room for new thoughts. The patient and analyst create a partially fictional trauma, a reconstruction of the ego through its deconstruction. *Death Proof* depicts a similar process; however, while here the trauma is devised through a fiction, in analysis a fictional restructuring arises out of a traumatic experience. The film may bring out uncomfortable feelings for the viewer because it prolongs the moment, permitting her to repeatedly "remember" the actors' bodily fracture through a different (fictional) view each time. This parallels the therapeutic exchange, which provides a comfortable space for a patient to witness and recreate an accident from several angles and allows for its psychical integration. And in mirror therapy, the amputee can recreate her phantom, while also recognising its fracture: she can fictionalise her illusion to gain more control over it. Thinking about psychoanalysis, mirror therapy, and fiction in this way, provides a new understanding how we engage with feelings of psychosomatic fragmentation through social or artistic media, and how this can have an impact.

For Winnicott, it is through this analytic process that the patient begins to trust that the analyst will not let her fall and may slowly release her fear of and desire for annihilation. By learning to find her own objects of desire, the analysand may form a strong enough ego to integrate and withstand the analyst's (inevitable) failure or refusal to appease her. Thus, it is through the analyst's example that the patient may alter her self-definition, learn to reach towards the environment, and begin to decrease the pressure of the breakdown "that is carried round hidden away in the unconscious" (Winnicott 1974, 90). In this way, the analyst acts as a transitional object, a combination between illusion and a physical reality that disillusions the subject from her False Self and towards a more unified bodily ego. One member of "Fighting It" suggests the importance of having a space to open a dialogue about fracture. He states: "being able to talk about it with people who know exactly how you feel is usually a huge relief. You are not alone" ("Fighting It"). Winnicott's model and Tarantino's film, therefore, offer nuanced views regarding feelings of psychosomatic fracture in BIID and PLS, and why and how the mirror-box is healing.

In sum, the mirror-box acts as a transitional object that can have a similar effect of integrating the psyche and soma. As Marike Finlay (1997) states, "psychoanalysis, for Winnicott, by recreating [...] a transitional zone and mirroring can recuperate that sense-of-being-as-a-subject" (66), and mirror therapy recreates one's whole and fractured body to recuperate one's (physical and mental) sense of being. The mirror-box demonstrates a physical form of a theoretical concept. I now want to turn to an example of one individual Georges Perec who begins to cope with feelings of fissure through a different, though related, act of self-definition and self-reflection—writing. I will focus on how this is embodied and signified in his semi-autobiography *W or The Memory of Childhood* (1975).

Note

1 Although Winnicott does not focus on the role of the father in containing and holding the child, the father is a carer, and thus also responsible. For more on this see Michael Jacob's *DW Winnicott* (1995), Gillian Wilce's *Fathers, Families and the Outside World* (1997), and Judith Trowell and Alicia Etchegoyen's *The Importance of Fathers: A Psychoanalytic Re-evaluation* (2005).

References

Bollas, Christopher. *The Shadow of the Object: Psychoanalysis of the Unthought Known*. New York: Columbia UP, 1987.

Death Proof. Directed by Quentin Tarantino, performance by Kurt Russell, Zoe Bell, Rosario Dawson. Dimension Films, 2007. DVD.

Finlay, Marike. "Post-modernizing Psychoanalysis/Psychoanalysing Post-modernity: For Maria Kapuscinska." *After Post-Modernism Conference*. Montreal: McGill University, (1997), no pagination.

Jacobs, Michael. *D.W. Winnicott*. London: Sage Publications, 1995.

Kuhn, Annette. *Little Madnesses: Winnicott, Transitional Phenomena and Cultural Experience*. London: I.B. Tauris, 2013.

Lebeau, Vicky. "The Arts of Looking: D.W. Winnicott and Michael Haneke." *Screen*, vol. 50, no. 1, 2009, pp. 35–44.

McFarland, Thomas. *Romanticism and the Forms of Ruin: Wordsworth, Coleridge, and the Modalities of Fragmentation*. Princeton: Princeton UP, 1981.

Perec, George. *W or The Memory of Childhood* [*W ou le souvenir d'enfance*, 1975]. Translated by David Bellos. London: Collins Harvill, 1989.

Phillips Adam. *Winnicott*. London: Penguin, 2007.

Richards, Val, and Gillian Wilce. *Fathers, Families, and the Outside World*. Karnac Books for the Squiggle Foundation, 1997.

Strathman, Christopher A. *Romantic Poetry and the Fragmentary Imperative: Schlegel, Byron, Joyce, Blanchot*. Albany: State U of New York, 2006.

Shurr, William H. "Once More to the 'Woods': A New Point of Entry into Frost's Most Famous Poem." *The New England Quarterly*, vol. 47, no. 4, 1974, pp. 584–594.

Tarantino, Quentin. Interview. "Quentin Tarantino on Death Proof." *YouTube*. Web. 15 March 2011.

Trowell, Judith, and Alicia Etchegoyen. *The Importance of Fathers: A Psychoanalytic Re-Evaluation*. London: Routledge, 2002.

Winnicott, D.W. "Fear of Breakdown." *International Review of Psychoanalysis*, vol. 1, 1974, pp. 103–107.

9
ALMOST ARTIFICIAL LIMBS
Perec's *W or The Memory of Childhood*

Georges Perec's *W or The Memory of Childhood* opens with the words:

> In this book there are two texts which simply alternate; you might almost believe they had nothing in common, but they are in fact inextricably bound up with each other, as though neither could exist on its own, as though it was only their coming together, the distant light they cast on each other, that could make apparent what is never quite said in one, never quite said in the other, but only said in their fragile overlapping.
>
> *(1989, n.p.)*

Through gaps, memories, fragments, facts and fiction, this semi-autobiography embodies a reconstruction of the author's childhood. The book is composed of two parallel texts, each of which, he tells us in the above-quoted sentence, is bound to the next; each only exists through its other. The story of Perec, in other words, must only be told through something outside itself. If, moreover, a process of reflecting through another may help an individual, *W* exemplifies this process. Through language, fiction, and what I suggest is a psychoanalytic process, *W* traces Perec's desire to tell his story, and in so doing, to reconstitute his past, present and like the phantom limb sufferers who place their limbs in the mirror-box the way he feels. The following chapter will explore the author's journey and its affinity to apotemnophilia and PLS, beginning with a brief account of Perec's life.

Behind the text: Perec's life and work

Georges Perec was born in 1936 to Jewish immigrants Icek Judko and Cyrla Szulewicz Perec. David Bellos points out in his biography *A Life in Words* (1993) that the name is related to Peretz, which in Hebrew means to "break forth". His name is thus inseparable from his work, which concerns the ways in which identity, history, and language are structured through a break, through something unknown. Returning to Winnicott's theory, a traumatised subject is formed through fracture, suggesting an affinity between Perec's way of perceiving and representing the world and that of the traumatised subject. Those with PLS and BIID are also defined through a break; however, here it is not symbolic (the name "Perec") but physical. Correspondingly, Perec's rupture is not only symbolic but seeps into the physical: it not only stands for the author, it is a part of his body and work. I will be unpacking these connections through Perec's semi-autobiography, because here he explicitly attributes rupture to the traumatic loss of his mother and father in the Second World War[1] when he was a child, which he was too young to remember. *W*, I will argue, traces Perec's way of working through trauma, which cannot be separated from his experiences in psychoanalysis.

Perec began analysis at a very young age because he was plagued not only by physical illnesses throughout childhood, but by psychical ones, as indicated by a sketchbook his cousin found. Since the sketchbook was composed of drawings of fractured athletes, weapons, and vehicles (which would later provide the foundation for a fictional island called "W" featured in *W*), his cousin grew worried and sought out a psychotherapist (a fact that Perec had forgotten but learned later in life). In 1956, he took up psychoanalysis three times a week with Michel de M'Uzan, and in 1971, with J.-B. Pontalis,[2] ending his sessions in 1975. "How did Perec himself determine that his analysis was complete?" asks Bellos. "His judgment must have been connected with the composition, the publication, and the reception of *W*, but in ways that can perhaps never be entirely elucidated" (Bellos 1993, 562). Perhaps Bellos is referring to the fact that *W* indirectly charts and enacts his experience in psychoanalysis. As Bellos points out, psychoanalysis parallels (but is not to be conflated with) his writing: "[w]riting was not a substitute for psychotherapy, he declared wisely, nor was psychotherapy a prerequisite for good writing" (Bellos 1993, 193). It influenced not only his work, but also his life, engendering beneficial effects, such as offering him the "permission" to pursue his dream to write. His texts, therefore, cannot be separated from his psychoanalytic growth, both of which reflect a space of unanswered questions and infinite puzzles that acknowledge this uncertainty, while also aiming towards cohesion.

Paul Schwartz (1988) sums it up clearly: "The fictional universe of Georges Perec yearns for completeness. The not yet completed Perec puzzle strives to order its pieces, to eliminate the cutmarks, in order to recapture an Edenic, virginal wholeness" (113). This resonates with those with BIID and PLS, as they demonstrate a different physical and immediate yearning for completeness through fictional means, a desire to eliminate a feeling of fragmentation through an image of wholeness. Contrary to some individuals who have BIID or PLS, Perec writes his incompleteness, he shares the cut marks through his work by breaking up linearity. Through "[l]ost traces, fragmentation, the obsessive ordering of time and space" (Schwartz 1988, 112), he plays with language to disclose its underlying negation and meaninglessness. Thus, reading Perec can be a truly puzzling experience, where the reader is faced with, and partially partakes in, the author's own literary and personal discoveries. Indeed, this self-reflexive act of writing is not unique to the author: it is characteristic of the postmodern movement in which he is often included. His work resists categorisation, aside from his involvement in the Oulipo group, a gathering of writers and mathematicians interested in using constrained writing practices in a particular way.[3] In so doing, Perec magnifies the mundane and trivial occurrences of everyday life, things, and thought. Reflective of both conditions, his text conveys the fracture behind assumed wholes, which *W* suggests stems from his own feelings of fragmentation. However, while those with BIID and phantom limbs unintentionally have psychosomatic disturbances involving false unity and rupture, Perec begins to write himself out of pain. He states: "literature is not an activity separated from life. We live in a world of words, of language, of stories" (Perec 2008, 250): in writing trauma through forms of literary rupture, the author is part of language. This concept is central to *W*: the author's and characters' identities and bodies often collapse into their names and linguistic representations.[4] In elucidating these connections, he asks that both he and the reader question what language means and how we construct meaning. He writes: "[w]e don't have to disengage from the world or want it to elude us simply because, in given circumstances, in a history that is ours, we may happen to think we will never be able to grasp it" (Perec 2008, 261). In fact, this is what can make literature so important: it can speak to the inability to know. Moreover, can literature, Perec wonders, help transform one's understanding of self, the world, and history? *W* hinges upon this question because here the author writes his traumatic past through literary rifts; he can only alter his past and self by acknowledging that he can never grasp what happened to him. As a result, his physical and psychical wounds are drawn out of his body and into text, the most prominent wound being that of his mother's departure.

It is this loss that forms the foundation for *W*, which chronicles the author's journey towards self-discovery. The semi-autobiography represents and materialises his attempt to remember the immemorial trauma of his parents being taken away during the Holocaust. Since he was too young to understand the loss that continues to haunt him, the author attempts to capture traces of the past, which he continually modifies, raising the question as to how this process may alter his identity and feelings. In using a fragmented language, he also invites readers to break their preconceived representations of self and other. *W* takes readers on a journey of self-definition through self-erasure, as Perec attempts to write his past by exposing its impossibility. The novel is divided into two parts, separated and connected by a parenthesised ellipsis. Each half follows two stories that alternate chapter by chapter. The first is a fictional story of Gaspard Winckler, a young boy who is lost at sea. This is written alongside an account of fictional and factual traces of Perec's past and that of his parents, told through stories, photographs, and memories. *W*'s second half describes a fictitious dystopian island named "W", which is governed by an Olympian, competitive, and tortuous system. This narrative runs parallel to a continuation of the author's imagined past.

I now turn to a slightly more detailed description of the narrative, starting with the story of Gaspard Winckler (semi-fictional version of Perec).[5] In Part I, an unknown doctor contacts the narrator, Gaspard Winckler. The doctor tells Winckler that the body of a sick boy with his name was lost in a shipwreck. The narrator is called upon to help find the boy because when he deserted the army he was given the boy's identity. Based on one of his childhood drawings, the fictional island "W" features sport as its singular goal, an ideology implemented by government officials. Athletes must win battles to work their way up a social hierarchy and ultimately survive. This social structure is founded upon a vision of common unity, enforced by figures of authority: "the Laws of W [...] wanted to give the impression that Athletes and Officials belonged to the same Race, to the same world, as if they were all one family united by a single goal" (Perec 1989, 153). We will soon revisit this notion of false familial unity, and although it will be discussed in relation to Perec's own memories, its presence on the island highlights the inseparability between social and personal perception, action, and reaction.

The BIID and phantom limb phenomena also depict how illusory notions of unity structure the self in relation to the environment in a real-world (as opposed to literary) scenario. However, this real-world scenario is also brought out through the metaphorical island, which suggests that the type of ideology outlined here (based on "unity") is dangerous. The system on "W" is run by binaries (with divisions between superiors and inferiors), and this system is doubly fortified through the island's physical geography (its villages are divided between winners, losers and outcasts), thus emphasising the relationship between physical and social position. Like the phantom limb and BIID individuals, whose bodies mismatch a communal concept of unity, on "W", physical and bodily structures are informed by the social world. Though the winners predominantly govern these rules, the educational system also plays a role in shaping individual mind-sets through (often physical) punishment (which we see echoed in Perec's own memories of school). What is central is that psychical moulding is inseparable from the physical or, as he writes, "life, here, [on "W"] is lived for the greater glory of the Body" (Perec 1989, 67). This initially utopian world, we soon discover, is actually a dystopian one that allegorises the Second World War concentration camps. Since in a very different way, BIID and PLS also elucidate how societal bodily ideals can hide underlying destruction (although I stress that I am not comparing apotemnophilia and PLS to the concentration camps or the author's traumatic war experience, but merely elucidating a link through his novel), I will explore ways in which communal symbols/ideas/wholes bear physical affects, and how this is connected to the theme of trauma in W.

Falling through trauma

W traces how Perec's childhood in a war-torn world without parents left him feeling physically and psychically wounded and lost. I now want to examine how the way he talks about trauma (and emphasises his bodily reaction to loss) parallels the trauma described by Winnicott and the BIID and phantom limb individuals.

"Properly speaking", writes Kristy Guneratne (2006), "the origin of trauma is in the body" (36). Freud explores this idea in *Beyond the Pleasure Principle* (2009 [1920]), which examines why individuals repeat unpleasant experiences, and why they unconsciously desire something (the nightmares of war neurotics, for example, or people in psychoanalysis who repeat painful mistakes). Here he describes a child he saw playing what he calls the "fort-da" game, where the child causes a reel on a string to disappear and reappear, each time it disappears saying "o-o-o-oh", which Freud reads as "fort" (gone) and joyfully shouting "da!" (there) when it reappears. According to Freud, this simulates the child's desire to control its mother's departure and return. The unpleasant experience of the reel's/mother's disappearance, in other words, is repeated for the joy over its reappearance, and furthermore for "bringing about his [the child's] own disappearance" (Freud 2009, 3).

It is this kind of early experience that Freud suggests is carried into the transference. Like the child, the patient "is obliged to *repeat* the repressed [painful] material as a contemporary experience" (Freud 2009, 3), a "compulsion to repeat". *W* (which repeats the story of Perec's mother's departure) can be connected to the reel/transference, where a new scenario supplants a loss. Freud focuses on the physical nature of this painful and paradoxically satisfying recurrence. Finally, the hide-and-seek aspect of the "fort-da" is portrayed in the text's ability to hide the author's past (as it opens with the statement: "I have no childhood memories" [Perec, *W*, 6]), while also seeking his memories throughout. These notions will later be unpacked in relation to what the BIID and PLS sufferers' drives reveal about the author's experiences. What I am interested in is the question: how does *W* illuminate their bodily erasure? To begin exploring this question, I will draw some links between Perec's traumas and those of the individuals with PLS.

Three times in the novel, the narrator mentions a parachute in conjunction with the moment he last saw his mother. In the first he explains, my "mother buys me a comic entitled *Charlie and the Parachute*: on the illustrated cover, the parachute's rigging lines are nothing other than Charlie's trouser braces" (Perec 1989, 26). The second:

> [s]he bought me a magazine, an issue of *Charlie*, with a cover showing Charlie Chaplin, with his walking stick, his hat, his shoes and his little moustache, doing a parachute jump. The parachute is attached to Charlie by his trouser braces.
>
> *(Perec 1989, 54)*

Lastly, the memory is altered from an image of Charlie to one of Perec himself jumping:

> in 1958, when, by chance, the military service briefly made a parachutist of me, I suddenly saw, in the very instant of jumping, one way of deciphering the text of this memory: I was plunged into nothingness; all the threads were broken; I fell, on my own, without any support.
>
> *(Perec 1989, 55)*

The passages above portray a connection between the metaphorical and physical, the fictional memory and the real impact it had upon the author (Georges Perec was a military parachutist). As Eleanor Kaufman (1998) puts it, "a physical sensation reflects his inner experience of plummeting without support through the war years" (2), and also reflects the impact of his mother's disappearance. Falling is again brought forth in the narrator's description of an accident. He explains that as a child he once injured another boy's face by dropping a ski, the boy reacted by scarring the narrator with his ski pole. This, the author states, became an identifying characteristic: it physically marked his individuality. A defining somatic wound is also depicted through the disabled child Gaspard Winckler, who represents Perec's childhood. Finally, he repeats a memory of breaking his arm.

In the first version of leaving his mother, the narrator remembers having his arm in a sling. However, it is later revealed by his family that this memory may be false. The next memory reads:

> The Red Cross evacuates the wounded. I was not wounded. But I had to be evacuated. So we had to pretend I was wounded. That was why my arm was in a sling. But my aunt is quite definite: I did not have my arm in a sling [...]. On the other hand, perhaps I had a rupture and was wearing a truss, a suspensory bandage.
>
> (Perec 1989, 54–55)

The final passage explains that when the narrator was knocked over by a sledge, he broke his scapula. Although his family has no memory of this accident, the author asked an old friend, who responded that in fact it was not Perec, but the friend himself that had "an accident identical in every way" (Perec 1989, 80). If we return to the two conditions, we find a self-conception that closely resembles the author's. The narrator, those with PLS, and those with BIID have integrated a simultaneously broken and whole appendage, indicating a split between mind and body, a feeling of physical fragmentation that cannot be comprehended. To mend this fracture, those with BIID, PLS, and the author employ a completely subjective image that embodies a wound, a partially fictive version of self that both replaces and reproduces rupture. Thus, the Perec depicted in *W*, those with BIID, and those with PLS feel subjective pain that mismatches objective reality.

The author's wounded arm stems most prominently from the loss of his mother. Guneratne (2006) writes, "In his commentary, Perec suggests that this intervention represents the breaking of something else, presumably his contact with his mother" (34). This calls up the Winnicottian paradigm of trauma that connects maternal and physical loss. In "Fear of Breakdown" (Winnicott 1974) the child facing a traumatic absence has also "internalised" an unknowable feeling of rupture. If for Winnicott, this rupture relates to the parents' holding pattern, what can the notion of self-holding reveal about the broken feelings expressed by Perec and brought out by PLS and BIID? Central to these links is the idea of a fictional version of self-as-whole that was developed non-linguistically in relation to trauma, which is why I want to begin with a "memory" in *W*, where Perec was a (pre-linguistic) baby. It is based on "more or less on statistical details" but is also, he writes, "probably ascribable to the quite extraordinary imaginary relationship which I regularly maintained with my maternal branch" (Perec 1989, 30). The memory is written as follows:

> I was born in the month of March 1936. Perhaps there were three years of relative happiness, no doubt darkened by baby's illnesses (whooping cough, measles, chickenpox) [...] a future that boded ill. War came. My father enlisted and died. My mother became a war widow. She went into mourning. I was put out to a nanny [...].[25] I seem to remember she injured herself one day and her hand was pierced through.
>
> *(Perec 1989, 32)*

This is followed by the first description of the last encounter with the narrator's mother, who was on the train holding a Charlie Chaplin magazine. Here Perec draws a clear connection between familial loss and a physical disability (both his sickness and his mother's wounded hand), indicating that his own injuries are inseparable from hers. This can be linked to the split that in Winnicottian thought results from a lack of maternal holding, that physical and psychical rupture stemming from the mother's inability to hold the child in her mind and arms. Both this theory of trauma and Perec's memory convey a struggle with creating a cohesive identity in the world, which those with BIID and PLP enact. By writing these reactions however, the author decelerates the process, allowing the reader to learn more about the way in which it unfolds.

From a Winnicottian perspective, the narrator has experienced an environmental breakdown (mourning and the loss of both parents) that has left him with an ungraspable feeling of illness, a kind of "primitive agony" that we have also related to BIID and the phantom limb. In the above passage, the narrator's mother's hands were pierced (she was unable to hold him), and his future thus "bodes ill" (consequently perhaps, he could not learn how to sufficiently hold himself). This connection between maternal and personal injury is further emphasised in the footnote within the above passage (numbered 25 after "baby's illnesses"). To clarify, throughout the book, the author uses footnotes to add alternative stories and details to memories, layering new thoughts that modify the past, perhaps indicative of repressed experiences creeping closer towards consciousness. It is implied that Perec, like a patient in analysis, is beginning to acknowledge his repressed memories in partially fictional form. To return to the footnote (25), from the above-quoted passage, he writes:

> I still have, on most of the fingers of both my hands, on the second knuckle joints, the marks of an accident I must have had when I was a few months old: apparently an earthenware hot-water bottle, which my mother made up, leaked or broke, completely scalding both my hands.
>
> *(Perec 1989, 40)*

If the first passage did not elucidate that the narrator was injured from an environmental deficiency, this one does. An increase in clarity here also indicates that when Perec added the footnote, he was more conscious of his injury having been caused by the loss of his mother. Paradoxically though, its fragmented prose and ambiguity suggests that when the footnote was written, the author more thoroughly understood the impossibility of completely remembering what marked his body. What his text is bringing out, therefore, is its own role in representing and constructing what cannot be accurately remembered. In this imagined memory, the author perhaps did not know how to "make himself up" because his mother did not know how to "make up a water bottle", leaving him wounded and without sustenance.

Since the falsified memory in the book enacts his journey to "make himself up", the novel stands in, in a way, for the broken water bottle. It enables the author to go back and reconstitute himself because he was never given the chance to do so as a child. However, the process is not easy. Returning to Winnicott, the child who does not know how to hold herself through a transitional object is left to reproduce a falsely cohesive version of self. The passage above suggests an embodiment of this fictive unity because the water bottle "completely" scalded his hands: for him, the rupture had to be "complete". In this context, the word "complete" suggests a traumatic splitting, in which the experience of fracture is buried in the unconscious, which the conscious mind appears to know nothing about: this is reflective of the traumatic splits of BIID and phantom limb individuals. Thus, the Perec writing the text may be gesturing towards a traumatic split embodied by the Perec in the novel. Moreover, the split described here is not only psychical but also physical, which is indicated in another story of his bodily fracture.

The author writes that he was knocked over by a sledge when ice-skating:

> I fell backwards and broke my scapula; it is a bone that cannot be set in plaster; to allow it to mend, my right arm has been strapped tight behind my back in a whole contraption of bandages that makes any movement impossible, and the right sleeve of my jacket flaps emptily as if I had really lost an arm.
>
> (Perec 1989, 79)

Again, a feeling of rupture that remains stuck in an image of unity alludes to the author's difficulty with self-holding with holding up his trauma, his past, and his body. This passage also conveys how Perec's struggle with false wholes extends to his use and conception of language. Although it is similar to the water-bottle scene in which the narrator cannot hold himself, I suggest that the broken arm memory involves a step towards independence. Here, the appendage is strapped and bandaged: although the boy is injured, his arm is held up by something. The jacket flaps emptily "as if" he had really lost an arm, revealing a growing awareness that Perec's hands are not completely scalded and that his fingers are not missing, but that his arm does exist, and can begin to heal.

Indeed, this image of a flapping empty sleeve bears a resemblance to both limb syndromes, it being a limb that is not there. And furthermore, the memory itself is a kind of phantom: although he felt the pain of a rupture, it did not objectively exist. Is the author then, in a way, writing his phantom/BIID limb, his fracture? Recall that earlier, we explored an email written by someone with BIID, who claimed that he was going to cause "an accident" by cutting off his own limb. When read next to the passage above, is the author not also causing himself an accident, albeit through the past instead of the future, and through his book? Instead of cutting a limb, is he writing its removal? It seems as though, resembling (yet fundamentally different from) those with phantom limbs or BIID, Perec feels broken and wants to see this absence, which he approaches through writing. In so doing, he suspends those frustrations with feeling fissured that BIID and PLS demonstrate in a physical form. *W* is not only metaphorical, then, but penetrates the physical, which is conveyed in one passage that draws out the bodily feelings experienced in the author's trauma, which, I suggest, reflects Winnicott's description of primitive agony.

To begin unpacking this thought, I will develop how the author's memories can be related to Winnicott's (1974) concept of primitive agony, focusing on what he calls a feeling of "falling for ever" (104). For Winnicott, this feeling of reaching out for something that is not there, of feeling un-integrated and as though one is psychically and physically falling, is linked to the loss of his mother. When we read *W* alongside this theory, Perec's parachute fall reflects a return to the primitive state of absolute dependence or, as Kritzman writes of *W*, "the falling into nothingness without support suggests the inability of the child to separate from the mother" (Kritzman 2005, 196). While those with PLS and apotemnophilia suffer from a feeling that echoes Winnicott's description of primitive agony, Perec describes a similar feeling through a metaphor that centralises the body. For him, it involves a paradoxical feeling of weight and weightlessness. Winnicott (1965) writes that without "good-enough active and adaptive handling the task from within may well prove heavy, indeed it may actually prove impossible for this development of a psycho-somatic inter-relationship to become properly established" (61). In other words, the weightlessness of falling and not being held is heavy. Carrying one's broken body is a traumatic experience that Perec's image of parachuting also depicts, because parachuting entails a loss of psychosomatic control (the individual is directed by gravity), closeness to death, and a feeling of heaviness. As Schnitzer (2004) writes, "[n]ormally considered a life saving device, which we often conceive of as floating gently in the air, here the parachute appears as a heavy burden to carry" (111). BIID and PLS demonstrate a physical outcome of a traumatic rupture that is analogous to this parachute falling. Those with BIID are weighed down physically by an extra limb, though they feel that it should be absent. Those with PLS are physically free of the extra limb and yet psychically weighed down by its invisible presence. These phenomena, therefore, exemplify how individuals may (in a different way) unconsciously carry paradoxical notions of self in reaction to fragmented feelings. Thus, sufferers from apotemnophilia and PLS show us an immediate and bodily demonstration of the ideas covered in Perec and Winnicott's more theoretical works. Up to this point, we have discussed the links between the narrator's experience of trauma, "Fear of Breakdown", BIID, and the phantom limb. I now want to expand upon these connections through an image in *W* that opens up a different reading of how the author copes with the desire for cohesion, specifically through family and language.

Enwombed in familial fiction

Perec writes:

> I am three. I am sitting in the middle of the room with Yiddish newspapers scattered around me. The family circle surrounds me wholly, but the sensation of encirclement does not cause me any fear or feeling of being smothered; on the contrary, it is warm, protective, loving: all the family—the entirety, the totality of the family—is there, gathered like an impregnable battlement around the child who has just been born (but didn't I say a moment ago that I was three?).
>
> *(Perec 1989, 13)*[6]

This passage takes place among several other fragmented memories, which he admits to having altered through imaginary details. Why, I want to ask, is this "memory" fictionalised in this way? Does this ideal familial unity gesture towards the author's need to grasp on to something whole as a starting point for his imagined past and its reconstitution? Adam Phillips (2007) writes that, "the beginning of a feeling of existing and feeling real [...] depends upon a basic relation to the experience of omnipotence" (133). The image above shows precisely this: the narrator is born into existence by creating a complete memory in rewriting his experience of childhood. Perhaps this works to reform an illusion of omnipotence that had never been fully developed. Lam-Hesseling (2002) writes of this scene: "[t]his intact family functions as a sign of reassuring wholeness, providing a subject with an idea from which it can derive feelings of cohesion and safety" (94). In light of Winnicott's model, this image of Perec as protected and safe is necessary to establishing his development. This stage takes place when the baby was one with the mother, in which "the infant takes from a breast that is part of the infant, and the mother gives milk to an infant that is part of herself" (Winnicott 1991, 8–9). This ideal moment, however, is underpinned with fear (of returning to that state), which this passage also conveys.

"The family was gathered", Perec writes, "like an impregnable battlement". Although this conjures an image of cohesion, a sense of being safe from intrusion, the word "battlement" evokes a sense of danger. Discomfort thus seeps through the pages of this comfortable illusion, happy omnipotence is always frustrated by its impossibility. This kind of contradiction does not stand alone. Moreover, in the beginning of the passage, the author writes that the sensation of wholeness does not frighten him; however, if fear were not a factor in the equation it would not have to be stated. Unity, then, obscures something frightening, and it is almost as though by discreetly signalling these dangers the writer was warning the baby (allegorising his forgotten past) of the upcoming trauma. Here Perec juggles a split between his current identity and his lost childhood through a contradictory and falsified text. He continues, "(but didn't I say a moment ago that I was three?)". His history is being altered as it is written: his memory changes with his words.

The author's desire to create a false image of wholeness in order to orient his identity and rewrite his fragmentation is not so dissimilar to the phantom limb and BIID recreations of self-as-whole. Just as Perec writes his unity through paradoxical sentences, individuals with the limb syndromes are whole through fragmentation. However, instead of drawing this out through literary fiction, it is already, in a sense, drawn in to the those with PLS and BIID. Although the author and those with apotemnophilia and phantom limbs present many similarities, many with BIID and PLS lack control over their pain. Perec, however, is able to use language to mediate his (different, yet, parallel) feelings of psychosomatic dissonance. The importance of language in this process is emphasised in the above passage because newspapers encircle the narrator: his identity is wrapped in language (reflective of the dance in *The Red Shoes*). This plays a double role: it both distances the narrator from the familial illusion and draws the reader's attention to the page they are reading. The book, like the newspaper, separates (but also connects) the reader and author, raising the question of how language plays a part in individuality and dependence, subjectivity and objectivity, rupture and cohesion. The metaphorical island of "W" is also founded upon a struggle with forming dangerously unified social bodies in reaction to fragmentation. This system of thought, Perec indicates, has also shaped him. His struggle with wholes and fragments thus relates to an embodiment of environmental ideology. The metaphorical island and the two conditions in discussion demonstrate that if this is not explored, it might have detrimental effects. In order to elaborate this idea, it is important to examine how psychoanalysis plays a role in the author's linguistic bodily border, in his separation from "absolute dependence", and at how this is represented in *W*.

Notes

1 Although *W* hinges upon the experiences and effects of the Second World War, I will not be focusing on the Holocaust in this chapter because it is not central to the link I am making between psychoanalysis, the phantom limb, and BIID. However, it is essential to *W*, because this is what generated the personal and familial traumas in discussion. While many other writers have concentrated on the crucial relationship between Perec and the Holocaust (such as Joanna Spiro, Eleanor Kaufman, Lawrence D. Kritzman, Susan Rubin Suleiman and Andrew Leak), I am choosing to explore the psychoanalytic and somatic experiences Perec faced in a post-war context.

2 Michel de M'Uzan focused on psychosomatics and for him,

> the role of the mother as the facilitator of the capacity to represent shows indebtedness to the influence of Winnicott and Bion, the respective development of notions of holding or reverie and containment [...] influencing the work of André Green and Pontalis.

(Birksted-Breen 2010, 34)

3 These methods are most evident in two of Perec's most prominent novels: *La Disparition* [A Void] (1969), and *La Vie mode d'emploi* [Life A User's Manual] (1978). In the former he omits the letter "e", accomplishing many things aside from the sheer linguistic acrobatics: the creation of a new catalogue (of words without the letter "e"), a metaphor for the Jewish experience during the Second World War (in many readings), a representation of absence that productively engenders the novel's language and narrative, and finally, since Georges Perec's name is full of "e's", the letter's deletion points towards the author's own erasure. *Life A User's Manual* traces the lives and ideas of individuals in an apartment block in Paris, the writing composed of lists, word play, and many other constraints.

4 To clarify, I am not suggesting a conflation between persons and literature in Perec's writing of trauma: Perec is not interchangeable with the text. The danger in this collapse (especially in light of Holocaust writing), is best illuminated by Amy Hungerford, who raises questions regarding the ethics of theorists who imagine "texts as traumatic experience itself, thus transmissible from person to person through reading" (Hungerford 2003, 20). I am not arguing that the text itself is traumatic for Perec or for readers. I am looking at how Perec uses the text to reconstitute himself.

5 The name Gaspard Winckler was inspired by Paul Verlaine's "Gaspard Hauser chante", a poem based on Kaspar Hauser (a German youth who grew up in the isolation of a darkened cell). In 1973, before completing *W*, Perec had engaged in a project to transform this poem, "as if, by rewriting it, Perec could at last shed the lyric of the unloved orphan" (Bellos 1993, 524). I also will be referring to the narrator both as Gaspard and Perec, because there is a necessarily blurred boundary between the identity of the Perec in the book (also called Gaspard) and the Perec writing the book.

6 Yiddish is written in Hebrew letters, which is soon relevant.

References

Bellos, David. *Georges Perec: A Life in Words*. London: Harvill, 1993.

Birksted-Breen, Dana, and Sara Flanders. "General Introduction." *Reading French Psychoanalysis*. Edited by Dana Birksted-Breen, Sara Flanders, and Alain Gibeault, London: Routledge, 2010, pp. 1–51.

Freud, Sigmund. *Beyond the Pleasure Principle* [*Jenseits des Lust-Prinzips*, 1920]. Translated by James Strachey, General Books, 2009.

Guneratne, Kristy. "Left Behind: Memory, Laterality and Clinamen in Perec's *W ou le souvenir d'enfance*." *Romance Studies*, vol. 24, no. 1, 2006, pp. 29–39.

Hungerford, Amy. *The Holocaust of Texts: Genocide, Literature, and Personification*. Chicago: University of Chicago, 2003.

Kaufman, Eleanor. "Falling From the Sky: Trauma in Perec's W and Caruth's Unclaimed Experience." *Diacritics*, vol. 28, no. 4, 1998, pp. 44–53.

Kritzman, L.D. "Remembrance of Things Past: Trauma and Mourning in Perec's *W ou le souvenir d'enfance*." *Journal of European Studies*, vol. 35, no. 2, 2005, pp. 187–200.

Lam-Hesseling, J. *Whose Pain? Childhood, Trauma, Imagination*. Thesis. University of Amsterdam, 2002.

Perec, Georges. "Robert Antelme or the Truth of Literature." ["Robert Antelme ou la vérité de la literature", 1963]. *Species of Spaces and Other Pieces* [*Espèces d'espaces*]. Translated by John Sturrock, London: Penguin, 2008, pp. 253–269.

Perec, Georges. *W or The Memory of Childhood* [*W ou le souvenir d'enfance*, 1975]. Translated by David Bellos. London: Collins Harvill, 1989.

Phillips, Adam. *Winnicott*. London: Penguin, 2007.

Schnitzer, Daphné. "A Drop in Numbers: Deciphering Georges Perec's Postanalytic Narratives." *Yale French Studies*, vol. 105, 2004, pp. 110–126.

Schwartz, Paul. *Georges Perec, Traces of His Passage*. Birmingham: Summa Publications, 1988.
Winnicott, D.W. "Ego Integration in Child Development." *The Maturational Processes and the Facilitating Environment: Studies in the Theory of Emotional Development*. New York: International Universities, 1965, pp. 56–63.
Winnicott, D.W. "Fear of Breakdown." *International Review of Psychoanalysis*, vol. 1, 1974, pp. 103–107.
Winnicott, D.W. *Playing and Reality*. London: Routledge, 1991.

10

A PSYCHOANALYTIC VOYAGE

Perec and symbolic reconstitution

"I have no childhood memories", begins *W or The Memory of Childhood* (Perec 1989), a statement that paradoxically contrasts with its title (as, how can a text about childhood memories begin with none?). Already we are privy to the structural conflict of the text: through fiction, the author is searching for what has been deleted. I want to look at how this journey is represented through one storyline (of Gaspard Winckler and Otto Apfelstahl), while also examining how the author's experience in psychoanalysis is interlinked with his literary and personal endeavour. As Bellos (1993) put it, like "psychoanalysis, autobiography involves the transformation of memory into narrative" (154), flagging up the inextricable link between *W* and psychoanalysis. Autobiography and psychoanalysis work together in the endeavour to define Perec's forgotten and traumatic past or, as Motte (2004) writes, he "materialises and inscribes upon the page the kinds of gestures that real anamnesis requires, that is, looking back, recalling and reconsidering" (61). Perec's trauma, reflective of BIID and PLS, involves an embodied response to brokenness. If the broken bodies Perec drew as a child illustrate this, the allegories within *W* suggest a more cohesive attempt to reconnect those figures. I will investigate how psychoanalysis is involved in this attempt by linking Perec's writings about psychoanalysis to Winnicott's theory of development.

For this I will be drawing upon "Backtracking" (2009 [1985]) and "The Scene of a Stratagem" (2008b [1977]), which describe the author's own experiences in session: the rituals, repetition, play, silences, physicality, relationship with the other, dreaming and fantasy, and the temporality involved in the "talking cure". In both texts, Perec discusses the correlation between speaking in psychoanalysis and writing in relation to his own self-definition. In his words: "I was going [to psychoanalysis] to seek to recognise myself and to give myself a name" (Perec 2008b, 164). In *W* we see this attempt to name what he cannot remember: his felt loss. And the phantom limb and BIID sufferers also struggle with self-recognition. Can Perec's journey, then, reveal something about the conditions: how their own struggle with bodily fragmentation and wholeness is connected to the need to recognise themselves? To open a linguistic reading of the kind of pain and repair involved in apotemnophilia and PLS, I will look at psychoanalysis within *W*. To begin this exploration, I will trace a story in Part I about the narrator and a lost boy, suggesting that through the processes of psychoanalysis and writing, the author is breaking down a false identity that has caused him physical and psychical pain. Since the story also illuminates the similarities between Perec's pain and that of individuals with BIID and PLS, I am interested in exploring how the literary journey he offers can be connected to the mirror-box treatment: in how semiotic reconstruction may affect the individual.

The story begins as the narrator Gaspard Winckler receives a letter with blank pages and "abstract symbols" such as a "hand that was simultaneously a root" (Perec 1989, 8). The letter, from a mysterious doctor named Otto Apfelstahl, requests that Gaspard meet him to discuss an unknown matter, which Winckler believes will change his life. Left feeling anxious, impatient and curious, Winckler searches for clues, but "found nothing" (Perec 1989, 11). This description mirrors the explanation of the psychoanalytic experience in the essay "Backtracking". Here he writes that in deciphering his own words in analysis:

> I skipped along the paths of the maze I had made for myself, following suspiciously legible signposts. It all had meaning, it was all connected, obvious and could be unravelled at will: signs waltzed by, proffering their charming anxieties. But beneath the ephemeral flashes of verbal collisions and the controlled titillation of the beginner's book of Oedipus, my voice encountered only its own emptiness.
>
> *(Perec 2009, 49)*

Perec indicates that his search for meaning and understanding began to unravel in psychoanalysis: the signs he was accustomed to deciphering only revealed their rupture. The empty signification described in this context is echoed in his writing: "I assume from the start that the equivalence of speaking and writing is obvious, just as I assimilate the blank sheet of paper to that other place of hesitations, illusions, and crossings-out, the ceiling of the analyst's consulting room" (Perec 2009, 45). Winckler's blank letter can thus be perceived as an allegory for the analyst's ceiling/the pre-written story. As perceptible in his encounter with the abstract letter, Winckler's search for meaning through signs only discloses its nothingness. The passage above similarly indicates that searches for specific psychoanalytical plots (such as the Oedipus complex) are blank, and yet, as it shows the author's "emptiness", it is paradoxically significant. Winckler's letter also reveals ambiguous signs that point towards something important. Therefore, the meaninglessness of signs does not negate their importance here; their nothingness may expose alternative forms of thought, which must be signified in some way. For instance, "a hand that was a root" may open up a reading of the corporeal nature of the author's self-exploration. The image suggests a search for bodily grounding, stability, and family roots. Revealed in these binaries between meaning and its impossibility is a split, which creates a double that is portrayed in the Winckler story and that can also be related to Winnicott's theory of trauma.

According to Winnicott (1965a), when the infant's environment has been insufficient, it

> develops a split. By one half of the split the infant relates to the presenting object, and for this purpose there develops what I have called a false or compliant self. By the other half of the split the infant relates to a subjective object, or to mere phenomena based on body experiences.
>
> *(183)*

Winckler's letter (an object) also indicates a split. The letter presented is given false meaning, while also conveying a nonverbal and a bodily affect (anxiety). This link illuminates the divide between the physical feelings and objective realities that is central to both limb conditions. Echoing traumatised Winnicottian individuals and Perec, those with PLS and apotemnophilia develop a way of coming to terms with what is not there. Put another way, the traumatised subject and many of those with alienated limbs reveal a split between the False Self that conforms to an idea of unity and the acknowledgment of a lack of unity. I now return to the Gaspard/Otto narrative to examine how the author begins to break down that False Self through a process that reflects psychoanalysis.

The story proceeds as Gaspard arrives at a hotel (to meet a doctor), where he encounters two bellboys with crossed arms, followed by a porter carrying two hefty suitcases and a woman holding a small dog. These images reflect those brought out in Winnicott's theory: arms holding not him but themselves, a heavy weight, and a helpless animal (reflective of an infant), enwrapped in a female's arms. The next image features a barman with wrinkled hands who is dragging his feet. Again, these are images of bodily weakness—an ambiguous illustration of feelings of being insufficiently held. Winnicott (1965b) states that the True Self may begin to have life "through the strength given to the infant's weak ego by the mother's implementation of the infant's omnipotent expressions" (145). If the barman stands for a part of the narrator's holding environment, he is too weak to strengthen Gaspard's brittle ego. The barman then offers Winckler a pretzel, which he refuses. Not only does this point towards a rejection of environmental imposition and protection of "inner" emptiness (as outlined in "Fear of Breakdown" (Winnicott 1974)) but also to a lack of personal definition. This is because, according to Bellos (1993), Perec's name (in Hungarian) is associated with the word "pretzel" (a pun the author toys with in several of his works). In a sense, therefore, he refuses his own name (his True Self).

The state of anxiety developed in this scene, I suggest, echoes the anxiety which brought the author to psychoanalysis. The connection is further solidified as he writes, Otto "was [not] late; neither could you say that he was on time"

(Perec 1989, 16), reflective of the psychoanalytic experience described in "Backtracking": "[t]here was something abstract in this arbitrary time, something which was both reassuring and fearful, an immovable and timeless time" (Perec 2009, 46). Though the two descriptions suggest a similar state, in "Backtracking" we directly learn about Perec's experience, while in the allegorical tale we are a part of it. *W* involves the reader in a timeless place where images do not make perfect sense, where his past is told, but, paradoxically, untold (imagined), where we are made aware that we are reading in the present something which was written in the past. Perec's writing points towards the fictional nature of language and memory. In this way, the reader approaches the author's search for his hidden "other:" the book itself is brought towards the material world.

The journey proceeds as Gaspard finally meets Otto Apfelstahl; immediately, he stops Gaspard from standing up "with a wave of his hand" (Perec 1989, 17). Thus, in just a short space, two hands are juxtaposed: in the frail barman and the more aggressive doctor, a physical change seems to be taking place. If this memory alludes to the author's hands having been formed through his mother's injury, perhaps the fragmented Otto story sets up a new pair of hands through which he may begin to restructure. Put differently, the layering of the book, its characters, and the analytic experience may all present stronger limbs to replace his mother's absence and help the author grow stable enough to begin digging towards his roots his "truer", silent self. Following nicely along with these thoughts, Apfelstahl asks Gaspard, "'[d]id you ever wonder what became of the person who gave you your name?' 'I beg your pardon' I said, 'not grasping'" (Perec 1989, 18). At this point, Perec cannot psychically or physically grasp his own identity. Like those with PLS who cannot control their phantom, and those with BIID who feel helplessly fractured, he has a problem with psychosomatic self-definition. In response, he questions the "ambiguity" of Otto's remark, to which Otto answers:

> I am not alluding to your father, nor to any member of your family or your community after whom you might have been named, as is, I believe, still a fairly widespread custom. Nor am I thinking of any of the people who, five years ago, helped you to acquire your current identity. I mean, quite straightforwardly, the person whose name you have.
>
> *(Perec 1989, 22)*

The first part of this statement may allude to a certain kind of self-discovery that aims to define specific familial narratives. What Otto offers is more nebulous: he wants to discuss the identity that Winckler has at that very moment, what hides behind his False Self. If for Winnicott, a trauma "cannot get into the past tense unless the ego can first gather it into its own present time [...] (assuming the auxiliary ego-supporting function of the mother)" (1974, 104), the exchange between Otto and Winckler exemplifies this time collapse. Instead of retreating to the past, Perec explores it within his current identity: with the analyst figure, in the book, and in the story itself. Thus, the author's experience of psychoanalysis, its representation, and the book itself all support his pursuit of a True Self, which is allegorised through Otto's suggestion to find Winckler's true identity.

Apfelstahl explains that after the war the narrator was given a false identity, the name of Gaspard Winckler, which had belonged to a sick boy (isolated, deaf, helpless, and dumb). Although the boy was taken to doctors, explains Otto, they discovered no injury, ascribing the illness "to some infantile trauma whose precise configuration unfortunately remained obscure despite examinations by numerous psychiatrists" (Perec 1989, 23). Given the context of this story, we may assume that this little boy stands for the childhood Perec has invisibly integrated and lost. The sick boy metaphor sheds light on those with BIID and PLS who also feel a non-diagnosable pain relating to a loss; a physical, inexplicable disability often leaves them to search for an explanation. In Perec's story, this allegory also points towards his own environmental lack. Otto tells the narrator that "the support organisation" that was to provide the narrator with an identity was killed before having set anything up and so, "[t]he organisation was at a loss" (Perec 1989, 23). The group of people who took care of the child were at a loss, because the Genevan official who was to deal with the boy's paperwork and passport died. Due to a loss of support, the narrator's own organisation was broken: the author developed a split upon being abandoned. Could this reflect the ego of the traumatised child who in Winnicott's eyes "organises defences against breakdown of the ego organisation" (1974, 103)? If the environmental organisation was at a loss, could Gaspard's (Perec's) ego have devised a defence against this breakdown such as a fake identity? Otto continues to explain that the child was taken on a yacht voyage with a group of others in the hope of improving his health. He explains that the crew searched

> ever more vainly for the place, the creek, the vista, the beach, the pier where the miracle could happen; [...] that there is, somewhere on the ocean, an isle or atoll, a rock or headland where suddenly it could all happen—the veil sundered, the light turned on.
>
> *(Perec 1989, 24)*

While the above-quoted sentence encompasses many strands of thought, first and foremost it is reminiscent of Perec's experience in psychoanalysis. He writes in "Backtracking" (Perec 2009): "you think that talking means finding, discovering, understanding, understanding at last, being illuminated by truth. But it doesn't" (44). Just as the author's search for clarity is shattered, so too is the crew's: "each of them clings to this illusion, until one day, off Tierra del Fuego, they are hit by one of those sudden cyclones which are everyday occurrences in those parts, and the boat sinks" (Perec 1989, 25). The crew's trauma is immediate and too fast to comprehend, whereas in psychoanalysis, in looking for "the image I was after [...] something like a crash in my memory set in" (Perec 2009, 50). While his description of analysis involves reflection, those on the ship blindly cling to a belief, indicating that his child-self could not face a traumatic situation. However, the psychoanalytic crash is beneficial: it is a crashing of protective identity, and moreover, one composed of words. He explains that in psychoanalysis,

> [w]hat had to give way first was my armour the hard shell of writing, beneath which my desire to write was hidden, had to crack; the high wall of prefabricated memories had to crumble [...] I had to go back on my tracks, to travel once more the path I had trod.
>
> *(Perec 2009, 52)*

Reflective of the Winckler story yet again, something here had to be destroyed in order for the author to take a linguistic journey back in time, through his "lost" past. Paradoxically, then, the crash in analysis, like the crashing of the yacht, left traces that began to unveil something hidden (not through a "light not turned on", but by one turned off) by opening more pathways and fragmented realities and illusions.

For Winnicott, it is the psychoanalytic breakdown experienced between the patient and analyst that leads to health. In "Fear of Breakdown", Winnicott (1974) warns that analysis may go wrong if the "analysing couple are pleased with what they have done together. It was valid, it was clever, it was cosy because of the collusion. But each so-called advance ends in destruction" (105). If the analytic journey heads towards a specific and more linear narrative when dealing with this kind of trauma, suggests Winnicott, the falsely cohesive ego is merely replicating itself, similar to the BIID and phantom limb replication of cohesive bodily egos. Winnicott continues: "there is no end unless the bottom of the trough has been reached, unless *the thing feared has been experienced*. And indeed, one way out of this is for the patient to have a breakdown (physical or mental)" (Winnicott 1974, 105). The story of Gaspard traces the author's breakdown. Moreover, in writing this plot, the author enacts the thing feared: he must face the loss of both his parents and his split-off self in order to compose the story at hand. If those with BIID and PLS also cling to a fiction, I want to suggest that the mirror-box raises different questions about Perec's process of writing. First, I will examine how *W* functions in a way similar to the mirror-box, albeit linguistically, which opens an avenue to explore identity formations. If *W* is a metaphor for and embodiment of mirror therapy, it decelerates the mirror phenomenon because it linguistically stretches the act of self-reflection and reconstruction.

To return to the narrative, Otto goes on to explain that he does not belong to "the assistance organisation which made it possible for you [the narrator] to find, in this very place, under the cover of a new identity, a degree of safety [...]. But nothing could be further from the truth" (Perec 1989, 43). If seen as an analyst figure, Apfelstahl is suggesting that he cannot find the narrator's True Self; he cannot replace the assistance organisation (the family) that was unable to be there to begin with. The doctor seems to be revealing something that for Perec was central to psychoanalysis: that although he initially expected those fantasies and dreams revealed through the analytic process to become texts, they did not end up being the "'royal road' that I thought they would be, but winding paths taking me ever further away from a proper recognition of myself" (Perec 2009, 51). He was accustomed to habitually creating cohesive stories, and thus expected a unified answer from psychoanalysis. However, in self-reflecting in this psychoanalytic way in a way that, like the mirror-box, toys productively with habitual self-recognition the author did not recognise himself, but something beyond, something silent.

Perec writes that in the narrator's exchange with Apfelstahl, the doctor goes silent and Winckler noticed that the bar was deserted again. "I looked at my watch; it was nine o' clock. Was I still called Gaspard Winckler?" (Perec *W* 44). Here an absence creates a reaction, a moment of silence with another person causes a piece of the narrator's assumed identity to fall. Winnicott's (1965a) thoughts on analysis resemble and encourage this kind of exchange: "a period of silence may be the most positive contribution the patient can make, and the analyst is then involved in a waiting game" (189). In the mirror-box, a false identity also crumbles through a lack, the box holds up an empty space that erases the false image that the sufferers embody. If for them, a physical effect ensues, can we see a similar effect in Perec's description of psychoanalysis and the lost boy narrative?

> At every session I waited for him to speak. I was sure he was keeping something from me [...]. As if the words that went through my head flew straight into his head and settled deep inside it, building up over the sessions a neat lump of silence as dense as my speech was hollow.
>
> *(Perec 2009, 50)*

A lump of silence, hollow speech: these images physicalise a shared silence, which is dramatised by the fact that the author feels his words escape him and "fly into" the analyst's head. Winckler's experience is not so different: Otto's "voice seemed amazingly close, and his slightest word affected me directly" (Perec 1989, 45). Again, there is a relationship between the other, language, and the body, transmitted through an absence. He is physically affected by silence, as though unoccupied speech were creating bodily sustenance, which further implies an exchange/relief of bodily emptiness (the words in the author's "head" are transferred directly to the analyst's "head"). The two passages also stress the importance of language in the formation of his false identity, implying that a silence between self and other can uproot a linguistic self-formation. Similarly, the mirror-box uproots the amputee's form—the subjectively felt limb—by replacing it with an erasure, an image that, like Perec's writing and the analyst's silence, exposes its underlying void to affect the body. I now want to look more carefully at this empty silence that underlies speech and has the power to create psychosomatic change.

The originally blank pages of the text *W*, like the letter that brought Gaspard to Otto, and the silence in analysis, also acts as a blank space upon which the author is able to begin rupturing his unity. To approach this, the Gaspard story suggests, the author must fictionally write a traumatic past because it was never linguistically grasped to begin with. This message is allegorised through Otto's remark that a whaler "picked up a distress call from the *Sylvander* [the boat] but failed to establish radio contact with her [.... When we] tried to raise contact it was to no avail" (Perec 1989, 57). Gaspard, representing Perec's split-off childhood, has been abandoned: no one can hear a call of distress. In Winnicott's terms, due to a parental absence, the boy was left alone and "dropped" in the pre-linguistic state. Though the child would not have been conscious of this at the time, the trauma has formed that child. Thus, the author's felt fragmentation can only be written now: "[t]he only way to 'remember' [...] is for the patient to experience this past thing for the first time in the present" (Winnicott 1974, 103) (for Perec, through analysis and in writing). Through the blank spaces involved, the author may be able to establish a kind of contact he was unable to forge as a child, which parallels the mirror-box's empty space, as it allows the individual to establish visual contact with her absent limb by presenting it.

One case study by David Oakley and Peter Halligan (2002) exemplifies the likeness between one limb sufferer and Gaspard in this instance. The study examines a man (NB) with a phantom (right) hand, whose pain level went from "seven to zero" when he placed the existent (left) hand in a mirror-box. However, when "NB closed his eyes the sensation of moving his left hand was lost" (Oakley and Halligan 2002, 80). One hour after using the mirror-box, his phantom pain resumed, when the doctors began to employ a hypnotic-like procedure of producing a "general relaxation", by helping NB think of calming imagery. Shortly thereafter, the doctors instructed him to "[p]lease imagine, and then see, the mirror-box in front of you" (Oakley and Halligan 2002, 80). In a state of relaxation, NB was able to visualise the hand's reflection and reported a lessening and, after time, elimination, of the phantom pain. "NB said that the virtual mirror experience had felt 'real' to him, that it was like actually being there with the mirror and that he could clearly 'see' the mirror reflection of his right hand" (Oakley and Halligan 2002 80), suggesting that the phantom "was free to be shaped by environmental influences and NB's own emotional state" (Oakley and Halligan 2002 80). Although NB could not initially integrate the phantom limb's absence, he was gradually (with support from others in the world and the cleared space in his mind induced from the calming images) able to begin integrating the phantom's absence. In other words, he needed support from others to integrate his fragmentation, in order to establish visual contact with the absent limb in the present.

A similar kind of exchange is depicted in the novel when Gaspard thinks,

> I did not speak. It was as though, at this point in his story, Otto Apfelstahl expected me to give a reply or at least a sign of some sort, even if only an expression of indifference or hostility. But I found nothing to say. He too fell silent; he was not even looking at me.
>
> *(Perec 1989, 59)*

In a way we see a repetition of the narrator's/Perec's loss of contact in childhood; however, here it takes place in a different scenario where Otto/the analyst, though silent, is still present. In NB's experience, the second (hypnotised) procedure repeats the first, but this time, the patient is able to integrate the loss of his phantom because he is supported and given psychical space. The author, similarly, conveys that the words upon which he relies are meaningless, which draws awareness towards something beyond normative linguistic patterns. If this something points to a non-linguistic feeling of fracture, this feeling shows through in the anxiety in the above quotation from *W*. Everyday speech and habitual narratives are uprooted. In "Backtracking", Perec writes that in analysis he found that he had an "arsenal of stories, [...] fantasies, puns, memories, hypotheses, ... and ways of hiding" (2009, 49), hiding perhaps from that True Self, the fractured and silent other. Again, a conflict between his True and False Selves is conveyed; he is stuck with a shield of speech that papers over silence. Thus, the conflict is, in the words of Winnicott, that it is a "joy to be hidden but disaster not to be found" (1965a, 186). This conflict is one we have been relating to the mirror-box, writing, and psychoanalysis: by holding up a visible and invisible area at once, the individual can both hide and expose a sense of fracture. If this can enable a physical change, how does it work? How can attending to "lumps" of empty speech create both a bodily release and simultaneous sustenance?

While, of course, we cannot know, Perec's dialogue, in line with Winnicott's thoughts on psychoanalysis, suggests that these silent spaces may leave room for more spontaneous gestures to arise. In *W*, amongst the uncomfortable silences, the narrator took a cigarette and Otto had his "hand stretched out, offering a lighter flame" (Perec 1989, 59). A particular kind of object relation is occurring here: the narrator is not rejecting a pretzel with frail hands, he is accepting a lighter. This depicts a step towards accepting the other, and an example of another person's hands assisting him. In a maternal fashion then, Otto implicitly assists Gaspard in physically caring for himself between silences. "We remained silent like that for maybe five minutes", continues Perec, until Otto "break[s] an increasingly oppressive silence" with the words:

> [i]f we accept that a master will fail to perform the elementary but essential safety routine of taking his daily bearing only in the event of extreme disruption or something close to outright panic, then we are led of necessity to only one conclusion. Can you see what it is?
>
> *(Perec 1989, 59)*

In light of the allegory, this passage suggests that Otto's games creating a lack while remaining present and handing the narrator desired objects at particular times may help Winckler learn to "carry" himself in the present, to "take his own daily bearing", and lessen the fear of breaking down. Put another way, if Winckler/Perec can learn to accept that the other (Otto/the mother) will fail to perform every task, but that he will survive nonetheless, then one conclusion remains. To this, Gaspard answers, "I do not know" (Perec 1989, 59), a recognition of silence, of the unknown. Perhaps by facing his breakdown with an analyst, Perec can trust silence enough to withstand the urge to fill it with an "arsenal of stories". His empty speech has been exhausted, and all he can say is that he does not know. In tracing the story of his lost childhood, the author, it seems, is beginning to face a hidden void, strengthening his capacity to hold up a lack, just as NB was momentarily able to face his fracture by slowly feeling stable enough to imagine it. The mirror-box physicalises the author's process, because it too breaks self-construction through an empty space. Furthermore, in both circumstances, one's self-constitution is broken through an image of self-as-other: in the mirror-box, a falsely four-limbed individual and for Perec, through the analyst and the character Gaspard Winckler. In both the mirror-box and book, therefore, a feeling of fissure is rebuilt through an illusory figure that stands for something else. What I will examine now is: why illusion, and why fiction? Why and how does the mirror work for the phantom limb subject, and how do the author, the analyst and literature elaborate this process?

Symbolising the body

"Backtracking" commences with the words, "I had to write, had to restore in and through writing the trace of what had been said". Perec continues, "[w]hy choose to write and publish, to make public what was perhaps only ever named in the privacy of analysis?" (2009, 43–44). I want to explore this question here, why and how Perec writes, and how this might bear physical results. Is he, like Orpheus, "seduced from a desire that comes to him from the night" (Blanchot 1982, 174), who begins to write because he has no choice but to look into the dark? In *W*, Perec gestures towards a reason. He states,

> I write because we lived together, because I was [...] a body close to their bodies. I write because they left in me their indelible mark, whose trace is writing. Their memory is dead in writing; writing is the memory of their death and the assertion of my life.
>
> *(Perec 1989, 42)*

Indeed, like Orpheus, he is drawn to death. Since the loss of his parents left the author empty, he must write: since marked by a lack, he must define himself through a lack.

Thus, the author, those with BIID, and those with PLS all suffer from psychosomatic injuries that relate to a feeling of loss; and while the phantom limb and BIID individuals respond with a painful invisible border, he shows us a more psychical reaction. He begins to work his way out of this pain with a different kind of border: writing. Like the limb outlines, writing also creates a contour that lies between the mind and body, disclosing a different version of the two syndromes. As apotemnophiles may cut into their bodies to self-define, the ink cuts into the paper's vacancy. It simultaneously forms a new symbol, as apotemnophiles would be shaped anew after they are amputated, and as we see in the (often specific) outline of the phantom limb. These definitions depend upon a blankness, and for

Perec, psychoanalysis has a similar effect. He writes that in session, "there rose to the surface the words [...] with my eyes stranded on the ceiling and ceaselessly scrutinising the plasterwork for outlines of animals, human heads, signs" (Perec 2009, 52). It is as though this blank space on the ceiling revived the rupture in his childhood that initially caused him to draw those fragmented bodies that would provide the backdrop for the fictional island "W". If the author has been written through gaps, forgotten behind repetitious cohesive borders, it is the bareness of the analytic room and the untouched page that has allowed him to begin glimpsing at that fragmentation. If, as I have been arguing, *W* traces this journey, it is partially by bringing out the physical nature of this linguistic fracture.

This is particularly clear in one statement that immediately follows the scene in which the narrator was surrounded by all of his family and Yiddish newspapers (an image that I suggested paralleled the Winnicottian state of illusory omnipotence and linguistic wholeness). Here he explains that he pointed to a Hebrew character called "gammeth, or gammel", a character that is not in the Hebrew alphabet and thus false: it is a character that represents nothing and is emptied of meaning. He writes that it was "shaped like a square with a gap in its lower left-hand corner" (Perec 1989, 13). This image alters the previously quoted one (of the Yiddish newspapers) because here, the language with which he identifies does not encircle him, it has a gap. Moreover, in stressing the letter's physical shape, Perec brings meaning closer to the material. Since the character has a gap in its corner, it means nothing in content and is incomplete in form: it embodies what it stands for. It is implied that he also bears a physical sign of a gap, he identifies with this broken letter, he is named by an act of "breaking through". Although this may initially remind us of the those with PLP and BIID who are also somatically defined by rupture, it differs in that unlike those with the syndromes, in this instance, the author is able to write an acceptance of incompletion. This carries over into the reader's experience, because the author brings the reader towards a linguistic materiality, attending to how the characters on the page are linked to the actual text and to his body. Like "gammeth or gammel", the text both embodies and stands for a void: although it consists of no actual memories, it is a book of memories written through fragments. Rather than feigning cohesion, the textual object embodies a wound. In this way, the text not only shows feelings of repair, but almost acts as prosthesis, albeit one that helps Perec heal.

We have explored how the author's reparative process has been illustrated through an allegorical narrative and a symbol, a theme that is elucidated most clearly in one final repetition of the parachute memory. Though we have already explored this image as related to a traumatic drop, in the following passage, a different sense of this fall is conveyed:

> A triple theme runs through this memory: parachute, sling, truss: it suggests suspension, support, almost artificial limbs. To be, I need a prop. Sixteen years later, in 1985, when, by chance, military service briefly made a parachutist of me, I suddenly saw, in the very instant of jumping, one way of

deciphering the text of this memory: I was plunged into nothingness; all the threads were broken; I fell, on my own, without any support. The parachute opened. The canopy unfurled, a fragile and firm suspense before the controlled descent.

(Perec 1989, 55)

By pairing the falsified memory of having fallen and broken his arm with one of jumping from a parachute, Perec gives us a sense of timelessly dangling over a void, similar to his descriptions of psychoanalysis. The passage in this sense brings us closer to that space between words in the analyst's room, where his false identity began to crumble. In "The Scene of a Stratagem", (Perec 2008b) he writes that in the "movement" of analysis, "I" had to let "the rationalisations I had taken refuge in fall into dust [...]. Of this subterranean place I have nothing to say" (169). Parachuting, from this perspective, symbolises this fall beyond deceptively cohesive words. Those letters and signs through which Perec is built begins to shift, leaving him to drop through language. It is almost as though analysis has pushed him towards that gap in "gammeth or gammel" that was already written upon his body. He writes of analysis: "[i]t happened, it had happened it is happening [...]. Something has simply opened and is opening: the mouth in order to speak, the pen in order to write" (Perec 2008b, 162). Something has shifted, the void unfurling: the parachute opening. However, this "fragile and firm suspense" is not only an ominous fall to death, but a liberating jump towards it, a return to a death never experienced.

In "Fear of Breakdown", Winnicott explains that the patient in analysis must experience agony through the analyst's failures in order to begin overcoming the agony: "the patient gathers the original failure of the facilitating environment into the area of his or her omnipotence" (Winnicott 1974, 105). Parachuting in the above text dramatises this, illustrating the author's control over the failure through a fiction. The strings, like the analyst's transitional arms, carry the author through a death-like experience in a non-traumatic manner. Kaufman (1998) writes, "[w]hile the parachute fall is in one sense the fall into the void and the recognition of trauma, it is also a fall out of trauma and into life" (4). Thus, the fall, like "gammeth or gammel", embodies what it stands for: it is a fall out of trauma and into life and in writing. By suspending the fall, Perec, through writing *W*, is able to look into the dark, towards his ambiguous annihilation, at the gap through which he was written; and in this look, just as Orpheus was "lifted", a sense of freedom ensues. Like Orpheus's fall to the Underworld, Perec's is a liberating "fall into dust", into "this subterranean place" that opens language.

If it also echoes the analytic words and gestures that stand in for the carer's absent arms, perhaps this can lend more insight as to why the author imagines "almost artificial limbs" in connection to this fall. From a Winnicottian perspective: the breakdown in analysis moves the patient's trauma from the body towards the mind through the analyst's stand-in arms, those "almost artificial limbs" that act as a metaphorical and physical substitute. This metaphorical and physical substitute, he indicates, affects him and in a way becomes him: "gammeth or gammel", the book, and the psychoanalytic exchange. The author writes of the trauma faced in psychoanalysis: "I know that it happened and that, from that time on, its trace was inscribed in me and in the texts that I write. It was given to me one day [...] like a gesture" (Perec 2008b, 169). The analyst in this description opens an embodied linguistic darkness that, like Orpheus's gaze, "frees himself from himself [...] frees the work from his concern [....] *gives* the sacred to itself" (Blanchot 1982, 175). Shedding the flesh of his everyday language and identity through the analyst and book, Perec's wound is exposed and yet contained. This process calls up the mirror-box because it too sheds psychical flesh. It actualises those "almost artificial limbs": a non-physical prosthesis, a mere image of self-holding that has bodily effects. In both events, it is by suspending an absence through a presence (the absent memory through the book) that the individual can "[amputate] a phantom limb" (Ramachandran 1999, vii) to more comfortably integrate fracture. In both examples then, the symbol becomes physical, and in *W*, the author exposes the negation within symbols (that permeate into the physical) by breaking them apart.

This sentiment is elucidated most clearly in *W* when Perec playfully breaks apart the letter "X":

> [t]he starting point for a geometrical fantasy, whose basic figure is the double V, and whose complex convolutions trace out the major symbols of the story of my childhood: two Vs joined tip to tip to make the shape of an X; by extending the branches of the X by perpendicular segments of equal length, you obtain a swastika, which itself can be easily decomposed, by a rotation of 90 degrees of one of its segments on its lower arm.
>
> *(Perec 1989, 77)*

By simply rearranging signs, the author exposes their meaninglessness while simultaneously unveiling their importance (as these symbols are burdened with meaning and history). If the symbol itself can be easily decomposed, he implicitly asks, can its significance? If so, may a possible future attached to its signification also be altered? Again, language becomes physical. This symbolic fracture echoes the author's own psychoanalytic and linguistic breakdown that has evoked his negation. If this engendered somatic affects, can rupturing language have a similar outcome?

The mirror-box, I contend, extends the question because it too involves the image of a segment of an arm to release its phantom wholeness and expose its negation, which results in bodily change. By altering the symbols above, the author indicates that words are often read with closed meanings, and that an imaginary assumption between the sign and its significance dangerously leaves out thought. BIID and PLS illuminate this tendency to fill a lack with imaginary wholeness, and in causing pain they also depict the danger in this. However, if a swastika, according to Perec, can be decomposed if a segment on its lower arm is rotated, and the mirror-box decomposes the phantom appendage by rotating it, can these dangers also begin to decrease? I am not comparing a swastika to a phantom limb of course. I am simply seeking to draw a parallel between the reflection in the mirror-box and the author's discussion of symbols, which is most clearly drawn out in the above quotation. Can using symbols differently have material effects on a wider scale?

To bring these thoughts together, I want to turn our attention to how the text *W* itself carries symbolic fragmentation towards the world, and how it is materialised in the mirror-box. Since Perec draws the reader's attention to the physicality of the book and its symbolic presence, we are reminded of the transitional object, a replacement for the mother's arms. The text is a kind of transitional object, I suggest, because it stands for unity and its lack. It is bound as a complete object, and also composed of unknowns (the symbol's meaning, the author's intent, the reader's interpretation). Permeable in the reader and writer's hands, the text is both material and not: though a person can hold it, its meaning slips through her fingers. For Perec, it is this object that creates a sense of support, which helps the author carve himself into the world and away from the traumatic feeling of dependence and falling.

The text also acts as a transitional object because it draws an outline between the "me and not-me", and helps the author avoid the drive to create a falsely unified outline that we see echoed in the two conditions. It helps the child Perec grow towards independence and psychosomatic integration in the present. This is partially due to its ability to communicate but not completely which allows the author to bring his private thoughts towards the world, while also keeping them open through fissured language. It is through this openness that his True and ambiguous self can remain hidden. "Perec even suggests", writes Spiro (2001), "that when it comes to knowing his past [...] he was like a child playing hide-and-seek, who doesn't know what he fears or wants more: to stay hidden, or to be found" (133). Like the BIID and phantom limb subject, his pain isolates him from the environment, because it magnifies the feeling that can never be understood, both by the author himself, and by others.

Just as the mirror-box brings the imaginary self towards the material world to be more thoroughly seen and understood, *W* brings Perec's painful fragmentation towards more communal understanding. In his own words: "it is language that throws a bridge between the world and ourselves, language that transcends the world by expressing the inexpressible" (Perec 2008a, 262). Throwing a bridge between that fearful fall and the environment, language holds up his split-off self to help Perec move towards the healthier individual illustrated in Winnicott's framework, who has the desire to "not [be] communicating, and at the same time wanting to communicate and to be found" (Winnicott 1965a, 186). *W* allows the author to hide and seek at once. He both finds that lost child by writing him, and yet preserves this impossibility this hidden self by fictionalising him. In sum then, Perec is brought to life by and through the text, while remaining hidden behind its fictional nature, and the phantom limb is brought to life in the mirror-box, while its fragmentation remains intact. Thus, it seems as though an absence reflected through fiction has, in some circumstances, the ability to decrease the need to form a painful whole. By recognising that a lack cannot be erased, the pain or danger of attempting to do so may decrease.

References

Bellos, David. *Georges Perec: A Life in Words*. London: Harvill, 1993.
Blanchot Maurice. *The Space of Literature* [*L'espace littéraire*, 1955]. Translated by Ann Smock, Lincoln: U of Nebraska, 1982.
Kaufman, Eleanor. "Falling From the Sky: Trauma in Perec's *W* and Caruth's Unclaimed Experience." *Diacritics*, vol. 28, no. 4, 1998, pp. 44–53.
Motte, Warren. "The Work of Mourning." *Yale French Studies*, vol. 105, 2004, pp. 56–71.
Oakley, David A., and Peter W. Halligan. "Hypnotic Mirrors and Phantom Pain: A Single Case Study." *Contemporary Hypnosis*, vol. 19, no. 2, 2002, pp. 75–84.
Perec, Georges. "Backtracking." *Thoughts of Sorts* [*Penser/classer*, 1985]. Translated by David Bellos, Boston: David R. Godine, 2009, pp. 43–55.
Perec, Georges. "Robert Antelme or the Truth of Literature." ["Robert Antelme ou la vérité de la littérature", 1963]. *Species of Spaces and Other Pieces* [*Espèces d'espaces*]. Translated by John Sturrock, London: Penguin, 2008a, pp. 253–269.
Perec, Georges. "The Scene of a Stratagem." ["Les lieux d'une ruse", 1977]. *Species of Spaces and Other Pieces* [*Espèces d'espaces*]. Translated by John Sturrock, London: Penguin, 2008b, pp. 165–174.
Perec, Georges. *W or The Memory of Childhood* [*W ou le souvenir d'enfance*, 1975]. Translated by David Bellos. London: Collins Harvill, 1989.
Ramachandran, V.S. *Phantoms in the Brain: Human Nature and the Architecture of the Mind*. London: Harper Perennial Estate, 1999.
Smock, Ann. "Introduction." *The Space of Literature* [*L'espace littéraire*, 1955]. By Maurice Blanchot, translated by Ann Smock, Lincoln: University of Nebraska, 1982.
Spiro, Joanna. "The Testimony of Fantasy in Georges Perec's *W ou le souvenir d'enfance*." *The Yale Journal of Criticism*, vol. 14, no. 1, 2001, pp. 115–154.
Winnicott, D.W. "Communicating and Not Communicating Leading to a Study of Certain Opposites." *The Maturational Processes and the Facilitating Environment: Studies in the Theory of Emotional Development*. Oxford, England: International Universities Press, 1965a, pp. 179–193. [First published 1963]
Winnicott, Donald. "Ego Distortion in Terms of True and False Self." *The Maturational Processes and the Facilitating Environment: Studies in the Theory of Emotional Development*. New York: International Universities, 1965b. pp. 140–152.
Winnicott, D.W. "Fear of Breakdown." *International Review of Psychoanalysis*, vol. 1, 1974, pp. 103–107.

11
CONCLUSION
(...)

W or The Memory of Childhood opens with the epigraph:

> In this break, in this split suspending the story on an unidentifiable expectation, can be found the point of departure for the whole of this book: the *points of suspension* on which the broken threads of childhood and the web of writing are caught.
>
> (Perec 1989, n.p.)

This short passage about a split, a departure, and suspension allude to an ellipsis that divides and connects *W*'s two halves. Although ambiguous, it also points towards specific ideas within the text, which resonate with the dilemmas of those with apotemnophilia and phantom limbs. The intention here is to contrast the textual split of the ellipsis with the embodied discontinuity experienced by individuals with these conditions, looking at how the ellipsis is a literary, as opposed to bodily, carving out. To repeat, the central dilemma in the limb syndromes involves a traumatic rift between a fractured and whole sense of self. Perec conveys a similar struggle in his text, personified in the adult narrator who signifies Perec's Other (Gaspard), and the lost child who represents Gaspard's Other both the child lost at sea, and the forgotten child Perec pieces together in the text. This painful split, as I have explored, stems from a childhood obscured by a fragmented and war-torn environment, and is ultimately triggered by the departure of the narrator's mother. The narrator has embodied this rupture, and (as indicated in the quotation above) it is this break, this departure, that lays the foundation for the text.

I have suggested that this split illuminates the psychosomatic split suffered by apotemnophiles and those with PLS. Furthermore, both syndromes echo *W* in demonstrating how a struggle to apprehend a rupture may manifest itself upon the body. In this context, the ellipsis can be perceived as a way of bridging the novel's content and the limb phenomena: since it is placed in the centre of *W* it not only represents but embodies the fracture signified in the text. It also separates the book into halves and thus reflects a rupture echoing what those with BIID and PLS embody, albeit in a less painful and self-destructive manner. It is the parenthesis around the ellipsis that reflects a desire to contain an ambiguous absence, as perceptible in the limb disorders. David Bellos (1993) suggests that "brackets normally signify that what is inside them does not belong to the structure of what is outside" (549). Put another way, the parenthesis forms an outline of absence that, perhaps, can counter the drive to create a painful, false sense of unity. While apotemnophiles attempt to sever parts of their bodies away from the world to create a specific lack, and those with PLS are driven to contain a particular form of fracture through a self-created border—as Stephen explained, "I can't affix any borders to me" (Sumner 2015, 44)—Perec is shaping a self-created border through the text to alleviate the painful pressure of his bodily and psychological wounds.

Judith Butler (2013) writes: "if traumatic events make giving an account difficult or impossible, or if they produce elision or ellipsis within a narrative, then it would seem that precisely what is not spoken is nevertheless conveyed through that figure" (182). In the light of this statement, we might conclude that the ellipsis in *W* also stands for the impossibility of forming a cohesive narrative from traumatic events. Although the author could have manufactured a story of his childhood to fill the gaps as those with apotemnophilia and PLS invest their rupture with a cohesive fantasy of self *W* reveals the impossibility of its completion. In other words, sufferers from these syndromes seem to actualise a loss rather than symbolising an overpowering feeling of rupture. Perec, on the other hand, has begun to write himself out of something similar: he has created a symbolic version of loss based on real lived experiences, stories, and photographs. Through a combination of illusion and reality (by using illusion and fiction to suggest that there is no cohesive reality), Perec symbolises the kind of loss that those with BIID and PLS experience. In revealing precisely what is not conveyed, the ellipsis encapsulates the impossibility of creating a cohesive notion of self in just three full stops. It also signifies the novel's paradoxical title: the *Memory of Childhood* told by a narrator who has "no childhood memories" (Perec 1989, 6). In a way, the memories of the narrator's childhood exist as the ellipsis exists: as an embodied absence that cannot be entirely expressed. And this is partially due to the traumatic loss of the mother.

In his article "The Work of Mourning" (2004), Warren Motte suggests that the ellipsis in *W* acts as a replacement for the memory of, and information about, Perec having seen his mother for the last time. However, since this is impossible to remember, "what he puts in its place, escaping from language as it does and suspended as it is, clearly points towards something that remains well beyond language and perhaps beyond thought, too" (Motte 2004, 62). For Motte, the two pages upon which *W* hinge represent an absence that cannot be conceived in thought. Furthermore, an ellipsis, according to Jenny Chamarette, "foreground[s] materiality [...], and draws attention to our own (interrupted) perceptual apprehension and comprehension of the text. Ellipsis slips between materiality and metaphor, overflowing the signifying relationships of the written text" (Chamarette 2007, 35). Thus, the ellipsis in *W* might be not only a representation, but also a symbolic manifestation, of Perec's internal psychical gap, which was left by a parental loss. In the words of Lawrence Kritzman, "[t]he traumatic loss of Perec's parents fractures not only his life but also his memory and inscribes on his body a series of irreparable wounds. Typographically the text marks this gap" (Kritzman 2005, 192). From this angle, the narrator has been constituted through an absence that is embodied within the text's ellipsis. These two pages, therefore, can be seen as an extension of the author's body; perhaps (to recall Perec's statement) an "almost artificial limb". When read in this way, the ellipsis physically and symbolically stands in for a lack.

If Winnicott's "Fear of Breakdown" (1974) suggests that a transitional object may allow for the reparation of such a loss, I propose that this process is perceptible in the form and content of *W*. "What is crucially at issue" in regard to the ellipsis, writes Motte, "is the parental touch, the act that emblematizes and guarantees everything else that Perec longs to recall in a past with which he is so bleakly out of touch" (Motte 2004, 63). I want to extend this thought in light of Winnicott's theory, to suggest that the ellipsis also signifies the mother's/narrator's missing arms. The individual in Winnicott's model is stuck with a void generated by a psychical/physical "drop" (a lack of parental holding). A painful fracture is consequently embodied, creating a split between the mind and body, self and other, which I have linked to Perec's text in both form and content, because this reading provides a different way of viewing BIID and PLS. In Winnicott's theory, such a lack of mental integration could give way to the creation of a False Self (a falsely whole and hollow ego), which Perec exemplifies in his narrative of society and of his own life. Since formally, Perec's fragmented prose exposes this formation of empty unity, *W* attends to an inextricable link between linguistic (symbolic) and human formation, which those with BIID and PLS bring to a lived reality. In reacting to an absence with a painfully false formation of unity, these individuals demonstrate how our conceptual analyses can be extended to bodily drives, and to immediate physical enactments.

Winnicott's transitional object provides a healing element to these ruptures, by offering a degree of control which enables the subject to negotiate presence and absence, unity and its lack, the self and other. By reconstituting the mother's missing arms, the transitional object can ostensibly help individuals integrate the mind and body. In translating bodily needs to the external world, the transitional object functions in a way similar to language and assumes the structure of the written text. In order to enable integration, Winnicott suggests that another individual (specifically, an analyst) should stand in for the mother's arms to help the individual build a stronger ego. We have seen this process most clearly represented in *W* through Gaspard's exchange with the doctor. I also suggested that writing the book was itself a therapeutic process that enabled Perec to translate this lack to the symbolic realm, providing a degree of cohesion without denying a lack. In these ways, the text works as a transitional object. The parenthesised ellipsis cements this idea because, like the transitional object, it is both present and absent: it is in the text,

Conclusion   169

and yet reveals its linguistic lack. It is both unified and dispersed, as it captures an endlessness between parentheses. And like the transitional object, it is part of Perec and other to him the text that he has written is now out of his hands. I suggest that by inscribing this transitional object, this figurative extra limb in the field of the textual and the symbolic, the author may more successfully contain its endlessness, and thus, his own fragmentation. Moreover, the ellipsis not only splits the text (reminiscent of a traumatic split), but also binds its two halves. From this angle, the ellipsis is not only reflective of a transitional object, it is a transitional object. This is important because it reflects the limb disorders: both the apotemnophile and the individual with a phantom limb are coping with a psychosomatic fracture. As Peter explains, "that stupid leg was still on my body [... I] sea[r]ch[ed] for perfection" (Mensaert 2011, 65). However, as Stephen demonstrates, the mirror illusion can enable a sense of psychosomatic integration and release a drive towards wholeness. Thus, the mirror-box not only represents a transitional object, it constitutes a transitional object. Not only does it symbolise self-as-other by presenting an image of self-as-whole, it can also replace a painful lack with an alleviating one. Although mirror therapy cannot alleviate BIID sufferers' pain, since it is the converse of PLP, the process of mirror therapy provides insight as to how this kind of psychosomatic phenomenon can be understood.

To further investigate, I will review the ways in which Perec's working-through is depicted in *W*, by returning to his statement: "[a] triple theme runs through this memory: parachute, sling, truss: it suggests suspension, support, almost artificial limbs. To be, I need a prop" (Perec 1989, 55). These three points of suspension (parachute, sling, and truss) call up Perec's epigraph: a reference to the ellipsis that also links to the "almost artificial" limb. The parenthesised omission, in this way, presents an illustration of Perec's empty sleeve. The ellipsis thus brings that image of a broken appendage that materially and metaphorically exposes its lack of original wholeness closer to a physical reality. This image does not connote a helpless break, but a suspension of fracture that allows for a slower integration: the arms of another help carry the author through the fall. Put another way, this elliptical suspension signifies a kind of strap that holds the two sides of the book together and the bandage that holds up Perec's ruptured limb. The truss here is connected to the language within the book that suspends Perec's lost childhood, the (quoted above) "*points of suspension* on which the broken threads of childhood and the web of writing are caught".

By materially and symbolically holding up the presence and absence of fragmentation and unity at once, it helpfully makes conscious a painful split related to a desire for original wholeness. The ellipsis, like the transitional object, *W*, and the mirror box, reveals a manifestation of the link between the textual signifiers and the physical syndromes in discussion. The ellipsis points towards an exchange between the body and mind, and the subjective and objective senses of self, reflective of Perec's concept of language, "language that throws a bridge between the world and ourselves, language that transcends the world by expressing the inexpressible" (Perec 2008, 262). The mirror-box presents a manifestation of this ellipsis, and of these reflections on rupture and wholeness, thus bringing these theories towards a lived reality, and the bodily conditions towards a linguistic, non-biomedical examination. This kind of bridge is thus reflective of this book, as it too holds up a space between the known and unknown.

The links drawn in this book, therefore, demonstrate that certain feelings of psychosomatic fissure can be altered through a particular kind of symbolic representation that simultaneously holds up a presence and absence. While I do not suggest that BIID and other instances of rupture can be cured by the kind of symbol I have been discussing, these relationships help us think about how we cope with the kind of feelings described by those with apotemnophilia and PLS. I have reflected upon psychoanalysis and literature concerned with bodily rupture, and the way in which we engage with and symbolise felt absences. While the lack of complete understanding of BIID and PLS has been problematic in the biomedical field, I have discussed various statements and testimonies of those with the conditions in relation to more abstract theories. This book, like the mirror-box which involves a material and non-material reflection, has taken two physical disorders, and individuals' written experiences of these disorders, and reflected upon them through more abstract ideas and concepts to develop an indeterminate, yet pointed conclusion: a disturbing need to control a sense of one's own completeness can be mediated through a process of reflection, a kind of reflection that both exposes one's fragmentation and keeps it intact.

References

Bellos, David. *Georges Perec: A Life in Words*. London: Harvill, 1993.
Butler, Judith. *Parting Ways: Jewishness and the Critique of Zionism*. New York: Columbia UP, 2013.
Chamarette, Jenny. "Flesh, Folds and Texturality: Thinking Visual Ellipsis via Merleau-Ponty, Hélène Cixous and Robert Frank." *Paragraph*, vol. 30, no. 2, 2007, pp. 34–49.
Kritzman, L.D. "Remembrance of Things Past: Trauma and Mourning in Perec's *W ou le souvenir d'enfance*" *Journal of European Studies*, vol. 35, no. 2, 2005, pp. 187–200.
Mensaert, Alex. *Amputation on Request*. London: lulu.com, 2011.
Motte, Warren. "The Work of Mourning." *Yale French Studies*, vol. 105, 2004, pp. 56–71.
Perec, Georges. *W or The Memory of Childhood* [*W ou le souvenir d'enfance*, 1975]. Translated by David Bellos. London: Collins Harvill, 1989.
Perec, Georges. "Robert Antelme or the Truth of Literature." ["Robert Antelme ou la vérité de la littérature", 1963]. *Species of Spaces and Other Pieces* [*Espèces d'espaces*]. Translated by John Sturrock, London: Penguin, 2008, pp. 253–269.
Sumner, Stephen. *Phantom Pain: A Memoire: It's All in Your Head*. Bloomington: Archway Publishing, 2015.
Winnicott, D.W. "Fear of Breakdown." *International Review of Psychoanalysis*, vol. 1, 1974, pp. 103–107.

INDEX

Page numbers in *italics* denote figures.

absent limbs 3, 14–15, 20, 26–7, 57, 77, 101, 158; *see also* limbs; *see also* arms; *see also* legs
accidents 12, 29, 43, 50, 52–3, 61–2, 116, 120, 128–9, 132–3, 135–6, 143–4, 146; *see also* false accidents
aggression (in the baby and growing child) 77, 119
agony of body and spirit 107, 121, 123, 125, 162
Aisenstein, Marilia 4, 34, 45, 80–4
alien hand syndrome 9
allegories 56, 99, 151–2, 155, 159
"almost artificial limbs" (metaphorical and physical substitute) 162–3, 168–9
ambiguous signs (gaining meaning from past history) 72, 152
amputated individuals 3, 19, 33
Amputation on Request 41–2
amputations 3, 5, 7, 9–12, 15, 17, 20, 22, 25, 30, 41–3, 47, 49, 51–3, 116; bodily 13, 32, 56, 78; foot 52; left leg 6, 17, 42–3, 53; and limbs 5, 7, 10, 15, 41, 49; and self-amputation 11, 41, 43; successful 20
amputees 6–7, 12–14, 16, 20, 26, 29, 41–2, 51, 56–7, 66, 70, 80, 83, 94, 99–102; dismemberment 71; image when using the mirror-box 55; sense of self 27
analysand 57, 71–2, 84, 136
analysts 26, 49–50, 56, 58–9, 69–70, 72–3, 79–80, 82–3, 125–6, 134–6, 152, 156–7, 159–60, 162–3, 168; cinematic 128;
classical Freudian 125; and images 80, 160; non-medical 43; and patients 57, 73, 80, 83, 125, 134, 157; post-Freudian 29; and psychoanalysis 56, 69–70; role of 84; supporting an individual 135
anatomical identity 8
anatomy 8, 11, 118, 124
Andersen, Hans Christian 106, 108
annihilation 96, 98, 113, 120–1, 123, 131, 133, 135–6; ambiguous 162; experience of 121; infant's 133; somatic 49
anorexia 8, 123
anxiety 16, 48, 66, 76, 121, 153, 159; archaic 117; castration 25–6; dream 72
Anzieu, Didier 4
Apfelstahl, Otto 151–2, 154–8
apotemnophiles 12, 17, 33, 42, 51, 78, 91, 160, 166–7, 169
apotemnophilia 62, 65, 68, 98–9, 108, 111, 121, 128, 138, 141, 146, 148, 152–3, 166–7, 170
appeasing 25, 62, 93–4, 109, 119, 130, 136; images of unity 98; losses 93; mind and body 62; psychosomatic pain 24, 62
appendages 20, 48, 93–4, 109–10, 122, 143, 145
Armless (film) 6
arms 9, 14, 20–1, 51, 56, 61, 89, 92, 106, 109, 119, 126, 143–5, 162–3, 169; absent 19, 162; broken 61; lower 163; missing 168; mother's 164, 168; new 61; partner's 110; transitional 162

Index

art 6, 33, 96, 106–7, 111–13, 132
Artaud, Antonin 3
artificial limbs 138–9, 141, 143, 145, 147, 161, 169; hands 10, 14; legs 17
artists 89, 99, 101, 112
assistance 54, 59–60, 156; and carers 60; organisations 156; quiet 54, 59
athletes 141; *see also* sport
authors 28, 61, 95–6, 102, 124, 139–40, 142–8, 151–64, 167, 169; and images 95, 147, 152, 160, 163; and narrators 143, 155; and texts 96, 143, 157, 163; traumatic war experiences of the 141

babies 24, 55, 57–8, 61, 77, 90–3, 116–19, 125–6, 144, 147–8; illnesses of 144; and mothers 93, 117; process of integration in Winnicott's model 57; and transitional objects 58, 125; traumatised 62, 117
"Backtracking" 151–2, 154–5, 159–60
Barthes, Roland 95, 102
BDD *see* body dysmorphic disorder
Bell, Zoë 133–5
Bellos, David 139
BIID *see* body integrity identity disorder
"biological body" 32
Bion, Wilfred 77–8, 91
Birksted-Breen, Dana 24, 77
Blanchot, Maurice 31, 34, 45–7, 54–5, 83, 89, 91, 93–103, 107–9, 111–13, 131, 160, 163; concept of literature 98, 103, 112; essays 30, 99–100; and his essay "Orpheus's Gaze" 30, 99–100; notion of language 55, 110; and the space of literature 110
blanks (state) 28, 79–80, 84, 117, 152
bodily fragmentation 120
bodily rupture 96, 110, 122–3, 132–3, 170
body acting as a carrier 80
body dysmorphic disorder 7–8
body identity 32
body image 7, 10, 32, 68, 100, 108, 122
body integrity identity disorder 3–13, 21–6, 28–34, 41–5, 65–74, 76–9, 81–4, 89–94, 97, 99–102, 119–24, 129–30, 132–4, 139–48, 154–6; amputations 94; appendages 109–10; conditions 52, 96, 122; and experiences of early onset 6, 90; and the focus on a body image 7; individuals 96, 141, 160; patients 8, 10–11; and phantom limb replication of cohesive bodily egos 156; and PLS experience 167; and PLS foreground psychosomatic dissonance 24; and pretenders in the community 6; and the subject's perception of self 124; sufferers 7, 9, 25, 41, 81, 100, 108, 120–5, 129, 151, 169; surgery 9
"Body Integrity Identity Disorder—First Success in Long-Term Psychotherapy" (study) 12
body language 76
"body phantom" 90–1
body representation 11
body schema 16–17, 19–20, 32
Bollas, Cristopher 59–60, 131–2
borders 22, 61, 79, 95, 167; moving 79; painful invisible 160; personal 77; self-created 167
boys 26, 141, 143, 155, 158; and appendages 145; and false identities 155; and families 143
brain 3, 7, 10, 14–15, 17–21, 56, 65–8; adult 21; tumour patients 10
"breakdown" 34, 49, 116–19, 121, 123, 125, 128, 130, 132–3, 135–6, 155–6, 159, 162; author's 156; environmental 144
Brooks, Peter 70–3
burning (sensation) 14, 53–4, 91
Butler, Judith 167

calming imagery 158
capacity 23, 32, 119, 160; to alter the analysand or reader 71; analyst's 59; and the patient's need to counteract his dismemberment 71; and psychoanalysis 71
Capgras syndrome 9
carers 49, 57–60, 117, 119–20, 122, 125, 134, 162
Caruth, Cathy 27–8
case studies 17, 42, 45, 61, 73, 80, 82–3, 158
cases 3, 9–11, 44, 52, 56, 66, 79–80, 82, 96; analytic 81; documented 6
"castrated mother" 79
castration 8, 25, 32, 78–9, 82–3, 92, 94; anxiety 25–6; experience 93; incomplete 100; symbolic 94
cathected objects 58
CBT *see* cognitive behavioral therapy
Chaplin, Charlie 142, 144
childhood 6–8, 50, 70, 72–3, 76, 136, 138–9, 141, 147, 151, 158, 161, 163, 166–7, 169; development and breakdown 118; lost 148, 160, 169; memories 142, 151, 167; narrator's 167; ridden with neurotic disorders 72

Index

children 25–6, 48, 51, 57, 68, 72–3, 78, 82–3, 90, 93, 117–21, 139, 142–7, 155, 158; growing 119; lost 164, 166; traumatised 155
Christie, Ian 111–13
clenching (sensation) 14, 53
cognitive behavioral therapy 19, 66
Cohen, Josh 82, 96, 101
cohesion 96–7, 128, 131, 139, 147–8, 168; feigning 161; illusory 91; psychosomatic 59; tenacious 32
communication 14, 24, 42, 45, 47–8, 51–2, 55, 58, 62, 110, 118; establishing complete 109; non-linguistic 25
Complete Obsession (film) 6
concentration camps 141
conditions 3, 5–7, 9–10, 24–5, 43–4, 65–6, 68–9, 71, 74, 76–7, 89, 91, 93, 98–100, 164; bodily 4, 23, 170; medical 22; neurological 10; postmodern 30; preliminary 22
control 4–5, 20, 48, 58, 82, 95, 109, 116, 120, 122–3, 129, 136, 142, 168, 170; of emptiness 82, 122–3; omnipotent 58, 134; psychosomatic 146; of rupture 123
Cooper, Dan 5
Cotard's syndrome 10
cramping (sensation) 14
Critchley, Simon 46, 55, 96

dangers 147–8, 163–5
dead bodies 47–8
death 43, 46–9, 82, 96–8, 101–3, 107–8, 110–12, 120–4, 128–35, 146, 160, 162; ambiguity of 112; experiences of 46, 131; fearing 135; partial bodily 47–8; re-experiencing psychical 124; unknowable 122
"The Death of the Author" 95, 102
Death Proof (film) 34, 128–37
"defence organisation" 122, 124
defences 77, 82, 84, 122–3, 129–30, 155; patient's 135; protected 129; psychotic/borderline 80
delirious patients 80
delusions 9, 25–6, 67, 77, 79, 84, 93, 100, 108, 113, 122, 132; concerning elements of BIID and PLS 74; of Freud's concept of psychosis 74; and mirror therapy 25, 67; and psychoanalysis 67
de Man, Paul 96, 106–7, 110, 122
denial 17, 48, 77–8, 113; and body schema 17; and castration 78; and hallucinations 78; of the lost limb 17
Derrida, Jacques 43, 44

destructive acts 3, 77–80, 98, 116, 119, 141, 156
diseases 12, 29, 80
dislocated limbs 3; *see also* limbs
dismemberment 71
The Dismemberment of Orpheus 30, 89, 99–103, 107–8, 110–12, 160, 162
disorders 4, 8–10, 12, 23, 66, 170; body dysmorphic 7; and phantom limbs 23; *see also* mood disorders
dissonance 3, 41, 117; cognitive 10; psychosomatic 120, 148
doctors 21, 43–4, 48–51, 62, 141, 153, 155–8, 168; aggressive 154; internet 44, 50; mysterious 152
Doidge, Norman 67, 100
"Doubtful Arms and Phantom Limbs: Literary Portrayals of Embodied Grief" 31
dreams 72–3, 78, 80, 82–4, 91–2, 96, 139, 156; and illusions 67, 91; and the mind 67; patient's 72; and psychanalysis 67
drive 8, 25, 62, 71, 73, 76, 112, 120, 123, 125, 129, 133–4, 164, 167, 169; amputational 46; dialectico-Sadistic death 110; human 71; individual's 120; painful 34; paradoxical 21

Eagleton, Terry 67
ego 76–7, 91, 118–19, 121, 124–5, 128, 131, 133, 135–6, 154–5, 168; coherent 91; compensation 93; empty 122, 130; integrated 129; organisation 130; structured 133; traumatised 129, 135; works 91
Elliot, Anthony 73–4
ellipsis 111, 166–9; encapsulates the impossibility of creating a cohesive notion of self 167; parenthesised 140; points towards a exchange between the body and mind 169; text's 168
empirical science 66, 68–9, 72
emptiness 48, 68, 120–3, 128–9, 152; bodily 157; control of 82, 122–3; helpless 132; inner 153; structural 121
environment 7, 12, 16–17, 57, 59–60, 77, 79, 90–1, 93, 117–19, 123, 125, 162, 164, 166; deficiencies 145; early 116; infant's 153; lack 133, 155; vagaries 123; women's 129
Eurydice 99–101, 103, 107–8, 110
Evans, David 32
exchange 4, 61–2, 154, 157–8, 169; analytic 83, 125–6, 131; linguistic 23, 48, 68, 73–4; patient/analyst 132

experience 17, 45–50, 60, 69, 71, 78, 80, 90–1, 97–8, 116–18, 120–3, 128–9, 131–3, 139, 147; analytic 154; bodily 24, 45; cinematic 112–13, 133; conscious 92; contemporary 142; cultural 58, 126; of death 47, 129, 131; early 142; familiar 56; of feelings 62, 132; of fragmentation 48, 123, 126; infant's 60; male 9; psychical 62, 94; reader's 161; subjective 17; viewer's 135; of women 32
expression 14, 42, 45, 47, 51, 67, 70, 83, 89, 132, 158; linguistic 51, 109; omnipotent 153; physical 23, 31; symbolic 68

failure 24, 46–8, 68, 93, 125, 136, 162; analyst's 125, 162; environmental 117; reader's 95
"False Self" 119, 136, 153–4, 159, 168
families 42, 44, 54, 59, 141, 143, 147, 154, 156, 161
fantasies 3, 6, 22, 55, 67–8, 74, 77, 83–4, 91–3, 106, 118, 151, 156, 159; cohesive 167; early childhood 74; geometrical 163; hidden 80; primal 83; unconscious 76, 80
father figure 129–30
fathers 78–9, 92–3, 108, 130, 139, 144, 154
fear 7, 12, 48, 50, 81, 113, 117, 121, 125, 132, 136, 147, 159, 164
"Fear of Breakdown" 48, 57, 116–17, 120–2, 126, 128–30, 134–5, 143, 147, 153, 156, 162, 168
Felman, Shoshana 27–9
fetish (Freud's notion) 25–6
fictional 3–4, 42, 52, 109, 133, 136, 139–40; individuals 28; nature 52, 97, 154, 164; re-enactment 73, 126; reconstruction 53; representation 42; self-image 99; self-reconstruction 50, 53; works 27, 33–4
"Fictions of the Wolf Man" 72
"fictitious coherence" 91
"Fighting it" (Yahoo Group) 5–6, 69, 92, 100, 136
films 6, 12, 33, 106–8, 110–13, 126, 128–36; *Armless* 6; *Complete Obsession* 6; *Death Proof* 34, 128–37; *Quid Pro Quo* 6; *The Red Shoes* 34, 103, 106–13, 148; *Whole* 6
fingers 41, 78, 80, 124, 144–5, 164
Finlay, Marike 136
Flanders, Sara 24, 77
Flor, Herta 15–16

foot 16, 43, 52; amputations 52; artificial 10; false 10; illusion 66; massages 134; rubber 10
Foucault, Michel 103, 115
fracture 93–4, 97, 99, 101–2, 109, 123, 126, 128–9, 131, 133, 136, 139–40, 159–60, 167, 169; bodily 9, 30, 92, 136, 145; experience of 121, 145; feelings of 48–9, 132; linguistic 3, 161; painful 52, 168; physical 28, 133; psychosomatic 24, 31, 136, 169; symbolic 163
fragmentation 5–6, 24–5, 28, 30, 44–5, 89–92, 102–3, 112–13, 121–2, 128–9, 131–4, 139–40, 148, 158, 169–70; bodily 4, 25, 70, 91, 134–5, 152; disordered 118; haunts traumatised subjects 129; incomprehensible 50, 61; individual's 122; linguistic 34; literary 31; painful 164; physical 143; psychical 23, 60; psychosomatic 18, 62, 69, 136; symbolic 164
freedom 102, 106, 110–12, 162
Freud, Sigmund 22–3, 25–7, 29, 32, 46–8, 56, 65, 68, 72–4, 76–8, 80, 82–4, 90, 113, 142; case study of the "Wolf Man" 72, 78–9, 83; concept of a fetish 25; concept of a neurosis 25; concept of psychosis 74; concept of the uncanny 47, 89; psychoanalysis 46, 56; psychology 73
friends 17, 42–4, 51, 54, 59, 61, 130, 143
friendships 51, 130
"From the History of an Infantile Neurosis" 72
Frost, Robert 142, 143
functions 9, 23–4, 46–7, 58, 62, 90, 109–10, 122, 156; biological 4; decentred 67; ego-supporting 134, 154; informative 79; intacting family 147

gender 8–9; dysmorphia 9; identity issues 8; reassignment for transsexuals 9, 11; roles 32
gender identity disorder 8–9
gestures 59–60, 97, 110, 119, 130, 133, 151, 162–3; ideal familial unity 147; primitive 126; spontaneous 118, 159
GID *see* gender identity disorder
girls 106, 129–30, 132–3
GMI *see* graded motor imagery
goals 9, 11, 16, 46, 53
graded motor imagery 19, 66
Green, André 34, 74, 77–81, 83–4
grief 17, 31–2
grieving 32
Grossberg, George T. 66

Grosz, Elizabeth 32, 67
groups 5–6, 10, 65, 69, 133, 155; internet 44; literary 95
Guneratne, Kristy 142–3

haemorrhagic rectocolitis 80, 82
Halligan, Peter 158
hallucinations 25, 78–80
Haase, Ullrich 108, 115
Hart, Kevin 101, 111
Hassan, Ihab 30–1, 100
healing process 19, 23, 25, 50, 54, 71, 82, 132, 136
health 52, 116, 118, 155–6, 164; and independence 128; mental 11; and psychosomatic integration 117; and separation between mother and infant 117
Hill, Leslie 94–5, 110
history 6, 27–9, 31, 72, 82, 98, 139–40, 148, 163; comprehensible 72; and linking to social concerns 29; and patient's life 72, 136; traumatic 82
Holocaust 29, 140
The Holocaust of Texts 28
human knowledge 91–2
human personality 118
humanities 6, 8
humour 120
Hungerford, Amy 28
hypochondria 32
hypotheses 14, 16–17, 159; neurological 10, 15–16; pain memory 15
hysteria 22–3, 32, 47
hysterical body 22–3

identification 16, 55–6; physical 16; spatial 56
identity 5, 8, 10–11, 49–50, 52, 95, 102, 107, 110, 128–30, 133, 139–40, 148, 154–5, 157; cohesive 144; current 148, 154; disorder 7; empty 123, 128; false 122, 128–9, 152, 155, 157, 162; formations 156; new 133, 156; protective 156
illness 4, 12, 24–6, 45, 50, 66, 80–1, 139, 144, 155; mental 12, 50, 66; patient's 80; physical 45, 139; psychosomatic 24–5; somatic 24, 80–1
illusion 20, 26, 58, 62, 66–8, 70, 83–4, 93–4, 106, 108–11, 126, 136, 152–3, 155–6, 167; creating 59; familial 148; infant's 92; of pain *19*; psychological 68
illusory 19, 24, 55, 58, 60, 62, 121, 125–6; cohesion 91; limbs 3, 122; objects 25, 62; wholeness 56, 92

images 14, 20–3, 32–4, 46, 55–6, 90, 92–3, 97, 101, 109–13, 132, 145–7, 153–5, 160–1, 169; calming 158; discordant 97; false 93, 148, 157; fictional 113; individual's 94
imaginary 55, 61, 90, 93–4, 102, 110; anatomy 32, 90; bodily frame 79; limbs 3, 62; relationships 144
imagination 22, 54, 59, 61, 67–8, 70–2, 110; human 74; and illusion 67; and the mirror-box 67–8; and psychoanalysis 67–8
immortality 96
imperfect bodies 6, 12, 32–3
In Prosthesis 33
independence 59, 72, 93, 117, 121, 133, 145, 164; and health 128; infant's 117; from the mother 93; women's 135
individuals 3, 5–11, 20–1, 23, 25, 34, 41, 47–8, 51–3, 68, 70–1, 90–2, 120–1, 123, 142; amputated 3, 19, 33; bodies 14, 122; maturational process 117; supportive 60; weak 51
infancy 48, 76, 90, 94, 120
infans 90–3, 99–100, 102, 107, 110; non-linguistic 110; ruptured 94
infants 7, 48, 55–7, 59, 76, 98, 117–22, 129, 131–2, 135, 147, 153; bodies 119; and the environment 77, 118; and language 55, 76; and transitional objects 58, 119, 121, 131
injuries 144–5, 154–5
institutions 43–4
integration 10, 49, 57–8, 168; mental 168; psychical 136; psychosomatic 24, 57, 62, 116–17, 119, 123, 126, 164, 169; symbolic 94; in Winnicott's model 57
internet 43–4, 51
interpretations 27, 32–3, 59, 73, 80, 82–3, 130; and fantasies 84; infant's 92; and patients 84; reader's 164
itches (invisible) 14, 56

Jones, Ernest 23
Joyce, Angela 121

Kaufman, Eleanor 143, 162
Keats, John 130–1
Klein, Melanie 23–4, 76, 116
knowledge 9, 57, 95
Kolb, Lawrence 17
Krasner, James 31
Kritzman, Lawrence 168
Kuhn, Annette 60

176 Index

Lacan, Jacques 34, 55–6, 89–95, 97, 100, 108; concept 92–3, 108; model 90–1; theory 56, 90, 93, 97, 102, 108
Lacanian 94, 108; ego 95; lens 99; mirror 91; paradigm 91; perspective 98; symbolic order 97, 107
LaCapra, Dominick 28–9
language 4–5, 23–4, 26–8, 30–4, 44–8, 50–8, 60–2, 76–7, 79–81, 83, 92–101, 109–10, 138–40, 161–4, 167–9; everyday 96, 98, 102, 110, 163; fissured 164; fractured 89; fragmented 99, 140; impersonal 103; indecipherable 109; Maurice Blanchot's notion of 55, 110; Perec's concept of 169; pre-verbal 59; rupturing 163; subjective 83; transparent 96; use of 47, 51, 76, 148
lap dancing 130
Laplanche, Jean 67
Laub, Dori 27–9
LeBeau, Vicky 90
legs 9, 14, 17, 33, 42–4, 47–9, 51–2, 54, 56, 89, 106, 132, 169; and mirror therapy 20; and pain 44; and phantom limbs 20; and wooden legs 33
Lemma, Alessandra 118
Lemos, Aaron 14
lenses (inverting images) 12–13
Lermontov, Boris 106–8, 111–13
letters 42, 152–3, 157, 161–3
Leys, Ruth 28
limbs 3–7, 9–16, 20–1, 29–31, 33, 41–2, 48–9, 62, 68, 96, 100, 102, 108–9, 122, 146; affected 11; alienated 10, 153; amputated 11, 13, 15; conditions 67, 110, 153; disjointed 92; disorders 167, 169; existent 4, 17, 27, 54, 58; extraneous 3, 17, 21, 41, 146, 169; literary 31, 34; missing 41, 67; pain 33, 56; phenomena 67, 167
Lingis, Alphonso 30
links 9, 23, 27, 31, 33, 42, 45, 69–70, 72–3, 81–2, 126, 131, 141–3, 147, 169–70; alleviated 124; inextricable 151, 168; mental 117; Pankejeff's borderline example 56; psychic 77; strong 43
literary limbs 31–4
literary theory 8, 33–4, 94
literary works 4, 31, 33, 65, 101–2
literature 4–8, 12, 26–8, 30–2, 34, 46, 54–6, 65–74, 80–4, 93–5, 97–9, 102–3, 109–10, 112–13, 140; first slope of 46–7, 55, 96, 109; linking with the body and the mind 5; and Maurice Blanchot 98, 103, 112; postmodern 28, 30

loss 14–15, 17–18, 32, 60–2, 92–3, 95–6, 99–100, 107–8, 122–3, 132–3, 135, 140–6, 155–6, 159–60, 167–8; bodily 15, 26, 60, 84, 121; environmental 119; familial 144; parental 168; physical 60, 100, 126, 143
love 49, 103, 107–8, 131

MacLachlan, Malcolm 17
madness 31, 97, 101, 103
Malle, Bertram 15, 66–7
"The Man From Burma" 45, 77, 79–85
maps 10, 15, 42; body image 100, 122; of the brain 15, 67; mind's 59; new 59; sensory 19
material world 16, 21, 154, 164
McDougall, Joyce 24
McFarland, Thomas 131
McGeoch, Paul 6
mediation 32
medication 10–12, 21, 54, 62, 67
Melzack, Ronald 15
memory 15, 17, 22, 26–7, 31, 33, 73–4, 78, 80, 82, 138, 140–4, 146–7, 159–62, 167–9; absent 163; author's 146; borrowed 50; broken arm 145; creating 84; falsified 69, 145, 162; fictional 143; fragmented 147; historical 98; repressed 144; trace 73
Mensaert, Alex 41–2
mental health 11
mental illness 12, 50, 66
mental institutions 43–4, 50–2
mental processes 82
Merleau-Ponty, M. 32
mind 3, 5, 21–2, 24–5, 47, 49, 59, 61, 65–8, 70, 73, 77, 84, 119–21, 126; and body relationship 3–4, 12, 15, 20, 25, 32, 42, 48, 54, 60–3, 65, 67–8, 117, 119, 168; child's 119; conscious 22, 145; individual's 59, 120; mother's 119; open 54; psychotic 74; states of 26; unconscious 73–4
mirror 4, 12–13, 18, 21, 41, 53–62, 68–9, 90–2, 95, 97, 101–2, 111, 158; description 152; Lacanian 91
mirror-box 18, 20–1, 23–7, 65–9, 73, 80–1, 83–4, 94, 97–103, 110–13, 125–6, 135–6, 156–60, 163–4, 169–70; acts as a metaphor for transference 4, 27, 136; breaks up an idea of unity through a symbol (of the invisible limb) 71; demonstrates how fictional images of self and self-as-other can change realties 113–14;

mechanism 134; phenomena 4, 93, 113; therapy 84
mirror-box treatment *18*
mirror illusion 3, 5, 20, 22, 26, 62, 68–9, 71, 92, 169
mirror image 20, 26, 33, 55–6, 58, 60, 62, 71, 90–1, 93, 98–101, 107, 112; fantasy 55; Lacan's 55; Stephen's 58; symbolises a phantom delusion 60
mirror phenomenon 61, 156
mirror reflection 56, 90, 158
mirror stage (concept) 55, 89–91, 93, 107, 110
mirror therapy 4–5, 18, 18–27, 65–9, 73, 80–1, 83–4, 94, 97–103, 110–13, 125–6, 135–6, 156–60, 163–4, 169–70; acts as an example of the way in which we are formed through signs 5; experience is both "cool and uncanny" 56; functions in a similar way to Winnicott's model of psychoanalysis 60; parallels a notion of language 42; recreates one's whole and fractured body 136
Mitchell, Juliet 23
mood disorders 4, 8–10, 12, 23, 66, 170
mothers 26, 50, 57–8, 60–1, 78, 92–3, 107, 117–18, 129, 131, 134, 139, 142–7, 154, 167–8; and carers 119; and children 26, 118, 143; implementation of the infant's omnipotent expressions 153; and infant 117; omniscient 135; penis 26, 78
mourning 17, 144, 167
movement 16, 22, 27–8, 32, 57, 72, 101–2, 109–10, 119, 131, 133, 145, 162; body's habitual 16–17, 126; continual 101; control phantom 18, 20; of eye or hand 34, 94; free 95; imagining hand 19; leg's 17; physical 126; productive forward 29; social 6

narratives 70, 72, 135, 154
narrators 141–5, 147–8, 152–3, 155–7, 159, 161, 167–8; and apotemnophiles 166; and authors 143, 155; and false identity 155; mother's hands 144
negation 45, 78, 80, 96–7, 100, 112, 139, 163; abstract 78; frames and enables representation 78
negative hallucination 76–9, 84
neurological hypotheses 10–11, 15–16
neurological models 72
neurons 16
neuroscience 65
neurosis 22–3, 25, 32, 74
newspapers 107, 109, 148

Nietzsche 111
non-congenital phantoms 56
non-existence 123, 135
Nortvedt, Finn 14, 17, 41
"nothingness" (concept) 46, 55, 101, 122, 129, 142, 146, 152, 162

Oakley, David 158
object relations theorists 23
object relations theory 16, 76–7, 116
objective reality 58, 79, 143, 153; *see also* illusion
objects 17, 19–20, 23–4, 57–61, 79, 92, 98, 109, 117–20, 131, 136, 153, 159, 164; correlative 119; cultural 126; external 116; introjecting 77; natural 95; subjective 153; textual 161; unimpinging 136
O'Connor, Flannery 33
Oedipus complex 25, 152
omnipotence 118, 122, 147, 162; and fear 147; illusion of 118–19, 125, 147, 161; and transitional objects 122, 125
Orpheus 31, 101–2, 107
"Orpheus's Gaze" 30, 89, 91, 93, 95, 97, 99–100, 103, 112, 163

Page, Vicky 106
pain 14–16, 18–21, 41–3, 45, 47, 49, 51, 53–7, 61–3, 68–70, 78, 112–13, 117, 121–4, 163–5; appeasing 62; bodily 21; burning 21; causes of 62; chronic 66; cure for 68, 132; emotional 24, 61; eradicating 65–6; free periods 18; and itching 14; levels 158; memories 15; neuropathic 19; non-diagnosable 155; pre-amputation 15; psychical 61, 152; psychosomatic 54; relief 21; subjective 143; understanding of 67–8
painkillers 44
Pankejeff, Sergei 72–3, 78–9
parachutes 142, 146, 161–2, 169
parachuting 146, 162
paradoxical relationships 20–1, 25, 48, 58, 78
paralyses 20, 22, 42, 44
parents 7, 25, 50, 78, 140–1, 143–4, 156, 160, 168
Paris School of Psychosomatics 24
patients 6–7, 9–12, 17–22, 45, 49–50, 56–7, 59–60, 66–7, 71–3, 78–84, 120–1, 125–6, 133–6, 156–9, 162
penis 78
perceptions 21, 77, 92, 95, 97, 124; bodily 30; new 58; personal 141

Perec, Georges 50–2, 60–1, 138–48, 151–69; childhood 141, 143; image of parachuting 146; life and work 138; mother's departure 142; and symbolic reconstitution 151; traumas 142, 151

perspective 46–7, 76–7, 79, 84, 90–1, 129, 131–2, 162; analytical 7; inter-subjective 14; literary 45; psychoanalytic 33, 67; Winnicottian 144, 162; woman's 9

phallus 32, 92–4

phantom 14, 16–17, 20, 25–7, 54–5, 66–7, 91–2, 94, 97, 100–1, 103, 109, 113, 134–6, 158–9; appendage 163; concept 92; delusion 60; feelings 16, 101; foot 57; non-congenital 56; sensations 4, 57, 66, 91

phantom limb syndrome 3–5, 12–13, 15–17, 20–2, 28–32, 69–74, 76–9, 90–4, 97–100, 120–1, 123–4, 141–3, 146, 151–6, 166–8; experience 167; foreground psychosomatic dissonance 24; lack control over pain 148; and mirror therapy 112; sufferers 21, 101, 132, 142

phantom limbs 5–6, *13*, 14–17, 19–20, 22–3, 25–6, 31–2, 41–2, 53–6, 90–8, 100, 111–13, 121–2, 140–1, 146–8, 163–4; conditions 76, 93–4; delusion 80, 122; disorders 32, 68; and hysteria 23; imagined 110; individuals 133, 141, 145; and mirror therapy 20, 26, 58; and pain 13, 53, 56; pain 14–15, 19, 21, 53–4, 56, 66, 68–9, 108, 111, 122, 144, 161, 169; phenomena 14, 111, 123, 141; sufferers 21, 32, 83, 91, 100, 113, 122, 124, 129, 138; syndrome 3–4, 12, 32, 76, 84; and trauma 27, 31, 56

phantom pain 14–15, 19–20, 41, 58, 158

Phantom Pain: A Memoire 60

phenomena 4, 13–14, 32–3, 41, 58, 70, 76, 93, 131, 146, 153; archaic limb 10; biomedical 22; non-physical 67

Phillips, Adam 26, 58, 120, 147

physical expression 23, 31

physical feelings 14, 54, 91, 132, 153

physical identification 16

physical illnesses 45, 139

physical reality 20, 90, 120, 136, 169

physiology 30, 118

PLS *see* phantom limb syndrome

poetry 73, 89, 113, 131

"positive one-ness" (Winnicott) 122–3

postmodernism 29–31

poststructuralism 28, 30, 131

"potential space" 58, 60

Powell, Michael 112

pre-linguistic state 110, 120, 158

Pressburger, Emeric 34, 103, 106–7, 110–11

primitive agony 121–2, 124–5, 128, 134–5, 144, 146

problems 3, 11, 24–5, 28–9, 43–4, 51, 60, 65, 70, 73, 81–2, 117, 154; bodily 31; mind-body 67; neurological 5; physical 83

process 23–4, 50, 56–61, 66, 68, 71–3, 80–1, 83–4, 134, 136, 138, 140, 144–5, 152–3, 168–9; analytic 136, 156; non-rational 68; psychological 107; therapeutic 168

proof 69, 129, 135

protective identity 156

psyche 21–2, 24, 45, 53–4, 56, 60, 62, 66–8, 74, 80–1, 83–4, 119, 121, 123–4, 126; care 25; disabled 24; woman's 32

psychiatrists 7, 44, 49, 65, 155

psychical 6, 15–16, 21, 48–9, 54, 66, 82, 93, 109, 139, 145, 168; activity 4; components 12; feelings 67; healing 50; sense 62, 118; wounds 22, 48, 67, 81, 84, 140

psychical integration 136

psycho-neurotic patients 125

psychoanalysis 4–6, 8, 12, 16, 22, 26–30, 32–4, 54–62, 65–74, 80–4, 124–6, 132–4, 139, 151–7, 161–3; and analysts 56, 69–70; Freudian 46, 56; in-depth 69; and the use language 71; Winnicott's model of 50, 60, 126, 133

psychoanalysts 34, 45, 49, 76, 82, 116, 126; and André Green 77; and Christopher Bollas 131; and Donald Woods Winnicott 7

psychoanalytic 4, 7, 15, 70–2, 81, 114, 163; approach 8; distress 81; exchange 26, 68, 125, 163; experience 152, 154; exploration 69; patient 27, 71; process 23, 50, 59, 138; project 73; support 58; transference 26

psychology and PLS 16, 16–18, 22, 67

psychosis 25, 32, 74, 76–7, 79, 93, 97, 108, 116, 124, 132; Freud's concept of 74; and Winnicottian trauma 121, 132

psychosomatic: change 157; cohesion 59; conditions 45, 66; cures 62; discord 25, 34; dissonance 120, 148; feelings 66; illnesses 24–5; injuries 54, 160; integration 24, 57, 62, 116–17, 119, 123, 126, 164, 169; self-definition 154; situations 81; split 61, 84, 166; symptoms 24–7

"Psychosomatic Solution or Somatic Outcome: The Man from Burma – Psychotherapy of a Case of Haemorrhagic Rectocolitis" 80
psychotherapy 12, 80, 139; and BIID 12–13; and body integrity 12; and medication 12; and self-amputation 12
psychotic 25, 76–7, 79, 93, 108, 124; mechanisms 76, 124; mind-set 79–80, 84; patients 74, 79; structure 93–4, 97, 100, 108; tendencies 117, 129

quadri-amputees 14
Quid Pro Quo (film) 6

Ramachandran, V.S. 3, 6, 10–11, 15–16, 18, 20–1, 54, 68, 163
Rapaport, Herman 31
re-experiencing 24, 48, 113, 120–1, 124–5; an embodied feeling of "death" 121; the feeling of traumatic fragmentation 48–9; primitive agony 122
readers 27–9, 61, 71, 83, 101–2, 131, 140, 144, 148, 154, 161, 164; dismembered 71; question what language means 140; textual 27
reading 4, 28, 31, 71–3, 81, 84, 95, 101–3, 133, 147–8, 152, 154, 168; and language 45; and mirror-therapy 98, 103; psychoanalytic theories 4; and writers 101
Reading for the Plot 72
reality 16–17, 26–8, 33, 52, 55, 58, 61–2, 67, 72, 74, 76, 91–2, 99, 109–11, 117; cohesive 167; external 77, 118–19, 124; fragmented 156; undifferentiated 111
The Red Shoes (film) 34, 103, 106–13, 148
relationships 21–2, 27–30, 33–4, 42–3, 55, 57, 60–2, 67, 69–70, 116, 118, 129, 133, 151, 157; analyst/patient 125; deceitful 129; early 59, 72; familial 59; flirtatious 130; human 47; painful 53; personal 107
representation 28, 32–3, 61, 77–80, 83, 96, 100, 109, 111, 155, 168; crisis of 27–8; hidden 80; linguistic 28, 140; mental 22; preconceived 140; subjective 77; symbolic 170
risks 69, 83–4, 124
"rubber foot illusion" 10, 14
ruptures 30, 49, 51–2, 71, 89–91, 99–100, 106, 112–13, 121, 129–32, 143, 145–6, 161, 166–8, 170; bodily 96, 110, 122–3, 132–3, 170; excessive 123; physical 108, 120; psychosomatic 27, 48, 128

"The Scene of a Stratagem" 151
scenes 60, 107, 109–10, 112, 130, 132–5, 147, 153, 161; sexual 8, 32, 73; spill over into the cinematic experience 113; of traumatised subjects 132
schizophrenics 31
Schmidt, Sebastion 6
Schwartz, Paul 139
Schweizer, Harold 71
science 7, 65–7, 69, 71, 73–4
Second World War 50, 60, 113, 139, 141
Segal, Hanna 24
Segal, Naomi 94
self 4–5, 53, 58–62, 67–8, 84, 90, 97–8, 101–2, 111, 118–19, 129–31, 140–1, 145–6, 156–7, 166–9; the bodily 23; compliant 153; double 47, 56; fragmented 77, 90, 108, 118; hidden 48, 164; imaginary 164; subjective 91; sustaining 60; unconscious 84
self-amputation 6, 11–12, 41, 43–5, 49–50, 53, 62, 66, 74, 98, 120, 124, 134; *see also* amputation
self-castration 79, 82; *see also* castration
self-destruction 48, 62, 123
self-images 123, 128, 130
self-recognition 90, 98, 151, 157
self-reflection 56, 136, 156
sensations 3, 13–16, 20, 42, 46, 53–5, 57–8, 118, 147, 158; burning 14, 53–4, 91; clenching 14, 53; conveying 47; fragmented 91; non-logical 42; obscure 91; physical 143; throbbing 14
sexual scenes 8, 32, 73
Sherman, Richard A. 66
silence 30–1, 59, 78, 82, 97, 100, 151, 157, 159; analyst's 157; empty 157; linguistic 30; oppressive 159; shared 157; trust 159; uncomfortable 159
Smock, Anne 99
Sobchack, Vivian 20
social dialectics 91–2, 97
space 58, 60, 79, 82, 97, 99, 101–3, 119, 125–6, 131–2, 136, 139, 162, 170; blank 157–8, 161; empty 82, 157–8, 160; fictional 131; negative 15, 84; transitional 128, 131
"space of literature" 97, 99, 110
spatial identification 56
speech 31, 34, 48, 80, 82, 84, 109, 157, 159; disturbances 22; empty 159–60; hollow 157; patient's 79; unoccupied 157
Spiro, Joanna 164
sport 141

stories 14, 41, 43–4, 49–50, 52–3, 69–71, 83–4, 109, 138, 140–2, 144–5, 152–6, 158, 160, 166–7; biographical 72; creating cohesive 157; fictional 116, 140; open-ended 71; pre-written 152
Strathman, Christopher 131
strokes 9–10
Subedi, Bishnu 66
sufferers 6–7, 9, 23, 26, 28, 91, 93, 97, 99–100, 119, 122, 124, 146, 157, 167; phantom limbs 21, 32, 83, 91, 100, 113, 122, 124, 129, 138; trauma 123; traumatised 129
suicide 5, 43–4, 111–12, 120, 123–4, 129
symbolic exchanges 27, 62–3, 90, 92, 94, 96, 98, 100, 102, 108, 110, 112, 114, 118, 120
symbolic form 27, 67, 71
symbolic meanings 22, 24, 80
symbolism 23, 23–4, 66, 70, 94
symbols 20, 23–4, 27, 33–4, 66, 68–71, 76, 80, 83, 92–3, 97–8, 101–3, 111–12, 161, 163–4; abstract 152; bodily 71; meaning of 164; new 160
symptoms 8, 10–11, 22–3, 47, 66, 73; bodily 22–3, 81; hysterical 22; somatic 22–3, 80
syndromes 5–10, 12, 14, 21–3, 28–9, 31, 41–2, 44–5, 62, 65–7, 74, 77, 79, 82, 160–1; alien hand 9; bodily 29; Capgras 9; Cotard's 10; physical 169

Tarantino, Quentin 34, 128
texts 27–31, 33–4, 44–5, 50, 54, 94, 96–7, 100–2, 138–40, 142, 145, 151, 156–7, 161–4, 166–9; falsified 148; fictional 4, 12; literary 26–7, 71; medical 44–5, 51; selected 42; written 43, 168
theories 7, 15, 17, 20, 24, 27–33, 54, 69–70, 77–8, 82–3, 117, 123, 144, 146, 170; postmodern 28, 30; poststructuralist 29, 51; psychological 15; psychosomatic 81; unified 24, 95
therapeutic relationships 59
therapists 12, 19, 21, 69
therapy 11, 19, 54, 56, 58, 60, 69, 73, 128, 132–3
throbbing (sensation) 14
tingling (sensation) 14
transference (concept) 26–7, 72–3, 125, 142
transitional objects 24, 34, 57–8, 60–1, 119, 121–2, 124–6, 131–3, 135–6, 145, 164, 168–9; environment 119; helping 119; and psychosomatics 24, 61; standing for the carer 125

transsexuality 19, 21
trauma 27–9, 48–9, 56, 73–4, 117, 120–1, 123, 125–6, 128–9, 132–3, 135–6, 139–45, 147–8, 153–4, 162–3; ambiguous 57; bodily 28; early 49; fictional 136; hidden 82; historical 28; infantile 126, 155; mental 48; multiple 53; patient's 162; physical 10; primitive 120, 135; studies 27–9; sufferers 123; theorists 27; theory 28; unknowable 124, 135
traumatic 34, 133, 145–6, 167, 169; accidents 22; experiences 23, 27–8, 49, 56, 73–4, 120–1, 136, 146, 161; fragmentation 48; losses 22, 139, 167–8; occurrences 117, 120; past 50, 140, 151, 157; state 48–9
traumatised 48–9, 53, 58, 62, 116–17, 120–6, 128–30, 132–5, 139, 153, 155; individuals 48, 58, 116, 122–3, 153; patients 49, 125, 134; subjects 48–9, 121, 128–9, 132–4, 139, 153
treatments 11, 14–15, 19, 21, 44, 67, 69, 73
"true self" (Winnicott) 118, 153, 155–6, 159
trusses 143, 161, 169

Underworld 89, 99, 101–2, 107, 109–10, 112, 162

viewers 112–13, 132–6
virtual reality box 18
virtual reality machine 68
Volatile Bodies: Toward a Corporeal Feminism 32

W or The Memory of Childhood 29, 34, 50, 136, 138, 151, 166–7
Weiss, Thomas 17
White, Amy 6
Whole (film) 6
wholeness 3–4, 6, 28, 32–4, 67, 70–1, 73–4, 78, 90–3, 97, 100, 103, 147–8, 152, 169–70; bodily 21; false 91; feeling of 20, 91; image of 90, 139; imaginary 91, 124, 163; physical 32; reassuring 147; temporary 71; virginal 139
Wills, David 33
Winckler, Gaspard 140–1, 143, 151–7, 159–60
Winnicott, D.W. 24–5, 48–50, 57–9, 61, 114, 116–26, 128–31, 133–6, 141, 143, 145–7, 153–4, 156–9, 162, 168; concept of analysis 135; definition of psychosis 124; description of primitive agony 146; essay "Fear of Breakdown" 48, 57, 116–17, 120–2, 126, 128–30, 134–5,

143, 147, 153, 156, 162, 168; state of illusory omnipotence and linguistic wholeness 161; and Tarantino's use of Romantic poetry 131; theory of trauma 34, 48–50, 59, 121–3, 128–9, 133, 139, 143, 151, 153, 168

Winnicott's model 57, 62, 116, 120–1, 124, 128, 130, 132–4, 147, 168; of psychoanalysis 50, 60, 126, 133; and Tarantino's film 136; of trauma 129

"Wolf Man" 72, 78–9, 83

women 22, 128–30, 133–4; experience rupture 134; and films 128; identities 129

wooden legs 33

wounds 48–9, 56, 74, 81–4, 129–30, 140, 143, 161; bodily 10, 80, 82; physical 21, 23, 25, 67, 83–4; psychological 25, 167

writing 27, 29, 96–9, 101, 103, 109–11, 116, 140, 148, 164